Enlightened
Office
Politics

Enlightened Office Politics

Understanding, Coping with, and Winning the Game— Without Losing Your Soul

Michael and Deborah Singer Dobson

American Management Association

New York • Atlanta • Boston • Chicago • Kansas City • San Francisco • Washington, D.C.
Brussels • Mexico City • Tokyo • Toronto

Special discounts on bulk quantities of AMACOM books are available to corporations, professional associations, and other organizations. For details, contact Special Sales Department, AMACOM, a division of American Management Association, 1601 Broadway, New York, NY 10019.
Tel.: 212-903-8316   Fax: 212-903-8083
Web site: www.amacombooks.org

This publication is designed to provide accurate and authoritative information in regard to the subject matter covered. It is sold with the understanding that the publisher is not engaged in rendering legal, accounting, or other professional service. If legal advice or other expert assistance is required, the services of a competent professional person should be sought.

Library of Congress Cataloging-in-Publication Data

Dobson, Michael Singer.
    Enlightened office politics: understanding, coping with, and winning the game—without losing your soul / Michael and Deborah Singer Dobson.
        p.   cm.
Includes bibliographical references and index.
ISBN 0-8144-7065-3
1. Office politics.   I. Dobson, Deborah Singer.   II. Title.

HF5386.5.D63   2001
650.1'3—dc21

                                        2001022068

Printing number

10   9   8   7   6   5   4   3   2   1

Dedicated to our siblings, with love

John Patrick Dobson
Lise Dobson Grisham
Barbara Singer King

Contents

Acknowledgments

The authors are grateful to Bill Capstack and Rod Jurado for their research support; to our editor, Ellen Kadin, for her vision of what this book could be and needed to be and for her tireless advocacy to help make it a reality; to Christina McLaughlin for her trenchant analysis and criticism; to Shelly Wert for her detailed editing; and to our agents, Elizabeth Pomada and Michael Larsen, for their thoughtful criticism and for their support and guidance.

Introduction

The Principled Person Meets the World of Office Politics

[F]or the children of this world are in their generation wiser than the children of light.

Luke 16:8

An Introduction to Principled Politics

Can you be an enlightened person and still play office politics? Can you live up to your own ideals as a principled person in the real organizational environment? For many people, there seems to be an inherent contradiction between what seems to be necessary for survival and advancement and what seems to be mandated by one's personal moral and ethical codes.

In fact, it's hard to imagine the concepts of being a "principled person" and "office politics" going together. Politics, in the minds of most people, is virtually the antithesis of principle. And office politics seems even worse: petty, often silly, oriented to personal gain at the cost of the organization as a whole. Unfortunately—and as you probably have already realized—this puts the principled person at a huge tactical disadvantage in the organization. You know the game of office politics is swirling all about you right now, but you feel that you're faced with a terrible choice: play and be effective, or save your soul and suffer for it. As the title of Harvey Mackay's best-selling book has it, you've got to "swim with the sharks without being eaten alive."

Fortunately, we believe that this is a false choice, or at the very least an unnecessary choice. While it's undeniably true that there are unprincipled players in the world of office politics and that there are tactics and strategies for office politics that can be downright immoral, it's also possible to be active and effective in your organization's political environment in ways that are principled and ethical. In fact, it can be wise, ethical, and, above all, necessary. Even more important, if you don't practice office politics the right way, you may be letting down your job, unit, and organization! As the quotation that begins this introduction implies, withdrawing from and refusing to understand the sometimes cruel realities of the environment in which you work and live is not helpful to the principled goals and ideas by which you want to live.

How to Be More Effective without Selling Your Soul in the Process

The purpose of *Enlightened Office Politics* is to help you, someone who strives to be a principled person, be effective in the real world of office politics without selling your soul in the process. Why should you want to do this at all? Because you already know that your ability to get things done, to achieve your goals, to create a more ethical environment that rewards and supports good behavior rather than political sneakiness involves your ability to work with the process as it really is.

Understanding the Reality of Office Politics

In order to help you maintain your principles and understand how to achieve your goals in an ethical way, we first look at the reality of office politics. Why does it exist? What's really going on? By reading this book, you'll learn that, while it is possible to make office politics a more constructive, positive, and useful activity, it's not possible to eliminate it altogether. You'll see why it's essential to understand the behavior and motivations of others, even when you disapprove of them. You'll learn about the essence of power in politics, and why being a principled person can turn out to be an enormous boost to your political power.

Why Do People Play Office Politics?

Motivation, as you'll see, is at the core of the political process. There are a variety of reasons why you might need to be a player in the game of office politics: learning how to choose the tactics that fit your personal values and also achieve your objectives, how to predict the likely tactics of others, and how to equip yourself with the tools to deal with them.

How Can You Learn What's Going On around You?

Office politics in some ways resembles a chess game. Pieces have power in themselves, but their relative positions on the game board really determine what's going on. A pawn is inherently a weak piece, but in the right position on the chessboard it can dominate the game and even achieve a checkmate. Our model of the Political Environment (see Figure 3-1) will provide you the tools you need to understand the dynamic and fluid environment and recognize that powerful pawn (or weak knight). One advantage of office politics over chess is that it is possible for pieces to change sides, and you'll learn ways to influence people to move to your side in the game of office politics.

People and positions and motivations all exist in an environment, and the landscape of your office or your industry has a dramatic effect on the political scene. You'll learn how to create a map of your political environment and learn to read that map to identify other leverage opportunities to achieve your goals.

All of these topics emphasize the level of your understanding and your insight into yourself and others. Understanding is always and inherently principled behavior. You can understand behavior and motives of which you may very well disapprove. Willful blindness is not ethical behavior; it's neglectful and inappropriate. But what do you do with that understanding?

Can You Seek Power without Losing Your Soul?

The part of office politics that often upsets the principled person most is the idea of seeking power. The quest for power is often thought of as inherently immoral, or, at the very least, shady. But that isn't true, or at least not necessarily true. In spite of the views of Lord Acton (who said, "Power tends to corrupt, and absolute power corrupts absolutely"), power can be harnessed in the service of higher goals. Responding to Lord Acton's dictum, U.S. Senator and presidential candidate Adlai Stevenson proposed "power corrupts, but lack of power corrupts absolutely." Being powerless does nothing to advance the goals of principle. Even such a staunch advocate of nonviolence as Mahatma Gandhi did not eschew power; he only chose the type of power that fit the principles and goals he set for himself.

You'll benefit from a deeper understanding of the nature of personal and organizational power, and from learning why your principles are more likely a source of strength than a source of necessary weakness.

Are There Enlightened Role Models for Office Politics the Way It Should Be Played?

While understanding what goes on around you is essential, it's not enough. You have to know how to actually play the game once you know the rules. What do office politicians (of all stripes and levels of principle) actually do? We'll look at role models of effective political behavior and how to identify the right role models in your organizational environment.

What Are the Core Skills of Enlightened Office Politics?

You'll learn that office politicians do their work by using three sets of skills that are normally not considered political but that are in fact political to the core. These skills are at the center of your actual ability to work effectively with the specific, tactical problems in the political environment. They are (1) your communications skills, (2) your skills in effective win/win negotiating, and (3) your understanding of planning and executing a political campaign. You'll learn how to develop and apply each of these skill areas in achieving the results you want.

How Can You Discover the Rules of the Game?

Insights about office politics (and politics in general) are often codified as rules, and you'll learn about the rules of the game in the final section of this book. It may be better to think of rules as guidelines rather than absolutes, because it's still up to you to discover how to apply those rules in the immediate tactical environment in which you live.

Why Are Some Organizations So Destructively Political?

It's clear from most of our everyday experience that some organizations have more of the negative behavior we think of as "political" than do others. There are several reasons for the difference.

First is the attitude that those at the top of the organization often have. If they practice the destructive form of politics, they set the tone and standard for the rest of the organization. We shouldn't be surprised—dismayed, maybe—when others practice the behavior that's been shown to be successful.

Second is the specific issue or objective at stake. When people feel passionately about one side or another of an issue, they tend to tug those in the middle toward one extreme or another. When the situation becomes polarized enough, communication begins to break down and the political environment turns progressively nasty.

The third reason involves the nature of the work and the organization itself. Henry Kissinger famously observed that academic politics is so bitter because the stakes are so small.

He's onto something. It's not about the size of the stakes, but rather about the difficulty of measurement.

We all believe that quality is a positive value, but conflict arises when quality is ill-defined. In fact, one way to determine how negatively political a situation is likely to become is to ask this question: How do we recognize high-quality performance? If there is a concrete answer to the question, negative political behavior tends to be limited. If there is only a subjective answer possible, negative political behavior tends to run rampant.

Objectively Measured Quality

Let's take a sales organization, for example. How can we tell who are the best performers? We measure the sales. There's little or no ambiguity about our rankings, and each person tends to know how he or she stacks up in the hierarchy. Such an environment can be highly competitive, of course, and can even be cutthroat at times. But the battle tends to be about objective criteria and how we can maximize our own performance. We might battle over territories or key accounts, but notice that it's much less likely we'll battle over personalities.

Similarly, the power possessed by each person is fairly easy to determine. If you won the sales contest for the last three quarters in a row, you have some clout you can use on behalf of your accounts, or to gain new accounts. If you've been coming in at the bottom 10 percent of the sales force, you have to trim your sails accordingly.

This environment has politics, but usually of a fairly clean variety. However, not all environments have such objective criteria to go by.

Subjectively Measured Quality

Everyone—educator and education critic alike—believes that quality teachers are crucial to success. But unlike sales performers, whose performance can be clearly and objectively measured, it's harder to determine by objective measurement who are the best teachers. Student performance? What about socioeconomic class, school location, discipline history, or hundreds of other variables? It's obviously easier to get good performance out of preselected gifted and talented students than from a class of troubled and disadvantaged youth, yet the argument could well be made that getting "C" work out of the latter group would demonstrate a higher level of teacher achievement than getting "A" work out of the gifted and talented students.

On the other hand, perhaps the work assigned to the gifted and talented group was so much more difficult, or the work assigned to the disadvantaged class so simple, that you could reach the opposite conclusion. Or it might well be that both teachers were outstanding or that they were measured by different criteria.

The problem here is not our unwillingness to come up with objective criteria; in fact, there are numerous systems purporting to provide objective measurement of teacher quality, each with its advocates. The problem is that one's philosophy, political or otherwise, tends to shape the measurement system. It's based on individual values, and different people hold different values.

Notice what this does to the political environment. Different people and different groups believe quite sincerely that they are the advocates of quality, yet they tug the organization in mutually exclusive directions. One's skill in politics—the human, messy, and personal side of politics—has an enormous impact on one's ability to advance these core beliefs and values. Someone who opposes our side is opposing quality (as we have defined it), and of course people who are against quality must have something deeply wrong with them. Our opposition becomes personal, and the personal becomes ugly.

Or, we live with amorphous performance standards, with each person individually deciding and acting on what he or she believes is quality. This can be quite legitimate. After all, there may in fact be multiple approaches all leading to good results. But what happens when there are a limited number of promotions or advancement opportunities available? How do we determine who is "best" for the job? Because we can't measure "best," yet must decide how to select people for such opportunities, we again turn to the personal and political process. The person selected is regarded by at least some others as less than legitimate in the new role, and we turn to the informal and political system to broker the next promotion in our favor.

The stakes are indeed large in such a conflict, but the behavior that results tends more toward the personal, petty, and bitter.

Lowering Negativity in the Subjectively Measured Organization

The tendency toward nastiness and negative political behavior in such organizations isn't necessarily fated, but it does take some positive action to reverse the trend.

First, determine whether the subjectiveness is inherent or whether a generally accepted and objective standard could exist. If you can create or implement an agreeable measurement standard, you change the dynamic substantially. Beware of the trap of measuring something because it's easy to measure rather than because it's of core relevance. You'll see some organizations putting enormous weight on punctuality not so much because the work is that time-sensitive, but rather because that's one of the few things they can measure on which everyone can agree.

If the subjectiveness is inherent, attitudes from the top have a dramatic effect on behavior below. Is there a spirit of inclusiveness of these differing sets of values? Alternately, has the organization's mission, vision, and values been stated so clearly and firmly that certain types of dissent are no longer possible? Both approaches can work.

Are people trained in negotiation and conflict management techniques to enable them to settle differences in a less negative or destructive manner? Is there management support and buy-in for using those processes when conflict erupts?

Are the criteria for advancement and promotion clear enough that those who seek advancement can figure out what to do to enhance their chances? If you don't want negative political behavior from people, they must have other avenues in which to advance their interests.

Top management support is crucial in reducing negative

political tensions, but your own performance, even at a lower level, can have an impact at least on behavior around you. Your own commitment to lowering the temperature and building consensus and your own practice of the positive political skills, which will be discussed throughout this book, will be a force for positive change.

How Can You Continue to Grow?

For further study, we provide an extensive bibliography that contains many fine references to aid you in your continued personal growth. When you find a reference in this book that strikes you as particularly helpful or insightful, let that be an incentive to discover still more about the subject. Office politics is one of those skill areas that you can work on for a lifetime and still not achieve mastery; it's a subject that rewards continuing study and continuing self-development.

Some books are designed for quick reference when you need a specific bit of information; other books are designed to be read all the way through. While this book is designed for cover-to-cover reading, numerous headings allow you to browse and focus your attention on the areas that are most fruitful for you. Use the index to link the content in the best way for your needs.

This book contains a variety of exercises. Most consist of questions for you to think about, and we give you space to write down your answers. It's more important that you use the exercises as opportunities to think than to necessarily write down comprehensive answers. The way office politics works has certain elements in common no matter where you are, but, at the same time, every organization and every situation is necessarily different. You want to customize your approach; to do that, think about the questions.

Whenever you are learning a new skill, and you are at the same time competing with people already experienced in that skill, it's not a good idea to try out your new idea on the toughest adversary in town. If office politics hasn't been your area of highest achievement in the past, go slow in using these techniques, especially if the organizational environment in which you work is a difficult one. Build on a foundation of small victories rather than shoot for the stars, at least in the beginning.

Office politics is important, and it is particularly important for the principled person who is working toward goals larger than just his or her own self-interest. Modern organizations need a spirit of organizational growth and transformation, and ultimately these can be achieved only through the political environment.

Chapter 1

What Is Office Politics, and Do You Really Have to Care?

How we live is so far removed from how we ought to live, that he who abandons what is done for what ought to be done, will rather bring about his own ruin than his preservation.

Niccoló Machiavelli, *The Prince*, 1532

Few subjects are more misunderstood or the source of more unnecessary pain than office politics. Have you ever thought —or said—things like this?

"I can't stand all the office politics in this company."

"It's not what you know, it's who you know."

"If you don't play the right games and eat lunch with the right people, you'll never get promoted."

If you think these assertions are true, well, frankly, you're right. If you think they are necessarily bad—well, they certainly can be.

One thing is certain: Office politics is inevitable in every organization with three or more people in it. And you know

1

you're faced with a choice: influencer or influenced, knowing or guessing, controller or controlled.

If you don't like this choice, you probably believe that you have only two options—to be an unethical, manipulative swine or to be a saintly but helpless victim of forces beyond your comprehension or control. That's the essential dilemma of the principled person when faced with the reality of office politics in the organization. If you think your only alternatives are to give up your principles or to surrender your effectiveness and your job security, no wonder you think you have only terrible choices.

In fact, being a principled person can make you more effective and more successful in the world of office politics, especially if you look at your situation in terms of your long-term goals and interests.

To play office politics the right way, the principled way, you first have to understand it. In these pages, you'll learn about the human dimension of politics, why it exists, and how it works.

You'll learn how to develop your own strategy for playing the game; for maximizing and using your power in ethical ways; for understanding the games and strategies of your peers, subordinates, and managers; and for surviving and prospering in this political world.

You'll learn how to develop your political skills and use them in appropriate, powerful ways.

And you'll learn how to get results.

Defining Office Politics

> Politics, n. A strife of interests masquerading as a contest of principles.
> Ambrose Bierce, *The Devil's Dictionary*, 1906

Most definitions of politics (or of any controversial topic, for that matter) reflect the moral outlook of the definer. The *American Heritage Dictionary*, for example, describes a politician as "one who is interested in personal or partisan gain and other selfish interests" and politics as "partisan or fac-

tional intrigue within a given group." But the root word "pol-
itic," from *Chamber's Concise 20th Century Dictionary*, means
"in accordance with good policy: acting or proceeding from
motives of policy: prudent: discreet."

Individual Motives

One of the sources of office politics is the inevitable conflicts
that arise among people in any organization. These disagreements may arise from any of the following situations:

- People have principled disagreements about policy and
  direction of the organization.
- People have different visions and goals.
- People have different personal and selfish interests.
- People have egos and like to have them recognized and
  stroked.
- People have different personalities to which others
  react in different ways.
- People remember their own and others' past actions
  and behaviors.

There's nothing very radical, or inherently unprincipled
or evil, in these statements; most people will easily acknowledge their truth: that people don't check their humanity at
the door when they punch in on the time clock.

Scarcity

Scarcity of resources is one of the major factors behind office
politics. From the days of the pyramids to the present, every
organization, company, or government has lived with the reality that there are far more desirable projects and activities
than there are resources to manage them. In other words,
work is infinite, but resources are finite.

Every time senior management gives you a dollar, or a
person, or a week, it becomes a dollar, a person, or a week
management can't give to someone else for something that
also has value. (In financial terms, this is known as "opportunity cost.") That sets up an unavoidable competition, as we

each strive to get the resources we need to accomplish our objectives, and the playing out of the informal competition is what we know as office politics. And if the organization is under stress or financial challenge, the struggle gets that much worse.

It also gets worse when what's at stake is competition for access to status, which is also a kind of limited resource. For most people, when their personal status is at stake, the kid gloves come off.

Office Politics Defined

Our discussion leads us to the following definition of politics:

> Politics: The informal and sometimes emotion-driven process of allocating limited resources and working out goals, decisions, and actions in an environment of people with different and competing interests and personalities.

This definition is intentionally neutral, as simply descriptive as we can make it. It helps us understand what we're about. Here are the key points of this definition amplified:

• *Informal and sometimes emotion-driven*. Office politics is separate from the formal organizational structure and involves human dynamics and emotions, in addition to facts and reason.

• *Allocating limited resources*. The ultimate outcome of office politics—and how success and failure are measured—is how the organization's resources, such as time, money, and people, are allocated.

• *Working out goals, decisions, and actions*. The purpose of office politics is to work out goals, decisions, and actions that can turn into reality. This often involves negotiation, compromise, and application of power.

• *Different and competing interests and personalities*. People have different ideas and desires about what should be done, some based on reason and analysis, some based on emotion or personal agenda. Personal likes and dislikes inevitably affect decisions.

Again, it's important that you notice that this definition is ethically neutral. It describes a process that is inevitable whenever people gather in any sort of organizational context.

Take this test to see if office politics exists in your organization.

1. Count the employees.

2. Does the number exceed three?

3. If the answer to #2 is "yes," office politics definitely exists in your organization.

Within this concept of politics, you can play many different ways for many different goals. Some tactics are unethical, others ethical. Some goals are unethical, others ethical. You must still use office politics as the vehicle to achieve your goals, because it's the ultimate arena in which the necessary decisions will be made and consensus achieved.

What It Means to Be a Principled Person

> Men of principle are sure to be bold, but those who are bold may not always be men of principle.
> Confucius, *Analects*, sixth century B.C.

The fact that you're reading this book suggests that you consider yourself a principled person. What exactly does that mean, and in what ways does that distinguish you from other people?

From where you stand in the organizational environment, there are five basic categories of people:

1. Unprincipled people
2. Differently principled people
3. Indifferently principled people
4. Extremists
5. People like ourselves—principled people

Unprincipled People

Of the five groups, unprincipled people are the easiest to understand. It is not that they have no focus or direction but rather that their focus and direction are oriented toward self-advancement. They are self-centered rather than principle-centered. They evaluate their choices and situation in terms of what maximizes benefit to themselves. Such people are not necessarily evil, although specific actions may be. They are amoral.

The unprincipled person is the one we most often think of when we think of office politicians as a type. Because their primary goal is self-interest, rather than the wider interests of the organization or of other people in the organization, unprincipled people may use a wide variety of manipulative, even sneaky, tactics to achieve their goals. It's hard to trust an unprincipled person, because that trust can be sacrificed at any moment if the unprincipled person receives a better offer or sees a better opportunity.

The unprincipled person often has a short-term focus, which follows logically from that person's overall objectives. Maximizing career success and personal aggrandizement normally involves a series of short-term tactical moves. Some are successful and some are not, but the skilled unprincipled person often has a way of landing on his or her feet.

Differently Principled People

The differently principled person operates from a set of deeply held and deeply felt principles, values, and objectives, but those principles, values, and objectives are very different from the ones you hold. They may well be wrong, destructive, even evil in your judgment, but it's important for you to understand that the differently principled person's beliefs are sincere. On a deeply polarizing topic (abortion, for example), it's clear that people on both sides of the issue who feel strongly about it are in fact sincere and principled, even though their views are diametrically opposed.

There are certain principles that differently principled people tend to have in common, and those are the basic ingredients we mean when we speak of good character. These principles include a commitment to such traditional values as fairness, integrity and honesty, human dignity, service, quality and excellence, development of potential, personal growth, patience, and nurturance and encouragement of others.

While the differences among principled people may not be able to be reconciled, we recognize principle in action through many of the behaviors and commitments we have cited.

Indifferently Principled People

Somewhere between an unprincipled person and a principled person is an indifferently principled person: one whose adherence to principle is nonexistent at worst and spotty at best. Frankly, almost everyone's adherence to principle is spotty at one time or another. Few of us are perfect in our principles; we let down the code of ethics we espouse and actively believe in. Often we rationalize away our failure; sometimes we acknowledge it and move on. Sometimes we resolve to do better in the future; other times we repeat the same failing over and over again.

Here is where the biblical maxim "judge not, lest ye be judged" comes most strongly into play. It's reasonable, appropriate, even necessary to have a clear vision about other people the way they are—their limitations and failings as well as their strengths and virtues. But with the human being, weaknesses and strength come in a single package; you can't have one without the other. It is not inconsistent with principles to accept and adjust to the weaknesses of others. After all, by and large we manage to live with ourselves in spite of our own weaknesses and failures.

Eschewing judgment is not the same as being unaware or blind to these problems. If someone is, for example, indifferently honest, it's appropriate to be skeptical of statements and claims that person makes. If someone is indifferently reliable, it's smart to think of backups and alternative strategies rather than to put your fate in that person's hands. If someone has trouble keeping his or her mouth shut, it's a good idea not to share important confidences. We don't want to overreact, but we do need to react appropriately. Perhaps an otherwise principled person has specific and predictable weaknesses and vulnerabilities. In those areas, we must be guarded and careful. In others, we can be more confident of the person's reliability.

Extremists

A subset of the principled person is the extremist. An extremist is necessarily and inherently driven by certain specific and core principles. For the purposes of this book, we'll define an extremist as someone who believes that his or her specific values or objectives are so important that they obviate the need or obligation to apply the principles of fairness, integrity, dignity, etc. Ends, in the mind of the extremist, necessarily justify the means.

Sometimes the difference between the principled person and the extremist becomes dangerously narrow, especially in their attitude toward compromise and negotiation. Deal making is at the very heart of politics. But how can you stand on principle and yet make a deal without selling out your values in the process? In our discussion of win/win negotiation in Chapter 8, you'll learn a variety of techniques for achieving a principled outcome while still negotiating a deal that satisfies the needs of the other person.

Avoiding Extremism

At the core of avoiding extremism, however, is a critical understanding: values are not necessarily compatible. The single-minded pursuit of one value has a tendency to undercut other values. A common example is honesty. We properly value honesty; we exalt it as a primary virtue. Our national mythology prominently features the legend of George Washington and the cherry tree. But, at the same time, we have the concept of "brutal honesty," the idea of the "little white lie," the "strategic misrepresentation" in negotiation, and many others. If you're too honest or honest in the wrong way, you can damage others and yourself for no particular gain. That doesn't mean we don't care about honesty; quite the contrary. We value honesty and we value human kindness—and the reality is sometimes they are in conflict. What we need is an ecological perspective, in which the most important thing is balance. Too much of one plant or animal destroys others; the right balance provides harmony. Things always relate to one another; nothing stands alone.

In the comparatively narrow world of office politics, it may be easier to keep that ecological perspective in mind. Should your company care about quality and customer service? Of course. But if it ignores the realities of finance or market share, it's likely to go out of business, which will hardly improve its quality and customer service. If, on the other hand, the company worries only about finance and market share and ignores quality and customer service, it will likely find itself in trouble sooner or later. The company needs a balance of virtues rather than the simple-minded pursuit of one at the cost of all others. That's not inconsistent with being a principled person. In fact, it's the basis for how the principled person can deal effectively with the world of office politics.

Principled People

We've implied a definition of a principled person in our discussion of the other categories, but now we need to describe that person more fully. Exactly what is a principled person, and how does that person differ from the other types?

A principled person, for the purposes of this book, is one with a commitment to principled behavior—integrity—at the core. The virtues we associate with a person of integrity are a good summary of the types of behavior and attitude we normally attribute to principled people. Principled people are honest, reliable, dependable, and professional. They do what they say they will do.

Principled people are individuals with a commitment to the organization for which they work. That means they have a shared vision of what the organization is and what it needs to be, and they are willing to commit themselves toward that goal even at the cost of their short-term advancement and success.

A principled person has the skills and drive necessary to advance those goals within the boundaries of good character. Without the skills, without the work, without the effort, principles are simply hot air. A real principled person knows that the work counts and demonstrates a good work ethic about long-term as well as immediate job efforts.

A principled person understands the relationship among the different elements of his or her life—commitments to the job and to the organization but also to family and loved ones, community service, and self-development and self-actualization. A principled person knows how to say "no" when it's appropriate.

Being a principled person, then, is not only a matter of commitment but a matter of work. It's not static, but rather dynamic. You can't be a principled person merely through good thoughts and good feelings. Being principled is normally not the easy way to achievement, but it is the best way.

Maintaining Good Character

As we'll continue to see in this book, the skill of diagnosis, of interpretation, of insight into the motives for different kinds of political behavior is critical as you choose your path across the political landscape. How do you react to different people and their goals? How do you defend yourself? How do you advance your values, your interests, and your goals while still living up to the standards of good character?

While it's important to be right on principle, on values, and in the ingredients of character, as you well know, right isn't nearly enough. The slogan "Might makes right" is most often used as a sarcastic expression that describes reality as we see it, and in that sense it's obvious that there's some practical truth in the slogan. It's descriptive. But character can also be a source of might. Stalin, when told that the Pope disapproved of some of his actions, is reputed to have replied, "And how many divisions does the Pope have?" Military divisions notwithstanding, there's still a pope, but there is no longer a Soviet Union.

Understanding, therefore, that "might" is a complex word that includes a lot of different areas other than *force majeure*, you must therefore also realize that to be effective in dealing with the various people and goals that exist in your organizational environment, it's not enough to be simply right—you must have the power to back up your positions.

Why You Need Power

The fundamental concept in social science is power, in the same sense in which energy is the fundamental concept in physics.
    Bertrand Russell, philosopher and mathematician

Success in politics involves the acquisition and use of power.

The principled person often has an ethical concern about power. Is it morally acceptable to seek power? To answer this question, let's use the engineering definition of power: energy that overcomes resistance and accomplishes work.

For example, you need gasoline to power your car. By itself, this is neither ethical nor unethical. How you get the gasoline is an ethical choice: You can buy it or you can steal it. How you drive the car is an ethical choice: You can drive safely or disregard the rules of the road. What you do with the car is an ethical choice: You can use it as an ambulance or in a drive-by shooting. But gasoline and the running car by themselves are ethically neutral. How you acquire and how you use power and the purposes for which you use your power are subject to ethical rules. The mere fact of power considered alone is morally and ethically neutral.

In the world of people and organizations, the same logic applies. You need power to get any work done.

How to Get Power

The secret of power is the will.
    Giuseppe Mazzini, Italian political thinker and revolutionary leader, 1831

Operationally, playing office politics means getting and using power. Power is ultimately about your ability to get things done, and those characteristics that help you get things done are the elements of power.

Political power is a complex matter. You've observed many people who can get things done, and you may have observed that they get things done in very different ways. There are many routes to power, and many ways to influence events. The Six Types of Power, shown in Figure 1-1, describe a model for developing your power and understanding the power of other people.

The Six Types of Power

• *Role* power is the power inherent in your position. If you're a vice president or a clerk, a member of the executive committee or the picnic committee, if you're in the marketing department or building maintenance, your position in the organization is one measure of your power.

Figure 1-1: The Political Power Model—The Six Types of Power

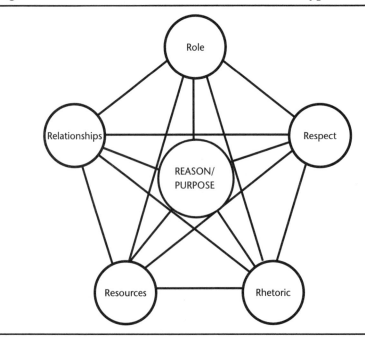

- *Respect* power is the power you get from the opinions others hold about you. If you're respected for your knowledge, your skills, your record of accomplishment, your personal integrity, you gain power. There is a negative version of respect power: fear power.

- *Rhetoric* power is the power you get from your communications ability. If you're persuasive, a good writer, able to speak publicly, a talented negotiator, you gain influence over others from that skill.

- *Resource* power is the power that comes from what you control. If you have the power to approve someone's budget, to decide which projects are funded, to decide who gets access to mainframe computer resources, or to select who goes on the business trip to Paris, your control of these resources translates into political power.

- *Relationship* power is the power that comes from whom you know and how you know them. If you're a golfing buddy of the chairman of the board, or the protégé of a vice president on the rise, or even friends with the right clerk in accounting, you get power on the basis of those relationships.

- *Reason* or *purpose* power is the power you get from being goal oriented. If you have a clear vision for your department or for the company, you automatically have more power and influence than someone who has no goal at all. This type of power is essential if you're going to be an ethical politician who isn't thought of by others as "political."

There are three key lessons you can draw from this discussion:

1. You don't have to be equally strong in all areas to be powerful.
2. These sources are interactive: Strength in one area influences all the others; weakness in one area detracts from all the others.
3. The core of power is in having a reason or purpose for its use and application.

What If You Decide Not to Play?

> When bad men combine, the good must associate; else
> they will fall one by one, an unpitied sacrifice in a con-
> temptible struggle.
> > Edmund Burke, British parliamentarian, 1770

But what if you don't want any part of the process of office
politics? Surely, if you do a good job, work hard, avoid political behavior, and stay honest and friendly, you'll be okay,
right?

Wrong. While we would all prefer to believe good work
speaks for itself, there's the problem of who defines what
good work is. There's the problem of determining how credit
is shared in a team environment. And there's the reality that
factors other than ability, skill, and effort influence the decisions about who gets promoted and who gets ahead. That's
why office politics—the informal part of the organization—is
unavoidable and inescapable.

Marilyn Moats Kennedy, one of the most respected au-
thorities on office politics, warns of the five myths of the
working world:[1] that hard work equals success (it depends);
that only incompetent people are fired (political and relationship failures are far more commonly the reason); that performance appraisals fairly assess performance (more often,
they measure personality, style, and fit); that office politics is
a nasty game played by bad people (while sometimes that's
true, that attitude promotes victimhood); and that you either
understand politics or you don't (absolutely false—you can
and must choose to recognize its reality and inevitability and
learn to be effective in it).

Deciding not to play office politics, unfortunately, simply turns you into a victim, someone who is helpless to respond or deal with the vicissitudes of the workplace. In
today's competitive environment, this can lead to a layoff, or
worse.

Don't choose victimhood when you can choose success.
Being a principled person necessarily means that you believe
your principles matter. Failure—especially unnecessary failure—means not only that you suffer but that the principles

and values you care about, the work you care about, and the people you care about do not advance. While a principled person normally doesn't seek out a fight, he or she should not shrink from one when it's necessary.

Note

1. Marilyn Moats Kennedy, *Office Politics: Seizing Power, Wielding Clout* (New York: Warner Books, 1980), pp. 24–48.

Chapter 2

Positive and Principled Reasons for Learning to Play Office Politics Like a Pro

You never really win anything in politics. All you get is a chance to play for higher stakes and perform at a higher level.

John Sears, American political strategist, 1980

Probably the worst reason to play office politics is for its own sake, although people do it all the time. For both ethical and practical reasons, you need to have your goals and objectives clearly in mind in politics. If, as we've observed, office politics by itself is morally and ethically neutral, then we use it as a means to achieve certain ends. We select goals and strategies to achieve those goals.

The Power of Purposefulness

In the Political Power Model (see Figure 2-1), the circle "Reason/Purpose" is in the center of the power grid, and that's

Figure 2-1: The Political Power Model—Reason/Purpose

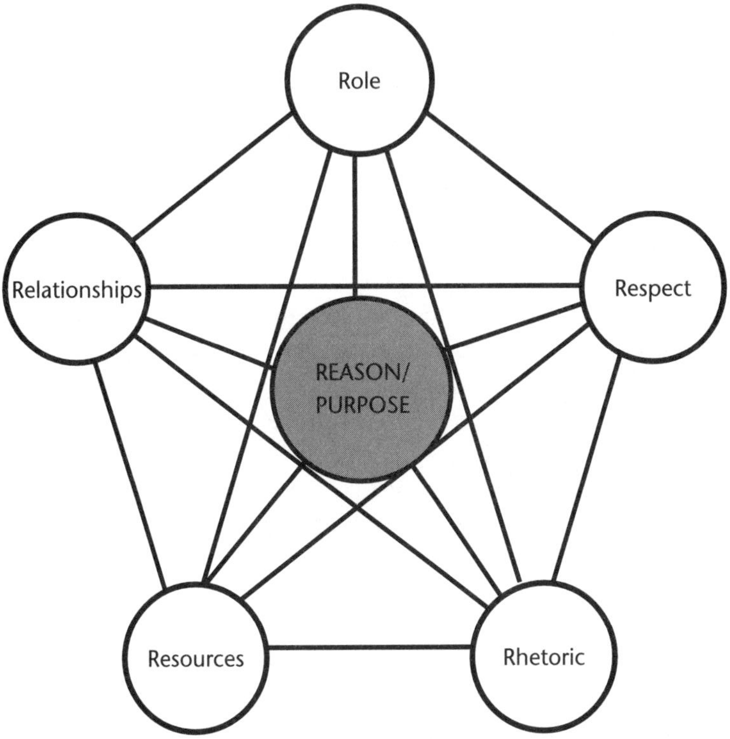

no accident. The people most often labeled "political" in the pejorative sense are those who play for the sake of playing, who are obviously "on the make," and who have no purpose other than their own narrow interests. We've defined those as unprincipled people, and they are probably the most common types you are likely to encounter in the organizational environment. They are quite common in most organizations.

Effective office politicians don't seem "political" in the common sense of the word, the sense that people use to distinguish between a "politician" and a "statesman." In terms of our definitions, the person labeled a "politician" is likely to be an unprincipled person, the person labeled as a "statesman" a principled person (or differently principled person).

(The extremist, on the other hand, is likely not to be seen as "political" in any sense, because he or she tends to disregard the political process whenever it doesn't quickly deliver the desired results.) Both politicians and statesmen use the same basic tools; the statesman is considered to be using them for a higher purpose and with higher ethical standards.

Fortunately, in many cases, helping the organization, the department, your boss, and your peers succeed is often a good path to promotion, power, and career advancement. The conflict between principle and politics is often illusory.

There are various reasons, both good and bad, to make office politics a deliberate part of your work life. You need to understand both the good and bad reasons: the good, because you want to know how to use them effectively, and the bad, because you know that others are motivated by them. To make matters somewhat more complex, the same category of motive can be either good or bad, depending on details. In the following section, we'll explore the world of political motivation.

Setting Political Goals

The secret to success is constancy of purpose.
Benjamin Disraeli, British Prime Minister, 1872

To be effective in using the tools of political analysis and power, you must be absolutely clear in your objective or objectives. There's nothing wrong with pursuing multiple objectives as long as they are related to and support one another and as long as your relative priorities among the objectives are clear.

As you consider the reasons you may engage in political behavior, whether or not you feel you're successful at it, remember that you also need to consider the reasons the people around you may be engaging in political behavior, both in support of and in opposition to your goals. The exercise at the end of the sections that follow will help you organize your thoughts.

TIP! When you write in this book (or on separate sheets of paper if you prefer) about political issues involving coworkers or bosses, it's a good idea to do this *outside* the office—candid assessments (especially if they're unflattering) have a way of getting back to the person they're about.

The reasons you and others may be (or in some cases should be) engaging in political behavior are diverse. They fall into a number of different categories, which we discuss in the sections that follow.

Organizational Goals

> Where there is no vision, the people perish.
> Book of Proverbs

Because the backbone of an organization is people, achieving the organization's mission, vision, and values is an inherently political act. Do you want the company to succeed? Do you want customers to experience quality of product and service? Do you care about the professional and organizational legacy you leave? These are reasons to choose to use political behaviors.

Do you really have to play politics to help the organization achieve its goals? Frequently you do, because not all of the people in the organization see their interests as the same as the organization's. Perhaps a management initiative that will improve quality, profit, and market share threatens to eliminate certain programs and directions—and jobs—in which others have invested a lot of their career and energy. You may be able to persuade others to see their interests as more in line with those of the organization—but sometimes you cannot.

To choose the organizational perspective as your goal means to select political tactics in line with the goal. Here is an arena in which you as a true principled person can shine.

By choosing integrity and honesty as a core tactic, by operating from a sense of organizational purpose, by aiming to have a positive impact where you work, by developing your skills and knowledge, you can make the all-too-common negative reality of office politics into a force for good. And it's been done time after time, in organization after organization.

Here's an example: Sam Walton of Wal-Mart received a letter from a Brazilian businessman who had purchased a discount chain and wanted to interview him about retailing strategies. "Only later," said the businessman, "did I realize he was as interested in learning from us as we were in learning from him. . . . Later we launched a joint venture with Wal-Mart in South America."[1] Walton was generous with his own knowledge and at the same time willing to learn and grow.

This is a "statesman" strategy for office politics. Before you adopt it, make sure there is an organizational vision in which you can believe. Remember, there are only three basic strategies for career fulfillment: (1) do only what you love, (2) learn how to love what you do, or (3) get the heck out.

ASSESSMENT OF ORGANIZATIONAL GOALS

Answer the following questions candidly about yourself and how you see others, using additional paper if necessary.

1. Do I have a vision for what this organization could and should be?

   _____

   _____

2. Is there an official vision for this organization (published as a mission statement or elsewhere)?

   _____

   _____

3. Is there a conflict between the official vision and the way people really live and behave? If so, describe it.

_____

_____

4. Is my vision in tune with the official vision of the organization as I understand it? If not, how does it differ?

_____

_____

5. Are there significant obstacles in the organization that may prevent its achieving its vision? If so, describe them. If the objections or obstacles come from specific people, name them and their positions.

_____

_____

6. How strongly do I believe in my vision or the organization's vision? What risks would I be willing to take to help it become actualized?

_____

_____

7. What is at stake for those (if any) who oppose the organization's vision or my vision? How will they gain or lose if I am successful? (This helps determine how hard they are likely to fight.)

_____

_____

Using the Exercise in Your Work

Vision—yours and others—is one of the key ingredients in leadership. Understanding the organization's vision, how it relates to your own, and how it is applied in practice helps you determine at the most fundamental level whether a good fit exists between you and the organization. If it doesn't, ask yourself whether a workable change, either in yourself or in the organization, is possible.

Within the organization, many people operate without a sense of vision or mission, or with one that is cloudy and unexpressed. They lose the ability to set goals and are far weaker in their ability to influence others.

Having a vision isn't automatic. For many of us, it requires thinking and self-analysis. Work on this and you'll find yourself stronger and better equipped to provide leadership at any level in the organization.

Project Goals

> Amid a multitude of projects, no plan is devised.
>   Publilius Syrus, 42 B.C.

Projects are political, and big projects are even more so.

If you've managed projects, you've probably noticed that you seldom, if ever, get the time, resources, people, and authority you need. Projects take place in an atmosphere of scarcity and politics, because projects necessarily compete with other projects for limited resources. No matter how valid and worthwhile your project goals happen to be, other project goals also have value and compete for the same pool of resources in the organization. Often, you can't possibly accomplish your objective without the willing and voluntary cooperation of others over whom you have no official control or authority whatsoever—the very definition of a political environment.

Your biggest opportunity to affect a project outcome is usually in the stage in which the project is defined, something most project managers overlook. A project is never simply an end in itself; it is a means to an end. Sometimes, it's a means to several ends held by different people, who tug the project this way and that, striving for advantage, while you, the project manager, are caught in the middle. These people are known as project stakeholders, and the skills of stakeholder analysis and stakeholder management are core competencies in project management.

Always consider the various goals people have for your project. Be on the lookout for any constituency devoted to keeping your project from success. Identify possible conflicts and tradeoffs among the disparate goals people have. Remember, if you manage the wrong project (one that doesn't achieve the goals people have set for it), even if you do so brilliantly, it's still a failure.

The related political problem is dealing with projects when you don't actually know the objective. Unfortunately, the answer is that you've got to dig. Look for implied objectives, ways the project ties into organizational or customer objectives—or, sometimes, the career goals of your manager. Prepare a list of objectives, and take it to your customers and managers; get their feedback, and refine the list. It's up to you to figure out how to succeed, on the simple grounds that if you fail, you are the one who will be punished.

ASSESSMENT OF PROJECT GOALS

Answer these questions to identify the political dimension and issues surrounding the projects for which you are responsible.

1. How would your boss define your current official role in managing your project? Is your official authority in writing, or informal?

---

2. What authority (if any) do you have to make or approve purchases, to negotiate and approve contracts, or to make other decisions that bind your organization legally or financially?

_____

_____

3. For each key member of your project team, does that person report to you in a formal sense? If not, what level of authority do
   you possess (e.g., able to fire, reprimand, dismiss from team)? Do
   any members of your project team outrank you?

_____

_____

4. Who is responsible for the creation of the plan, the approval of
   changes to the plan, the maintenance of the plan, and the making of work assignments from the plan? If not you, where do you
   fit in?

_____

_____

5. Do you have direct access to the ultimate customer or client for
   the project, or do you have to go through intervening management (internal or external)? Are you accepted by the customer
   as a technical authority? Do you regularly attend top-level meetings that impact the project?

_____

_____

6. At what point do you have to gain the approval of others higher
   in the organization to make project-related decisions? Do you
   have enough respect and acceptance from higher authority for
   your recommendations to be seriously considered?

_____

_____

7. List the key organizational players with concern for this project. Are there people in power positions who have agendas (hidden or clear) that affect the project outcome, resources, priority, or methodology?

_____

_____

8. What is the relative priority of this project compared with that accorded other projects within the organization? How do other organizational priorities affect your project?

_____

_____

9. What political or organizational interests are at stake in your project? Consider not only the overall organization but the effects on specific other departments and individuals, both positive and negative.

_____

_____

Using the Exercise in Your Work

A lack of awareness and understanding of the political dynamic surrounding your project is a key source of potential failure. By thinking through the answers to these questions, you will be far better prepared to manage your project, or if you determine that the political environment has already doomed your project, to protect yourself and organizational resources in the process.

Defensive Goals

> The defensive form of war is in itself stronger than the offense.
>
> Karl von Clausewitz, *On War*, 1832

Another common reason to play politics is that you see your-self in a highly political environment with others who don't have your best interests at heart. Unilateral disarmament is generally considered unwise. People who look like victims get treated like victims, or as Hawkeye Pierce said to Frank Burns in an episode of the 1970s TV sitcom *M*A*S*H*, "You invite abuse. It would be impolite not to accept it."

Do you have enemies who wish you personal ill? Does your boss dislike you? Is your environment filled with cut-throat tactics? You may be seeking improved political skills in order to defend yourself against others who are using their political skills against you. When we speak of a "political" organization in a derogatory manner, what we normally mean is one that is sick with office politics: negative, hurtful, destructive. "A sick environment," observes the political car-toonist Doug Marlette, "encourages the worst in all of us. When every cubicle is a battlement, every coworker a poten-tial enemy, it's hard to resist the undertow. . . ."[2]

The first defensive strategy is to maximize your informa-tion networks, both formal and informal. Knowledge, after all, is a key precursor to power. Knowing what's going on, being plugged into the rumor mill, knowing what others are saying behind your back are all critical to your success.

Develop your own spy network, and learn to be a spy yourself. But how can spying be principled, ethical, enlight-ened behavior? Like many of the tactics in this volume, there is a somewhat fuzzy line to be drawn between ethical and unethical methods of gathering information. On one side of the line is behavior that is clearly ethical. A significant part of the CIA's intelligence-gathering mission consists of subscrib-ing to just about every newspaper and magazine in the world and reading them to abstract key information. This informa-tion is available and published; it needs to be collated and analyzed to be useful. Clearly, the mere act of reading and collating publicly available information is hard to classify as shady, much less unethical.

Another spy tactic is to develop sources of information and relationships with people. Such relationships, like other forms of information gathering, can be either ethical or un-ethical, depending on how they are practiced. The key, as noted previously, has to do with your personal integrity and your commitment to organizational win/win success, which is described in more detail in Chapter 8. When you are working solidly for the interests of your organization, such relationships are more likely to fall on the side of principle.

On the other side of the line is behavior that is clearly unethical. Avoid certain underhanded use of intelligence, such as using your information to discredit a rival—unless, of course, the conduct is so far over the line that you can't *not* tell—cover up the truth, or bully others into compliance. Be aware that these behaviors are practiced by many people in the organization, and be prepared to defend yourself. (Always make sure you are familiar with the many games and tactics you might find ethically inappropriate to use, because you may need to cope with them coming from other people.)

A few additional strategies for improving your defensive position in the organization:

• Keep good documentation. A good strategy is to keep a daily work diary, but be careful to write only factual information in it, as opposed to opinions and ventings about unpleasant events. Also, keep good notes on the results of your intelligence activities so that you can see the bigger picture develop over time.

• Consider confronting unethical power seekers, in private and carefully planned, with the goal of negotiating a peace treaty. (You'll find a detailed discussion on negotiation techniques in Chapter 8.)

• Develop and implement a way to get regular feedback—an outside perspective—on your own conduct, in the areas of (1) performance, (2) accordance between the organization's principles and objectives and yours, (3) relationship problems, (4) role issues, (5) communications, (6) resource management, (7) vision, and (8) perspective. Ask people with organizational power how you can change and develop yourself as a candidate for future advancement and new roles.

• Above all, maintain a record of high integrity and good performance. If you do, many attacks on you will be discounted and not believed.

You'll find some analytical worksheets in this volume to help you organize your intelligence dossier and analyze the people in your work sphere.

ASSESSMENT OF DEFENSIVE NEEDS

Answer the following questions about dangers in your work situation that might require mounting an effective defense.

1. Do you have reason to believe that you look and act like a victim to other people? If so, what are the characteristics that make others think that? Can you modify those perceptions?

    _____

    _____

2. Do you particularly dislike certain coworkers, bosses, or subordinates and consider them personal enemies? If so, what is it about them that makes you feel that way?

    _____

    _____

3. Do others in the organization consider you a personal enemy or treat you as one? Why?

    _____

    _____

4. Is your organization particularly political in a cutthroat or nasty way? What specific incidents, situations, or people make you think that?

    _____

    _____

5. Do you often feel like an outsider in your own department or organization? What makes you feel that way? Is it voluntary or involuntary on your part?

_____

_____

6. Are you often the last one to know about impending job announcements, reorganizations, policy changes, and big corporate news? If so, do you seek out that information using the informal grapevine?

_____

_____

7. How good is your organizational spy network? If it is not good, describe any qualms you have about developing it. Are those qualms rooted in facts or your values, or are they more a matter of fear and uncertainty?

_____

_____

Using the Exercise in Your Work

Take charge of your own environment and resolve to be aware of your overall situation. An appropriate attention to self-defense is a necessary reality in organizational life. In business, decisions are taken for the good of the business and/or for the good of the power players in the business, and not necessarily for your own personal good. As you identify any deficiencies in your self-protective strategies, develop a personal action plan to make yourself more secure. Children are necessarily dependent on their parents, but it's a bad idea to get yourself into a parental relationship with your organization.

Career Advancement

> The trouble with the rat race is that even if you win
> you're still a rat.
>
> > Lily Tomlin, comedienne

In a study of more than one thousand people who experienced job failures, Marilyn Moats Kennedy found that only 25 percent of the people failed because they couldn't do the job technically. Of the remainder, 35 percent were incompatible with their bosses in terms of values or of work style, 25 percent could not get along with or win acceptance from their peers, and 15 percent left or were fired because they could not accept the values of the organization as they understood them.[3]

Issues of career advancement and even career stability can't ignore the informal organizational environment, the importance of human relations, the stylistic as well as substantive issues—in short, office politics.

Climbing the Management Pyramid

According to the traditional pyramid of management, there are more jobs available on the bottom levels than at the top (Figure 2-2). Think of the management pyramid as an elaborate game of musical chairs, with fewer seats available each time the music stops. After a while, you advance only if someone saves you a seat.

The first few promotion rungs on the ladder are strongly affected by ability—but even then, politics plays a role. Once you've passed the first few levels of promotion, everyone else in your peer group has also demonstrated competence. The marginal differences in actual competence are no longer the most significant element in getting your next promotion. Instead, people skills, relationship building, management skills, persuasive ability, and desire for the job are critical: in other words, skills related to office politics. The strategy of simply doing a good job and not playing politics in hopes that you will be magically singled out and rewarded with promotion is not a very reliable method—it's time to outgrow the "promotion fairy."

Figure 2-2: The Management Pyramid

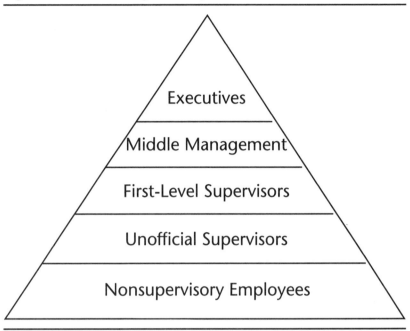

Executives

Middle Management

First-Level Supervisors

Unofficial Supervisors

Nonsupervisory Employees

One core area that requires political skills is the section marked "Unofficial Supervisors" in Figure 2-2. One of the most frustrating situations you may find yourself in is being assigned what are essentially supervisory responsibilities without being given the title, the authority, or the money. You may even think it is unfair, and, arguably, it is. However, it's common enough that a better way to think about it is as an audition for a later promotion. It's far more difficult to remove or demote someone after an official promotion; it's easier to let someone "try out" unofficially and then return the person to the ranks if it doesn't work out. When it doesn't work out, it's much less often a reflection of the job capability of the person than a reflection of that person's weaknesses in office politics skills.

Advancement Goals

Many people seem to be motivated by money, but that turns out often to be an unsatisfactory or incomplete explanation for their behavior. Money, obviously, allows the acquisition of material goods, but it can also be a way of keeping score of one's standing relative to that of others, a way to measure praise and respect, a method of achieving personal security, or any number of things depending on the individual. The "why" of money may be more important than the "what."

Similarly, most of us wish to be promoted in our careers, but a promotion is seldom an end in itself. For promotions as with money, the "why" may be far more important than the "what." We all learn eventually that the wrong promotion may make our situation worse, in spite of a raise, a new title, and an office with a window.

The importance of the following exercise is to focus on your motivations for career advancement in terms of the benefits you are seeking. With this knowledge clear in your mind, you can do a much better job of seeing the opportunities that may exist and focusing your career development strategies toward a goal that will truly satisfy you.

ASSESSMENT OF CAREER ADVANCEMENT GOALS

Identify the specific career goals you have and would like to pursue, and circle the relative importance from A (most important) to C (nice but optional).

1. Making more money	A	B	C
2. Having more power and influence over other people	A	B	C
3. Having more control over my work situation	A	B	C
4. Being more included in the process	A	B	C
5. Gaining status in the organization	A	B	C
6. Being recognized by others for my achievements	A	B	C
7. Expanding and improving my professional skills	A	B	C
8. Opportunity for travel	A	B	C
9. Showing others that I have what it takes	A	B	C
10. Pleasing or impressing a specific person (other than myself)	A	B	C

Additional Reasons

11. _____	A	B	C
12. _____	A	B	C
13. _____	A	B	C

Using the Exercise in Your Work

Success has to be self-defined. If you achieve someone else's idea of success, you'll still feel empty and unfulfilled. People who are clear about what they want find more options and opportunities to pursue those goals.

At some point, you will likely want to negotiate a raise, a promotion, or some other advancement or opportunity. You can only get something from what is available. If there's a promotion or salary freeze, for example, your options are necessarily limited. But what about the other things you want? When you give people a wider set of options that will meet your needs, you increase the likelihood of getting at least some of what you want.

Coping with Subjectivity and Dealing with Performance Evaluations

> The human understanding when it has once adopted an opinion . . . draws all things else to support and agree with it. . . . For what a man had rather were true he more readily believes.
>
> Sir Francis Bacon, English statesman
> and philosopher, 1620

Are you doing a good job? Who decides? How can you measure it? Do you and your boss or you and your employees see it the same way? Most of us would probably prefer that our evaluation be based on objective measurements, and certainly some of our job elements can be assessed using objective criteria. But normally not all job elements can be assessed that way.

An enormous amount of what happens in the workplace

is measured subjectively, not objectively. Intangible and un-expressed values, attitudes, styles, visions, and personalities affect how performance is defined and evaluated. It's not enough to say, "I do good work" without considering the factors that make different people define "good" differently.

There are inherent difficulties in performance evaluation, and that's why politics ends up playing a significant role. And don't forget that performance evaluation is not just done in the context of your performance appraisal but goes into the formation of others' judgment (bosses, peers, subordinates) about your performance year-round.

First, subjectivity is unavoidable in the process of evaluation. Much of what's evaluated can't be exactly counted or measured. In addition, the personality fit between boss and employee legitimately impacts productivity and results, and nothing could be more arbitrary or subjective than that.

Second, career advancement, salary increases, and sometimes job security itself are the outcome of the evaluation process, giving employees very high stakes in the outcome.

Third, performance appraisals can be a tool to achieve supervisory goals. Imagine that a supervisor who wants to get rid of an employee she or he considers a poor performer and that the same employee wants to transfer to another department, feeling that he or she is being unfairly treated by the supervisor. If the supervisor gives the employee a performance appraisal she or he believes accurately reflects the performance, the poor appraisal will likely scuttle the transfer. On the other hand, a satisfactory appraisal may get rid of the employee, which can be quite a benefit to both parties (and is of questionable ethics). Many different factors play into how supervisors end up appraising performance.

Understanding the subjective criteria and making sure you meet them to get good appraisals is another purpose of playing office politics.

It's important to manage the performance appraisal system creatively and effectively. Be proactive by keeping good records of your own work and your own accomplishments. Regularly brief your manager on what you've done and what you've accomplished, using a short memo for the purpose. Bring the memos with you at the start of the appraisal process, and assist the boss *not* in giving you a puff-piece evaluation but in writing a thorough and thoughtful evaluation by providing the necessary documentation. You'll both benefit.

ASSESSMENT OF SUBJECTIVITY CONCERNS

Answer the following questions about your work situation.

1. Do you have a written position description? If so, is it an accurate description of your real job? How does it differ?

_____

_____

2. Do you have written performance standards or goals? Is it clear how your performance will be measured? If not, what elements are subjective—the opinion of your boss or someone else?

_____

_____

3. Do you believe your boss has a good understanding of the issues and challenges you face in getting the work done? How do your understanding and your boss's differ?

_____

_____

4. Are you aware of any unexpressed evaluation criteria, especially items you would consider "little things," that have a disproportionate effect on how your boss perceives your performance?

_____

_____

5. Whether your last performance appraisal was positive or negative, did you believe it accurately reflected your real performance? If not, how did you see the differences?

_____

_____

6. Do you believe there is a lot of "playing favorites" in your department? How and where would you identify it?

_____

_____

7. What specific behaviors seem to get someone singled out either positively or negatively?

_____

_____

Using the Exercise in Your Work

Tax advisors recommend that you start your tax planning before the end of the year, because most of the strategies that can lower your tax bill have to be done in advance. The same logic applies to performance appraisals, which makes thinking through these questions particularly important. The biggest thing you want to avoid on a job description is being surprised. And the way to avoid being surprised is to be proactive in setting meaningful goals, discovering problems with plenty of time to solve them, and organizing yourself so that your manager has the best and most complete view of what it is you do and have done in the rating period. Use your answers to these questions to prepare yourself in plenty of time to take positive action.

Being Part of the Team and Working with Corporate Culture

> Almost all absurdity of conduct arises from the imitation
> of those whom we cannot resemble.
> Samuel Johnson, English lexicographer and critic, 1751

"Because everybody else does" is another reason for playing office politics; at least, it's a reason some people do. Sometimes we do it to imitate those whom we admire (or fear). Sometimes we do it to fit in. Notice that these are motives that often apply to the unprincipled person, because they often seem like the best way to meet his or her objectives.

The Harvard Medical School psychologist and consultant Steven Berglas observes, "You want to know how leadership works? Throw out the mission statements; don't bother with values statements; just look at how the company leader behaves and you'll know with 100 percent certainty how the employees will act and feel about their employer and their employment status."[4]

Some organizations operate in "win-lose" mode: there is a certain finite supply of goodies (raises, bonuses, good job assignments, promotions) to distribute among a fixed group of employees, and if one employee gets something, it means that another employee by definition does not. When this kind of thinking typifies the organizational environment, it's invariably done from the top down. When the behavior originates in top leadership, it's fairly predictable that the rest of the organization will go the way of the company in David Mamet's play *Glengarry Glen Ross*; in other words, politics of a particularly nasty variety. Discrediting opponents and grabbing for credit start to seem like good tactics for getting one's fair share (or more than one's fair share) of the pot. The "win/lose" organization is, unfortunately, not uncommon. When you're in it, you have a limited range of choices. If you don't fight, you lose. If you do fight, you lose integrity. Or, of course, you can quit.

Playing politics can also be about acceptance. "I don't even badmouth [others] for professional gain, but just to show I'm in the know, to get the person I'm talking to to like me," observed one manager.[5] Personal insecurity, a need to be liked, a need for inclusion all become reasons for political behavior.

If you find that you behave in political ways because of insecurity or the desire to fit in, be careful to avoid tactics that can produce the opposite result. Here's one more case in which principled, enlightened behavior is also practical behavior. For example, the tendency to gossip is very common, especially when you are trying to show that you fit in. Malicious gossip, among its other problems, frequently gets back to the person being gossiped about, with the result that you make an unnecessary enemy.

The desire to please and fit in with senior management is sensible at its roots, on the grounds that if you don't look like a member of the club, you probably won't be asked to join the club. Look out for the hidden agendas in this situation. Here's a true story:

> I was talking to my boss about my career potential one day, and he said, "You'll never be a vice president here no matter what you do."
>
> I was shocked. "Why not?"
>
> He said, "The CEO went to Yale, and there are six other Yalies who are directors or vice presidents. Not a single vice president failed to attend an Ivy League school—and you didn't. Nothing personal. I won't make vice president, either.
>
> A year later, he was gone. And a year after that, so was I.

The "hidden keys to the executive suite" differ from organization to organization. It's also possible to overcome them; while a lack of an Ivy League diploma would certainly be an obstacle in the organization just described, people get ahead all the time without having their tickets punched in the right place. You can change the rules of the game, but only through exceptional effort in some other part of the environment. Accomplishing this requires careful study and analysis.

ASSESSMENT OF "FITTING IN" GOALS

Answer the following questions about the political environment in which you work.

1. How ethical and principled do you believe your CEO is? What characteristics and behaviors make you have that opinion? If you identify ethical or principle gaps, what are they?

   _____

   _____

2. To what extent are the virtues and failings of the CEO mirrored in other top managers? Are there exceptions? If so, are those people "in the loop" or "out of the loop"?

   _____

   _____

3. Assess your immediate supervisor and second-level supervisor according to the previous two questions.

   _____

   _____

4. Is there competition for a limited supply of "goodies"? Describe the goodies and the competition.

   _____

   _____

5. Do you believe you need to be in the gossip loop to fit in? If so, have you ever made remarks about someone just to fit into the conversation?

   _____

   _____

6. Are there patterns and affinity groups among the more powerful members of the organization—same school, same race/gender/ ethnicity, same clothing styles, same hobbies and interests? What are they? Can you easily (and ethically) adopt them, or not?

_____

_____

Using the Exercise in Your Work

There are criteria in the unofficial organization that determine whether you're considered "part of the team." Because you frequently have at least some degree of control over many of these criteria, you need to know what they are and how they work. Thinking through these questions will help you figure out exactly what the game is, how you might fit in, and frankly see if you really want to play.

For the Sake of the Game

> A passion for politics stems usually from an insatiable need, either for power, or for friendship or adulation, or a combination of both.
> Fawn M. Brodie, *Thomas Jefferson*, 1974

It may seem strange that some people simply think office politics is fun and play the game for the sake of the game. Power is seductive, and some people accumulate it for the sake of having it. (This is also a typical motivation of an unprincipled person.) In fact, there's nothing wrong with enjoying the game; mastery of office politics—as, indeed, of most skills— comes easiest to those who truly enjoy it for its own sake. The problem comes when the enjoyment of the game and the lust for power become exclusive ends in themselves, devoid of ultimate or external purpose.

But as innumerable Western movies have taught us, the problem with being the fastest gun in the West is that people want to challenge you, and sooner or later someone will show up who's faster than you. On the other hand, if you put your gun in the service of a cause, then others can value and appreciate your mastery and support you rather than fight you.

"For the sake of the game" is not fundamentally a principled reason for playing office politics, but the truth is that sometimes what is positive is also fun. In other words, some people are principled and also enjoy office politics on the tactical, or game, level. If "for the sake of the game" is among the reasons you choose to play office politics, so be it. Make sure, however, that it is neither the sole nor the primary reason for playing. If it is, it will lead to constant temptation in the direction of unprincipled behavior.

It tends to be the case that people do not do well what they fundamentally do not enjoy at all. Your mental attitude toward the environment of office politics considered purely as sport or game can make you more or less effective at it. If you hate every aspect of it, you'll find it hard to be good enough. If you love it a little too much, you'll find yourself overdoing it. The following "political IQ" assessment will help determine the attitude with which you approach the game. If you fall into either extreme—"political pro" or "political innocent"—be careful because your attitude likely will have consequences for you within the organization.

ASSESSMENT OF YOUR POLITICAL IQ

Rate how the following statements describe you.

Characteristic	Strongly Describes		Somewhat Describes		Not At All
1. I believe the quality of my work speaks for itself.	1	2	3	4	5
2. Office politics keeps us from getting good work done.	1	2	3	4	5
3. I am a self-starter whose own high standards drive my work.	1	2	3	4	5
4. I believe emotions should play very little role in decisions.	1	2	3	4	5

Characteristic	Strongly Describes		Somewhat Describes		Not At All
5. I believe being right is more important than building relationships.	1	2	3	4	5
6. I believe that many people in management care less about quality than I do.	1	2	3	4	5
7. I believe authority and re-spect must be earned by those in power, not auto-matically assumed.	1	2	3	4	5
8. I would hate being thought of as a "brown-noser."	1	2	3	4	5
9. I pride myself on always telling the truth, regardless of consequences.	1	2	3	4	5
10. I would never gather power for its own sake.	1	2	3	4	5
11. I don't gossip or listen to gossip.	1	2	3	4	5
12. I believe people who play office politics are often less able or skilled.	1	2	3	4	5

Total Score _____

SCORE

49–60   *Political Pro.* You're deeply involved in the political process every day and in every way.

37–48   *Politically Savvy.* You understand and cope well with office politics, but it's not an all-consuming passion.

24–35   *Politically Aware.* You dislike the game but under-stand that it's real and necessary. You can take some political actions if you really have to.

12–23   *Politically Innocent.* You not only dislike office poli-tics; you believe it's neither necessary nor ethical. You believe your work speaks for itself.

Using the Exercise in Your Work

Developing a balanced perspective on office politics is one of the keys to playing the game. Depending on how you score in this exercise, you might decide that certain elements of your attitude require adjustment to make you more effective. If so, use the information and ideas in this book as ways to help you achieve an appropriate balance in support of your goals.

Analyzing Your Own Reasons

> Herein lies political genius, in the identification of an individual with a principle.
>
> Georg Wilhelm Friedrich Hegel,
> *The German Constitution*, 1802

Armed with this analysis, you are now ready to examine your own motives and goals for office politics. Consider all the possible motives; it's often the case that more than one applies. If a motive doesn't apply to you, consider whether it should; is there an organizational purpose to which you can aspire, a vision you'd like to make real? Consider whether the motives that honestly apply to you are compatible with being a principled person, or whether you need to rethink your own values and self-image.

As you do this, also consider the motives of others in the organization. Why are they playing or failing to play office politics? What does their choice of tactics represent? Are they principled, unprincipled, differently principled, or extremists—or some combination of these, depending on what's at stake on a given day?

After you complete that exercise, you'll learn more about the environment in which politics takes place: people and the organization.

ASSESSMENT OF YOUR REASONS FOR USING OFFICE POLITICS

After completing the previous worksheet (or at least thinking about your answers), assess your reasons for political behavior using this grid.

| | Importance of Goal to Me | | | | |
Motive	Strong		Medium		Weak
Organizational Goals	1	2	3	4	5
Project Goals	1	2	3	4	5
Defensive Goals	1	2	3	4	5
Career Advancement	1	2	3	4	5
Coping with Subjectivity	1	2	3	4	5
Fitting In	1	2	3	4	5
Enjoyment of the Game	1	2	3	4	5

When you understand other peoples' motives, you can often understand their behavioral and tactical choices. Using the information in this chapter, rate the key players in your organizational environment on the basis of your best assessment and best knowledge. Work at seeing the situation from their point of view, not yours, whether or not you agree with their point of view. Like it or not, people choose their behaviors on the basis of how they see the world, not of how you would have them see it.

Key Individual #1   Name: _____

| | Importance of Goal | | | | |
Motive	Strong		Medium		Weak
Organizational Goals	1	2	3	4	5
Project Goals	1	2	3	4	5
Defensive Goals	1	2	3	4	5
Career Advancement	1	2	3	4	5
Coping with Subjectivity	1	2	3	4	5
Fitting In	1	2	3	4	5
Enjoyment of the Game	1	2	3	4	5

Key Individual #2   Name: _____

| | Importance of Goal | | | | |
Motive	Strong		Medium		Weak
Organizational Goals	1	2	3	4	5
Project Goals	1	2	3	4	5
Defensive Goals	1	2	3	4	5
Career Advancement	1	2	3	4	5
Coping with Subjectivity	1	2	3	4	5

Motive				
Fitting In	1	2	3	4	5
Enjoyment of the Game	1	2	3	4	5

Key Individual #3   Name: _____

Motive	Importance of Goal		
	Strong	Medium	Weak
Organizational Goals	1 2	3 4	5
Project Goals	1 2	3 4	5
Defensive Goals	1 2	3 4	5
Career Advancement	1 2	3 4	5
Coping with Subjectivity	1 2	3 4	5
Fitting In	1 2	3 4	5
Enjoyment of the Game	1 2	3 4	5

Key Individual #4   Name: _____

Motive	Importance of Goal		
	Strong	Medium	Weak
Organizational Goals	1 2	3 4	5
Project Goals	1 2	3 4	5
Defensive Goals	1 2	3 4	5
Career Advancement	1 2	3 4	5
Coping with Subjectivity	1 2	3 4	5
Fitting In	1 2	3 4	5
Enjoyment of the Game	1 2	3 4	5

Using the Exercise in Your Work

As a result of these exercises, you have been able to develop a wider perspective of the political environment and the potential benefits and liabilities of your participation or lack of participation. Review the summary of your reasons. Are they in line with your values and goals, or do you need to consider adjustments?

Similarly, take a good look at the people around you. Each person acts according to his or her interests and aptitudes *as he or she sees them.* Until you see what the world looks like from the perspective of others, you won't have the power to influence them or defend against them when necessary.

We'll continue to take a look at the motives and behavior of others along with our own motives and behavior throughout this book.

Notes

1. Jim Collins, "The Long View: The Learning Executive," *Inc.*, August 1997, p. 35.
2. Doug Marlette, "Iago Lives!" *Esquire*, August 1997, p. 102.
3. Kennedy, op. cit., pp. 34–37.
4. Steven Berglas, "Entrepreneurial Ego: Liar, Liar, Pants on Fire," *Inc.*, August 1997, p. 33.
5. Marlette, op. cit.

Chapter 3

Knowing the Battlefield—The Shape of the Political Terrain

The kind of thing I'm good at is knowing every politician
in the state and remembering where he itches.
                    Earl Long, Louisiana politician, 1960

As we all know, the organizational environment, politically speaking, can be a dangerous place. Whether our motives for playing office politics are to help shape an improved workplace or simply to defend ourselves, we need to understand the dangers of our environment, where they come from, how they affect us, and, above all, what we can do about it. This kind of understanding is the first step in danger reduction.

If you happen to blunder into a minefield but the mines are clearly marked and you have an accurate map, you're not in terrible danger as long as you keep your eyes open and pay attention. On the other hand, if you're dropped into the same minefield wearing a blindfold, you'll likely be dead in a hurry.

For the principled person in the world of office politics, there are two essential reasons to understand the landscape of office politics. One is, of course, self-defense. As we've discussed, you need to understand tactics, motivations, and behavior that you would never personally use, because others use them.

The second reason is that understanding the terrain, the landscape of office politics, is actually at the root of a large amount of principled behavior. The noted speaker Tony Alessandra formulated the Platinum Rule: Don't do unto people as you would have them do unto you; rather, do unto others in the style and manner they prefer to be done unto.[1] Part of having good character is service, being supportive and helpful to others. To do this, you have to know what they want and why they want it; otherwise, you're not helping at all.

The organizational and political landscape shapes the motivations and behavior of the other players. This is the background, the terrain of office politics. Military leaders always study the terrain; the natural features of the battlefield, properly analyzed and exploited, are often the critical factor in deciding the victor. Again, whether your goal is offense or defense, you must know the terrain.

The actions and behaviors of the people in your political environment grow from a combination of their own goals and personalities and the situation in which you all find yourselves. This chapter and the next describe a model, the Political Environment, that helps you place human behavior in an organizational context (see Figure 3-1). Your mission is to use the ideas in this model to diagnose your organization and the people within it so that you can increase your ability to work effectively.

It's important to note that models aren't reality. Models are useful because—and to the extent—they provide a picture of your environment. Models are neither true nor false; they are either useful or not useful. We've developed a two-stage model for understanding the people and environment in which office politics takes place.[2] The first stage is to place the people in your environment into the overall organizational context, in the second state, you look at how this context affects their attitudes and behavior toward you.

Environmental Factors

The political terrain consists of six main factors:

1. *Change.* Is the company going through major growth or downsizing? Has there been a change in ownership or

Figure 3-1: The Political Environment Model

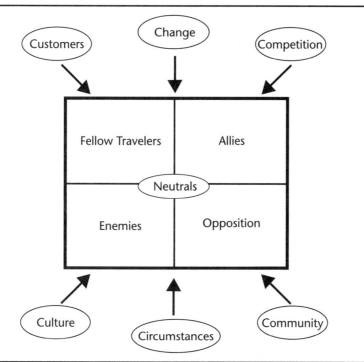

management? Has the company changed direction? Whether positive or negative, major change is always stressful. It motivates people to apply political strategies for self-protection and to manipulate the change itself.

2. *Circumstances.* Has a major crisis been resolved? Are you making or losing money? Have individuals in the organization had major disruptions in their own lives? Circumstances can include changes but encompass a wide range of environmental factors in and out of the office that affect behavior, especially in the political sphere.

3. *Community.* Is the industry one in which people from other companies frequently talk with one another or meet at trade shows or trade groups? Does the company have strong involvement in the local community? Are the personal politics of top management strongly expressed, whether liberal or

conservative? The organization is part of a community, and its values and issues translate into workplace behavior.

4. *Competition*. What's the competition like? Is it friendly or rough? Are your competitors bigger or smaller? Who sets the standards for the industry? Corporate rivalries can be emotionally intense, far more than facts may seem to warrant.

5. *Culture*. Did most of the power players in the organization attend the same school? Are there informal "dos" and "don'ts" that people have to respect? Do people normally stay late to get ahead? Is most business done on the golf course? Reading your company culture, both formal and informal, helps you understand political issues.

6. *Customers*. Do your customers have champions inside the organization? Are they large enough to write their own ticket? Have their needs changed significantly? Are relationships with customers close or distant? Customers can—and often do—become power players inside your organization.

These factors create and define your political environment.

Change

> There is nothing more difficult to take in hand, more perilous to conduct, or more uncertain in its success, than to take the lead in the introduction of a new order of things.
> Niccoló Machiavelli, *The Prince*, 1532

We know that issues of change and change management are frequent topics in the study of management, and that's because change has a dramatic effect on human behavior in organizations. As a result, change is a key political concept (Figure 3-2).

Change arguably brings out the worst in people, and yet change is the one certainty in the modern organization. The amount and type of change have an immense impact on individual behavior and the political environment. They may

Figure 3-2: Change

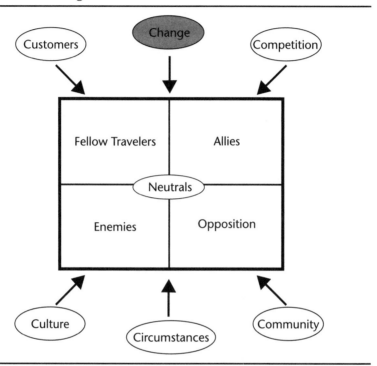

have a strong impact on your own goals and reasons for becoming more effective at office politics.

Types of Change Situations

Some common change situations you may experience include:

- Acquisition of your company by another company
- Introduction of a new department manager and/or a new leadership team to run the organization
- Implementation of a new management technique, from enterprise project management to reengineering
- Major disruptions in the economy and/or your market
- Implementation of new technology or change in existing technology systems

- Launch of a new project or product with significant impact on the bottom line
- Changes in laws and regulations that affect your business

Understanding the changes, who is affected by them, how they are affected, and how they see their choices and options is critical to understanding your political environment.

Fear and Benefits of Change

In what ways do people feel threatened as a result of change? Why are they so often fearful? This fear doesn't include only fear of job loss, though that's important. Consider too the fear of loss of specialized knowledge. A person whose self-perception rests on her or his detailed knowledge of the job can take quite a large ego blow if that knowledge is "overtaken by events." Specialized knowledge is often a source of personal power for individuals, and losing the relevance of the knowledge is the same as losing power—and face.

In what ways do people see the possibility of improving their situations as a result of change? Potential areas for improvement are not only opportunities for promotions or financial gain, though these, too, are important. Consider as well the personal one-upmanship and payback opportunities that become possible when shifts take place. It may be an advantage to Person A if Person B will suffer as a result of the change. Consider relationship-building opportunities and shifting alliances in the face of dramatic change.

Difficulty of Change

Why is change so difficult? Regardless of the nature of the change, whether it is a net positive or negative, whether it is voluntary or mandatory, the fact of change always has certain predictable effects. It helps to understand three essential principles of change:

1. All change creates some loss.
2. Change makes things more difficult in the short run.
3. The pain of change is guaranteed, but not the benefit.

Let's see how these principles might apply to a common change situation, the act of giving up smoking cigarettes. Many people agree with King James, who described smoking as "a custom loathsome to the eye, hateful to the nose, harmful to the brain, dangerous to the lungs, and in the black, stinking fumes thereof, nearest resembling the horrible Stygian smoke of the pit that is bottomless." If this were the whole story, people wouldn't smoke in the first place, and giving up smoking wouldn't be the challenge it so often is.

All Change Creates Some Loss

The first reality is that in most situations, good and bad are combined. There are inarguable negatives about smoking, but that doesn't mean there are no positives. For example, smoking is stress-relieving; it gives you something to do with your hands; it is a way of associating with others; you get longer breaks; and for some people, it tastes good. It also helps keep weight down and it's associated with certain images of cool and power, from Humphrey Bogart to FDR.

If you want someone to give up smoking cigarettes, it's not a good idea to dismiss these benefits as trivial or nonexistent. They're real, and they matter to the smoker. Remember, if there were absolutely no positives whatsoever to smoking, no one would smoke in the first place.

It would be nice if you could give up the negatives of smoking without giving up the positives, but you have to give them up as a package deal. And there is loss associated with giving up those benefits. When you're advocating or fighting for change, you have to be realistic about the benefits people see in the status quo. Trivializing them just makes people mad.

To manage this change more effectively, both in yourself and in others, here are some techniques:

- Create a list of the positive elements of the status quo to make sure you understand them fully. Identify po-

tential weaknesses in the positives, but don't deny the overall importance of the benefits.
- Offer sympathy and acknowledgment to the person or persons in the change situation about the losses.
- Make a list of the potential benefits of the change, and emphasize those, as well as the advantages of avoiding the negatives of the status quo.
- Encourage the person or persons in the change situation to have input into the change itself, because often a minor adjustment to the desired change can have the effect of substantially lowering change resistance.

Change Makes Things More Difficult in the Short Run

Regardless of the long-term benefits of giving up smoking, the short run is going to be difficult. The symptoms of withdrawal, the difficulty of changing habits, irritability, and weight gain carry with them real pain and discomfort, though the level varies with the individual. In the process of managing change, you have to be realistic about the short-term pain and discomfort and be prepared to cope with it. Tactics include motivational speeches and tools (support groups), behavioral techniques (snapping a wristband, substituting chewing gum), and management of the specific discomforts (nicotine patches). Again, ignoring the reality of the pain tends to be counterproductive. Try some of the following ideas:

- Analyze the difficulties inherent in the change. Are they short term (involving the period of change only) or long term (inherent negatives that result from the change, regardless of benefits)?
- Can the negative elements be reduced or eliminated? Sometimes a short-term program can accomplish some improvement; sometimes the change itself can be modified to reduce negative consequences.
- Provide an opportunity for venting and emotional relief, but keep it contained and focus on long-term positives.

The Pain of Change Is Guaranteed, but Not the Benefits

So, you finally give up smoking, walk outside to take a breath of fresh air . . . and you're run over by a Camel truck. Reasons to quit smoking include the chance for better health and longer life—but those benefits are influenced by factors in addition to whether or not one smokes. Giving up smoking certainly improves the odds, but that's not the same thing as providing certainty. With any change, you have to pay the price in full up front, and the benefit, because it lies in the future, is always less than 100 percent certain.

To enable the person facing the change to assess realistically what the benefits of the change may be, try these tactics:

• Be honest about the range of outcomes.

• Identify ways to increase the likelihood of achieving the desired payoff from the change initiative.

• Identify people who are the major source of skepticism, and try to reduce their influence or opportunity to reach the group as a whole. Help them discover a "What's in It for Me" (WII-FM) approach for themselves in the change. Often, buying off a key opponent can dramatically improve total outcomes.

Is this example an endorsement of continuing to smoke? Of course not. It's an example of what it means to face change, especially if you are the one who wants the change but someone else (your staff, for example) has to go through the change process. Change resistance is real, and it is rational behavior. Part of managing the political process of change is knowing what's going on within people.

LOOKING FOR CHANGE

Describe the changes that have taken place in your work environment over the past year.

1. _____

2. _____

3. _____

For each change, consider the following questions:

1. Who is affected by the change? (Include yourself if appropriate.)

_____

_____

2. How is each individual affected by the change? (Consider career impact, job security, feelings about different work assignments.)

_____

_____

3. Does anyone change his or her relationship to you? If so, how?

_____

_____

4. Is there going to be follow-up change to this one? (Describe the changes that may occur.)

_____

_____

5. Who are the major champions of the change? Who are the major opponents of the change? Which side has the most power and influence in the current environment?

---

6. How do you feel about the change, and what would you like to happen?

---

7. What political strengths do you have that can influence the outcome you want?

Using the Exercise in Your Work

Change management is one of the critical leadership skills in the modern organization, the subject of national best-sellers. The personal is the political, as the saying goes, and the political dimension of change management is something you overlook only at your peril. When confronted with a potential change situation, take a deep breath and go through the questions above, considering how they affect you and others, and using this insight to develop a workable strategy. You'll find that putting inchoate fears onto paper often makes them less terrifying, and that doing so may also point the way toward a good outcome.

Circumstances

When schemes are laid in advance, it is surprising how often the circumstances fit in with them.
Sir William Osler, physician and author, 1904

Figure 3-3: Circumstances

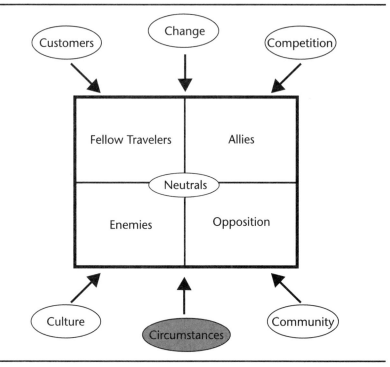

How people behave is partly a matter of their innate personality and partly a matter of the context, environment, and circumstances in which they are operating (Figure 3-3). You can't understand one without the other.

Nature of the Organization

While the extent and the nature of change in one's environment are important circumstances governing human behavior, there are other important circumstances that affect people's behavior, the pattern of their alliances, and the political environment of the organization. Is the company large or small? Is it the dominant business in its community, or only one of many? Is it located in a small town, a suburb, or a major city? Is it a family-run business, or are managers normally brought in from outside? Is it in a highly regulated industry or a lightly regulated one? Is it for profit, nonprofit, or public in nature? Is it in the government or the private sector?

Individual Circumstances

Look at the circumstances of the individuals involved as well. In one example, the president of a major corporation came from a poor background, while most of the vice presidents came from Ivy League colleges. This circumstance could play out in either of two ways: the president could use his or her position power to put down the Ivy Leaguers for any perceived failure or lack of "streetwise" or "school of hard knocks" education, or the president might harbor feelings of insecurity about her or his background and end up being bullied by his or her subordinates.

Either way, these nonjob-related circumstances will have a substantial input on the political environment, whose decisions are accepted, and how one gains influence in the organization. What's difficult here is that a single situation— educational or class differential between members of two levels of management—can lead to two different scenarios, with different implications for your best strategy.

Social Class

The entire issue of social class, especially in America, is a touchy subject, yet it has enormous implications for understanding and working within the political environment. One social commentator, Paul Fussell, writes: "When in early middle life some people discover that certain limits have been placed on their capacity to ascend socially by such apparent irrelevancies as heredity, early environment, and the social class of their immediate forebears, they go into something like despair, which, if generally secret, is no less destructive."[3] This is a painful reality, but more common than we suppose.

Action Strategies

You're not entirely helpless in the face of the class system or, indeed, the other circumstances that affect your environment and the people within it, but, as with most political issues, you must first accept those realities in order to move and prosper within them. Let's first explore ways to increase your understanding, which is the first necessary step, then look at ways to manage these circumstances more effectively.

UNDERSTANDING CIRCUMSTANCES

Identifying the key circumstances in your organizational environment is a difficult challenge. Think about the issues discussed in this section. If your relationship and the situation makes it possible, discuss the matter of circumstances with your mentors and allies; you may find important information that helps you make better sense of your environment. For each circumstance, consider the questions in the following worksheet:

1. What is the nature of the circumstance?

_____

_____

2. How does it affect the people in my environment?

_____

_____

3. Is the circumstance subject to change or alteration?

_____

_____

4. How does it affect me and others' perceptions of me?

_____

_____

Using the Exercise in Your Work

Where you stand often depends upon where you sit. Understanding human behavior—your own as well as others'—requires an understanding of the circumstances that surround them. We act in response to our environment. These questions have particular value when you're confronted by behavior or reactions that don't make sense to you. It's vital to understand the perceptions of others whether you believe them to be objectively valid or not.

Strategies for Working with Difficult Circumstances

We've discussed three major areas of circumstance: the nature of the company or industry, the circumstances of the individuals, and the role social class plays. Let's look at strategies for managing each.

Nature of the Organization

The first strategy for dealing with the nature of the organization is measuring your personal fit within it. Some people seek out and prefer being in large organizations; others are happier in small companies. Some people like a highly competitive environment that calls for being constantly at one's best; others prefer a more measured and balanced pace in life. It's unlikely that you can change the fundamental nature of the organization for which you work; the obvious option is to switch to a more appropriate organization.

The challenge, however, is that sometimes the organization has elements that suit you very well mixed with elements that clash with your personal style and values. There may be a substantial cost, perhaps an unacceptable cost, associated with departure, and there's also a cost in staying. What now?

1. Accept that you will need to endure a certain level of frustration or disappointment, because life does not always provide a perfect solution.

2. Make sure you understand clearly (putting it on paper is always valuable) exactly what tradeoffs you are making.

3. Take a close look at the overall organization to see whether there is another position, role, or opportunity that is either in existence already or that can be negotiated into existence. Examples include such strategies as negotiating work-at-home arrangements, special project roles, and intrapreneurship (creating your own new business unit within an existing organizational structure).

4. Consider whether the nature of your conflicts with the organization permits you to discuss them with your manager or others in the hierarchy. Frequently, this can open up doors that you might not otherwise be aware exist. Make sure that you structure your approach in terms of meeting the organization's needs so that you don't come across as a complainer.

5. Make sure you have a well-balanced life overall. It's very easy in our modern world to find your identity so deeply rooted in your work that any setbacks or discomforts contaminate your entire life. If other roles—family, social involvements, friends, hobbies—are available and satisfying, you'll find that an enormous amount of pressure is lifted.

6. Understand that a sense of powerlessness makes any situation more miserable than it would otherwise be. If you truly believe you have no choice and no options, that you must suffer whatever the workplace has in store for you, your stress level will be higher. One advantage of a regular program of savings and investment is to give you improved financial options—walk-away money. When you have a choice, you often don't feel compelled to exercise it; when you have no choice, that's often all you can think about.

Individual Circumstances

Conduct background checks on key players in any organization with which you work or do business. This can be done in a variety of different ways, from direct, friendly questioning to the kind of investigation a private detective might perform. The appropriate ethical concerns here have to do with both techniques and motives.

Motives come first. There's a crucial difference between

the act of "digging up dirt" on someone, which is investigating with the goal of finding something negative that can be used as a weapon, and the far more friendly act of learning about a person to enhance one's relationship. The second motive—learning about someone—is often part of good manners and can form the foundation of a positive, long-lasting relationship, as well as increase understanding of the person's goals and interests. This is completely appropriate from an ethics perspective, and the enlightened office politician will have this as a primary goal.

Then there is the issue of technique. Let's consider a variety of ethically appropriate methods of learning about someone. We've already considered the first, the technique of friendly direct questioning.

Next, take a look at publicly available documents. For example, many companies prepare a press release on each senior manager at the time of hiring or on the occasion of a major promotion. Ask to see them; there's normally no problem. Check the company Web site for bios of top managers. Check the Internet by doing a search of the person's name. He or she may have a personal site, may have a posted résumé on a job-search board, or may be listed in the membership of a particular association or organization. Check the archives of your local newspaper or any major professional or trade associations in your industry. Because this kind of information is offered on an open basis to the interested public, there's nothing wrong or even questionable in seeking it out.

What do you do with the information when you've gotten it?

First, use it to avoid putting your foot in your mouth accidentally. Something as simple as an insult aimed at the wrong college, region of the country, or hobby can create a conflict you don't want or need.

Second, use it to identify potential areas of shared interest. There's nothing wrong or hypocritical about finding a link with another person and using it as a way to open a conversation or dialogue. In one situation, a new manager discovered that the CEO and he shared an interest in the same hobby. In a casual meeting, he asked, "By any chance, do you know so-and so?" referring to someone well known to people involved in that hobby.

The CEO was surprised. "Why, yes! How do you know him?" And of such things are effective relationships made. This helps you stand out from the crowd, helps people see you as a human being rather than as simply another cog in the organizational machinery, and helps demonstrate other areas of skill you may possess.

Social Class

If you've identified social class barriers to your political success within the organization, take heart. While America certainly has a class structure, it is often based less on ancestry than on personal style. While the English are famous for "the old school tie," in which the pattern on one's tie literally identifies the public school one attended, in the United States class symbols are often more fluid and more adaptable. Nevertheless, you should remember that a number of organizations effectively insist that their senior-level staff look and act like they are members of the upper middle class.

Obviously, maneuvers like "dressing for success" and use of proper business etiquette do matter. Knowing the style signifiers of social class is useful as well. Unethical? Not at all. When you enter the world of work, you accept that only portions of your innate nature are appropriate there. Other parts of your nature belong to other parts of your life. People from a wide range of backgrounds must work together, and, to streamline the process, standard codes of conduct are developed. This is as much a part of good communication as good grammar. We present ourselves nonverbally even more than verbally, and demonstrating that you understand the rules and customs is not an unreasonable requirement.

Community

No written law has ever been more binding than unwritten custom supported by popular opinion.

Carrie Chapman Catt, founder of the
League of Women Voters, 1900

Figure 3-4: Community

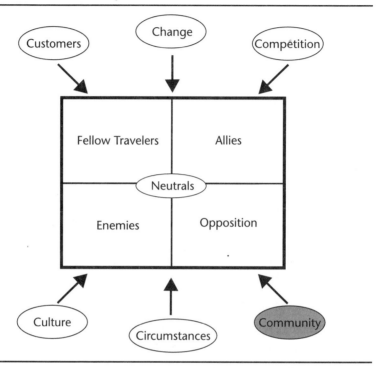

Separate from corporate culture, the concept of community limits and shapes your political environment (Figure 3-4). You belong simultaneously to various overlapping communities, as do your colleagues. These include:

- Your peer group within the organization
- Your industry peers, especially if your industry has regular trade shows or public events
- Your geographic community (local and regional) around your plant or office
- The geographic community (local and regional) of the organization headquarters, if different
- Your nation or, in a multinational organization, the national origin of the organization and its top managers
- Your socioeconomic class, race, religion, and gender

The journalist Joel Garreau theorized that the North American continent wasn't made up of the United States and

Canada, but instead contained nine separate nations, each with its own distinct economy, social values, traditions, histories, and cultures. While the boundaries of these nine nations aren't shown on traditional maps, if someone is from the Deep South or the Pacific Northwest or New England, that says something—though clearly not everything—about that person's character and values.[4]

Similarly, the concept of community in this context tells us that when we know where a person is "from" (both literally and figuratively), we know something of importance. In the same way that southerners and New Yorkers stereotype each other (though when you say "New York" it's important to distinguish whether you mean the city or the state), others pigeonhole you on the basis of their knowledge of your background. While that's often at the root of discrimination, you need to remember that this sort of stereotyping is common and goes on all the time. You have to recognize how and when it's being done to you.

When you do that, you can choose to play up the stereotype or counteract it, whichever you see as being in your best strategic interest; you also need to watch how you are stereotyping others to make sure you don't underestimate or wrongly evaluate another person. Harriet Rubin suggests ways to play off your own image or stereotype: "Become the very image, the total embodiment, of the opponent your enemy fears. . . . To act a role deliberately can shock the most complacent or intransigent opponent and most certainly will throw any antagonist into uncertainty."[5]

As a politician, Al Gore gained a reputation for being dry, didactic, patronizing, and wooden. As with many stereotypes, there was some truth in the perception, but not total truth. People are invariably more complex than a simple stereotype would suggest.

At the 1996 Democratic National Convention, Gore announced that he would do the Macarena. He stood stock still for a minute, then announced, "Would you like to see me do it again?" People are invariably surprised when you make light of your own stereotype—it's disarming.

Watergate figure G. Gordon Liddy took a woman to dinner to ask her to infiltrate a Democratic political campaign. She protested that her identity would not be secure, to which Liddy replied that only he would know and no one could force him to disclose anything he did not wish to share. When she demurred, he asked her to light her cigarette lighter and held his hand over it until the flesh began to char. Liddy writes, "Pale, Miss Stevens said she was sure I would never betray her, but excused herself as a candidate, invoking a just remembered plan to marry a Swiss airplane pilot in September of 1972."[6]

What's interesting about this is not only the playing up of the "tough secret agent" stereotype, but also Liddy's obvious awareness of the humor involved in his deadpan account of her rejection.

What did he accomplish, considering that the woman did not accept his offer to be a spy? He enhanced his reputation as a dangerous and unpredictable man, he ensured she would be unlikely to spread the story around or betray his attempt to recruit her, and, after all, it might have worked.

In the perspective of enlightened office politics, is this necessarily unethical or untruthful? Playing off a stereotype is like dealing with an image in a funhouse mirror. The distorted image is what the other person sees, and the image doesn't reflect reality—at least, reality from your perspective. Images are part of nonverbal communication, and a part over which we have little direct control. Playing with image and perception, though potentially dangerous, is necessary, because if you don't, you won't be perceived at all in an accurate fashion. And leveraging someone else's false opinion of you can be a form of judo, a creative way to get yourself seen in a new light.

THE COMMUNITIES OF YOUR ENVIRONMENT

You need to think about the interlocking communities to which you and your colleagues and your organization belong. How do they affect you and your strategies? How can you work best within them? Consider the questions in the following worksheet:

1. What professional/organizational communities do I live in?

_____

_____

2. What geographic and regional communities do I live in?

_____

_____

3. What personal communities do I live in?

_____

_____

4. If my organization is dispersed or owned by others, what different communities interlock with mine?

_____

_____

5. For each of the communities in which I live, how do their norms and stereotypes make others judge me? How do I judge them?

_____

_____

6. What are the positive and negative effects of these communities on me and on others?

_____

_____

7. How does this knowledge affect how I should behave and deal with others?

_____

_____

Using the Exercise in Your Work

Fish, it is said, don't notice that water is wet. We are not always aware of our communities, because they seem so naturally a part of who and what we are. But an awareness of them, especially the idea that we, and others, live in multiple communities simultaneously, is an important key to understanding them, and sometimes to deciphering the clues to certain behaviors. Use these questions to become more aware of this important factor.

Competition

> The battle of competition is fought by cheapening of commodities.
>
> Karl Marx, *Das Kapital*, 1867

There are two types of competition that affect your political environment: external and internal. External competition is the competition of the marketplace; internal competition is competition among individuals for promotion and perks and among departments for relative power and influence in the organization (Figure 3-5).

External Competition

Where is your company in its own market? Are you the market leader in your segment, are you in second place, or are you a minor factor? Do you have a corporate rival, someone with whom the competition is as much personal as business? Is your industry expanding or contracting? Do people rou-

Figure 3-5: Competition

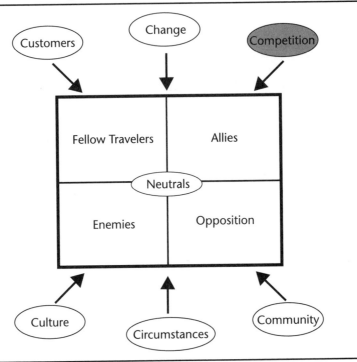

tinely move from company to company within the same industry, or is this not done in your business? Are you currently
winning or losing in the marketplace? How does the company's market image of itself relate to reality ("We're number
one!" when we're really number fourteen, for example)?

One key political issue is the appearance of loyalty. From
the perspective of business smarts, it's clearly better to overestimate than to underestimate your opponent. In the real
world, however, corporations often acquire an internal sense
of their greatness that is almost immune to reason.

"Sure, the competition is larger, but our people are better," you might hear. Quality of staff matters, but victory
tends to go to the larger outfit. As Napoleon said, "God fights
on the side of the heaviest artillery."

"Sure, they've been around and have a larger market
share, but our product is better." Tests proved conclusively
that New Coke tasted better than Coke Classic. Most authori-

ties give the Macintosh the quality advantage over Windows. Beta is technically superior to VHS. It doesn't matter. The truth that matters in the marketplace is the perception of the customer—and the customer isn't on your team.

The predicament you face is that people in your organization, especially in top leadership, often don't want to hear the truth. They want protestations of loyalty, and you have to deliver them if you are to have any credibility whatsoever. The delicate balancing act is between the necessity of parroting the party line and promoting the truth for the long-term health of the organization. Remember that if you want someone to understand the truth, you have to put it in terms she or he is willing to hear. That's a key marketing secret—and marketing your ideas, concepts, and directions is one of the essential elements of office politics.

Internal Competition

Internal competition can be personal in nature, such as a rivalry with someone in your division for career advancement, control of certain projects, or shaping of key decisions. Internal competition can also be interdepartmental—rivalries among different divisions or sections of the same organization.

When people use the term "office politics," they're often talking only about internal competition. As you've discovered, while internal competition is certainly a major part of office politics, it isn't all of it. With respect to internal competition, you need to focus on certain core competencies:

- Knowing what competitions exist, especially rivalries you're not part of but could spill over into your areas
- Knowing what your goals and objectives are, and having a clear plan to achieve them
- Knowing the political relationship of the people around you to the goals you have, and having appropriate strategies in place to deal with any obstacles
- Having a commitment to win/win outcomes, doing everything in your power to advance your interests in

such a way as not to cause unnecessary damage and make unnecessary enemies

COPING WITH COMPETITION

Evaluate the internal and external competitions in your environment and understand how they impact you by answering the questions in this worksheet.

External Competition

1. What is the real position of my organization in my industry?

---

2. How do people inside my organization (especially executives) perceive its position? What beliefs or claims do we make that aren't true (at least, not yet)?

---

3. Are there specific company rivalries that exist? Where did they come from? How serious are they? How are they expressed?

---

4. How comfortable is management about hearing bad or unfavorable news about us, or good news about our competitors? What happens to people who are candid?

Internal Competition

1. What rivalries exist between my division or work group and others? How serious are they? What is at stake?

   _____

   _____

2. What personal rivalries exist between my coworkers and others in the organization in which I am not personally involved? How serious are they? What kinds of tactics are used in that competition? How does—or might—the competition affect me?

   _____

   _____

3. What rivalries am I involved in? What issues are at stake? What are my goals, and what strategies are appropriate to meet them?

   _____

   _____

Using the Exercises in Your Work

There are few situations more dangerous than to be in a competition and unaware that you are competing. Even if you don't want to be in a given competition, being aware that you are is a precondition for being able to stop it, or get out.

If you are going to compete, compete effectively and in a way that fits your principles and long-term strategic values. Although it seems weaker to play by self-imposed rules, you gain so much long-term strength from being unwilling to bend to fit the mere demands of the moment that you profit, and profit enormously. Use these questions to ensure that you understand your circumstances and select the right strategy for competition, both external and internal.

Culture

> Even given the freest scope by their institutions, men are
> never inventive enough to make more than minute
> changes. . . . It is a commonplace that prophets have been
> put to death for the difference between Tweedledum and
> Tweedledee.
>
> Ruth Benedict, *Patterns of Culture*, 1934

The anthropological concept of "culture" involves certain
norms that develop among members of a group that is
thrown together over time. Culture develops primarily as a
result of proximity, and secondarily as a result of common
interests, styles, and goals. While not everyone within a culture subscribes to all its dictates, and some even reject the
culture in which they find themselves, the culture influences
each member nevertheless (Figure 3-6).

Figure 3-6: Culture

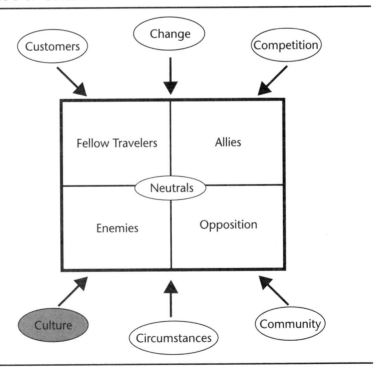

Corporate culture is one of the core issues studied by management experts, especially in focusing on such issues as quality. A mission or vision statement is a summation of the ideal corporate culture—which often differs from the real corporate culture, which acts in many specific and powerful ways to shape, limit, and focus its members. You will not succeed if you oppose your corporate culture too directly; the art of politics is the art of achieving hundreds of small changes against the larger backdrop.

This point actually applies to senior executives to a greater extent than is often supposed. While changing the corporate culture is often a key mission of a new executive team, it's harder than it looks, and a good many executive teams fail in the attempt, or settle for far less success than they hoped for. Systems have inertia, and, while executives have a significant impact on shaping corporate culture, they are not the only actors.

Vision and Values

Take a good, close look at any written vision, mission, or value statements produced by the organization or your division. While these are all too frequently hot air, there's usually some political insight to be had at some level. If you have one of those mission statements that includes words like, "Our mission is to provide world-class quality and unparalleled customer service as the leading producer in our market, while valuing the diversity of our workforce as key contributors to stakeholder value," ask yourself what is really meant. Remember the conflict between self-perception and company loyalty and the real market in which you operate. Is management talking to itself, is it developing a marketing slogan, or is there a real attempt to change what's going on in the organization?

When you listen to Ford's "Quality is Job #1" slogan, for example, what does it mean? It might mean a little of all three of the elements we just mentioned. If you're a Ford employee, though, you'll form your own impression on the basis of what actually happens when you identify a potential conflict between the goal of quality and other organizational goals, such as profit or project deadlines. If you say, "Quality is Job

#1," and make your decision accordingly, and your managers support you, then it's a statement about values. But if instead you are told, "Make it cheap, make it quick, and get it out the door," then you will likely conclude it's a marketing slogan—and your respect for the honesty and integrity of management tends to drop as a result.

Values statements talk about teamwork, honesty, openness, trust, integrity, diversity—all important concepts. Again, make sure you compare the reality to the statement. It's not a problem if the organization doesn't currently live up to its stated values if there is a commitment to change and grow, because one reason to have such a statement in the first place is to set standards to live up to. It is a problem if there is a fundamental and recurring mismatch between the stated value and the actual behavior, especially at management levels. This can be immensely destructive to trust and effectiveness in the organization.

Peer Pressure

In the movie *Big*, in which Tom Hanks magically turns from a fourteen-year-old boy into a grown-up and goes to work for a toy company, his first job with the company is as an order entry clerk. Excited and highly motivated, he's working very quickly, when the person in the next cubicle, played by Jon Lovitz, leans over the cube wall and hisses, "What do you think you're doing?"

Shocked, Tom Hanks replies that he's trying to do his job—is he doing it wrong? But that's not what Lovitz is concerned about. "Slow down! You're going to make the rest of us look bad!" And Hanks does, proving that corporate culture isn't exclusively the province of executive management. Peer pressure is alive and well, and it shapes the cultural environment in which you work.

There are various reasons for peer pressure. First, in every organization there are a few people who quit but don't leave. Mentally and emotionally, they have resigned from the structure, but they stay for the paycheck and the social relationships. Sometimes they stay out of a sense of desperation, and sometimes even for the sake of revenge. Such people have a choice—to see their negative situation as their own fault or to blame the organization or the system for their misery. It shouldn't be surprising that such people often see the cause of their problems as something outside themselves. Accordingly, on the evident management theory that two wrongs make a right, they seem to feel if they can make others as disgruntled and unhappy as they, then they are somehow justified in their situation.

An even more powerful reason for peer pressure is a sense of how the organization gives rewards and punishments. There is a Japanese saying that the nail that sticks up gets hammered down. When a schoolteacher grades on the curve, the success and initiative of one person can actually have a negative effect on others, and, quite naturally, those students tend to resent the high achiever. The fault here lies with the teacher, but it's the student who receives the punishment. Organizations often apply formal or informal performance benchmarks, and when they are perceived as too far out of line with average performance, even if they're reachable by those at the far end of the bell curve, the peer group takes action.

Finally, there's the well-known concept of "an honest day's work for an honest day's pay." This is generally taken as an exhortation to work hard, but often the employee perceives this as a two-way contract. A traditional joke in the Soviet Union was "We pretend to work and they pretend to pay us," and that reflects, unfortunately, how at least some employees see their workplace. People tend to have a sense of what level of pay is fair reward for a given position and performance expectation. If the fairness expectation of managers and employees are too far out of whack, employees tend to adjust their performance and output to achieve fairness through other means.

It's often the case that an extreme disparity in fairness perception has to do with what the quality guru Philip Crosby calls the Hassle Index of a company—a rating of how difficult it is to accomplish certain reasonable activities, such as getting a parking place at work, a meeting with the boss, a travel advance, a raise for a subordinate, or a new desk.[7] People in a "high-hassle" environment tend to feel they should be paid for being degraded, but of course management doesn't see it that way. The solution, of course, is to reduce the hassle, because paying people for the privilege of abusing them tends not to achieve productivity goals in the long run.

Status Symbols

The business expert Michael Korda points out that in an organization, there are symbols that define real issues of status.[8] In one organization, he discovered the Thermos Rule. Status among executives was defined by the kind of thermos sitting on their desk, from a dark brown plastic thermos with one glass for a low-level executive up to a gold-plated thermos with two glasses and a small gold-plated tray for a top executive.

Even stranger, the Thermos Rule was independent of any other rewards, perks, or status, because if you just went out and bought yourself a gold-plated thermos for your desk, that tended to indicate that you didn't understand the rules of the organization and were therefore unsuitable for further promotion and maybe were even making fun of everybody else. Korda concludes, "Symbols of power matter to people and they matter a lot."

The "office caste system" helps identify power and status. At Allstate Insurance Company, a fifty-page volume titled "Office Workspace Standards" lists exact office specifications for each level of management. The U.S. Code of Federal Regulations, Subpart 101-17.3, spells out details for federal offices. Not just size of office but size and material of desk and chair, windows—nothing is too minor.[9]

When the Smithsonian National Air and Space Museum moved from its old home into its new building in 1975, new furniture was acquired. The building manager found a very nice wooden desk that was being sent to surplus and decided he wanted it for himself. But the desk had belonged to an assistant director, and in the end the building manager was forced to give away that desk and buy a new one . . . of appropriate status. Before you condemn this as wasteful, make sure you understand the symbolic vocabulary. It's part of every organization.

The outstanding office politician knows the importance of keeping her or his eyes open at all times, looking for the symbolic vocabulary of the organization and knowing that symbols matter. Dress code matters, whether the organization is officially "casual" or not. During a discussion of dress code and status symbols, one seminar attendee angrily announced, "A $500 suit never accomplished a thing!" True. But the person wearing the $500 suit may well have gotten the opportunity to take on a project or launch a venture that the person wearing the golf shirt and khakis—or in some organizations the T-shirt and cutoffs—would never get.

Dos and Don'ts

Customs are powerful. Your corporate culture places firm and sometimes even absolute limits on your actions, your speed, and your methods. There are unwritten rules, with violations often punished, and ignorance of the law is no excuse. There are people on the fast track and others excluded from the start. There are special ties of loyalty, hidden group memberships, and the full range of cliques—just like high school in many ways. Some rules are the same in all the corporate cultures you're likely to see; others are unique to specific organizations. It takes detective work to uncover the hidden rules, yet mastery of those hidden rules is part of what is used ultimately to decide who is promotable and who is not.

Dress code is one example. Watch the powerful people, the leaders. You'll find that whether their dress is formal or informal, there are certain norms. If you don't follow those norms, you won't be joining that group.

Lunch is another example. In some organizations, eating at your desk shows you to be a serious person. In others, lunches are for morale building and networking; going to lunch with a large group makes you a member of the team.

Hours worked is still another example. Business guru Zig Ziglar once observed that you build a better reputation coming in early than staying late. Coming in early shows eagerness to get to work; staying late suggests you can't manage your time well enough to get it all done. True enough, but in some organizations, the serious people stay late . . . and network. That's where the political arena is, and if you don't get into that circle, you won't be a player.

Besides observation, the other important tool for learning about corporate culture is mentors. One little-understood secret about mentors is that they are the people who tell you the inner secrets of the organizational culture, these dos and don'ts that are so important. Remember, people who don't learn them don't get promoted, and most of the rules aren't published. How do you learn? Your observation will take you only so far; you need help for the rest. Your ability to get that help—to build mentoring relationships—is one of the hidden keys to promotion.

Finally, although we've observed that a new executive team isn't automatically going to be successful in changing a corporate culture, it will certainly and virtually immediately change some of the more superficial customs, and you should be prepared to search out these changes and adapt quickly. Such cosmetic alterations are a necessary part of the political environment, and few of them are so deep-rooted that they should outrage your ethical sense. If you're part of the old team in a new team environment, you may be considered guilty until proven innocent, and establishing your bona fides with the new team should be one of your highest priorities. Explaining patiently how "we tried that and it doesn't work here," even if true, is a quick road to reduced political influence. Cheerfulness, an open mind, and a willingness to listen are all skills that will help you survive when top management changes.

LEARNING ABOUT CORPORATE CULTURE

The corporate culture in your organization has official and unofficial elements, but learning to fit in is crucial. The questions in this worksheet should help you get a handle on what you need to know.

Vision and Values

1. If the organization or department has a written mission, vision, and values statement, write it here.

   _____

   _____

2. How truthful and descriptive is it? Do you see real commitment to it on the part of management? Is there progress toward those goals?

   _____

   _____

3. What do you see as the real vision and values of the organization as practiced today? (Avoid cynicism.)

   _____

   _____

Peer Pressure

1. What "work norms" are practiced by your peers and subordinates? What happens to people who violate them (e.g., excluded, made fun of)?

   _____

   _____

2. List both the positive and the negative types of peer pressure you observe in the organization.

   _____

   _____

Status Symbols

1. Observe people of high rank and low rank. What visible symbols, formal and informal, mark their status? Are there written standards for certain status symbols?

_____

_____

2. Which status symbols can be copied safely (e.g., wearing the right suit, playing golf or tennis)?

_____

_____

Dos and Don'ts

1. What are the informal laws of the workplace? What are mandatory dos and don'ts for people who want to get ahead?

a. _____

b. _____

c. _____

d. _____

e. _____

f. _____

g. _____

h. _____

Using the Exercises in Your Work

These status issues often strike people as silly and immature, and sometimes that's the truth. They are, nevertheless, real and have a potentially powerful impact on your organizational strategies. Use these questions to improve your understanding of these hidden rules of the game. If you're unsure about the answers, spend time observing others, asking questions of mentors or other knowledgeable and trustworthy people, or evaluating what seems to work and not work.

Customers

> When I see a merchant over-polite to his customers, begging them to taste a little brandy and throwing half his goods on the counter,—thinks I, that man has an axe to grind.
>
> Charles Miner, *Essays from the Desk of Poor Robert the Scribe*, 1830

Figure 3-7: Customers

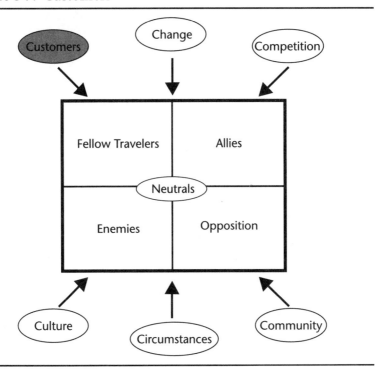

The customer-focused organization is the subject of innumerable books and articles in the quality movement (Figure 3-7). There is a political dimension to this as well, having to do with the relative power and influence of the customer inside your organization, through personal relationships, clout, size of contract, and other factors.

Customers with Clout

The savvy customer often plays politics, developing internal contacts in your organization to gain information and exercise leverage. It's a good way to get better outcomes. When you're the customer, do the same.

What this means from a political perspective is that all customers aren't created equal and that what you have to deliver for a customer may well have to vary on the basis of that customer's clout and relationships. You need to learn which customers take priority in the political environment, through observation and mentor relationships.

Customers, like everybody else, have personal quirks and styles. Some shout and demand to get their ways; others build friendships they can use. How you respond to, say, a shouting customer depends on who that customer is.

Consultants

There is a special customer relationship fraught with political implication: the management consultants and outside experts the company hires to advise it. There are a number of reasons organizations use consultants, and those reasons are both good and bad.

Sometimes, a consultant is called in because the company needs someone with special expertise that it doesn't have and needs in only a limited area. Sometimes a consultant is called in not so much because of special expertise but to provide objectivity—the ability to look at the situation without the filters and cultural barriers of insiders. These are good reasons.

Sometimes, however, a consultant is called in because the organization wants an outsider to do its dirty work, such as in a major restructuring or downsizing. Sometimes consultants are called in because such a high level of distrust exists between managers and internal experts that whatever the internal experts say is dismissed out of hand. In that situation, the internal people are often very frustrated when the consultant says what they've been saying for months or years, causing more long-term morale damage. These are more problematic reasons to bring in consultants.

A third category of reasons is primarily political in nature. Sometimes a top executive hires a specific consultant with whom he or she has a long-term relationship in order to have a personal ally outside the normal organization hierarchy. This can be highly beneficial or terribly destructive, depending on how it's handled.

You often don't have a lot of direct control over this situation, so the issue becomes how you cope with it. These tactics may help you:

1. *Tread carefully around an outsider.* That person may have access in the power structure you don't have.

2. *Remember that the new car smell goes away after a while.* In other words, a consultant fresh in the organization may have his or her every word considered gospel; after a while, the consultant may lose substantial status. Be patient.

3. **Build your own relationship with the consultant.** If the consultant finds you to be a supportive ally, this can often advance your status and credibility with management. But find out who the consultant is allied with. If that's the person, group, or power source you also want to be allied with, build the relationship. If not, remain personally friendly, but avoid an entangling alliance.

4. *Listen carefully.* It's too easy to dismiss a consultant as having little of value to contribute, but you may be surprised. You don't necessarily have to accept everything in order to get some value out of the relationship. And that's a win/win.

CUSTOMERS AND CONSULTANTS

The questions in this worksheet will help you analyze the political position and issues for your key customers and consultants.

1. Who are your biggest, long-term customers? How much of the business depends on them?

   _____

   _____

2. Identify the sources of power of your customers: relationships, money at stake, size of job, length of relationship.

   _____

   _____

3. What personal characteristics do these customers have, both positive and negative, that affect your relationship with them?

   _____

   _____

4. Does your organization employ any consultants? If so, who are they, and what are their areas of responsibility?

   _____

   _____

5. What sources of power, both formal and informal, do these consultants possess? To whom do they report?

   _____

   _____

6. What danger might these consultants pose to you? How can you work with them to minimize danger and achieve a win/win outcome?

_____

_____

Using the Exercise in Your Work

People have done themselves substantial damage by failing to understand the real role and position that customers and consultants have in the organization. From a customer service perspective, it's highly appropriate that customers do possess power, and it's certainly in line with good values and principles to support all customers, those who have political power and those who do not. Use these questions to focus your thinking about the relationships customers and consultants have with the organization, what consulting relationships may tell you about the motives and objectives of higher levels of management, and how these things affect you and your career.

Notes

1. Tony Alessandra, *Mastering Your Message* (audiotape) (Mission, Kans.: SkillPath Publications, 1997).
2. The authors acknowledge the inspiration of Peter Block's Relationship Grid for one portion of this model. See Peter Block, *The Empowered Manager: Positive Political Skills at Work* (New York: Jossey-Bass, 1987), pp. 131–151.
3. Paul Fussell, *Class: A Painfully Accurate Guide through the American Status System* (New York: Ballantine, 1983), pp. 8–9.
4. Joel Garreau, *The Nine Nations of North America* (New York: Avon Books, 1991).
5. Harriet Rubin, *The Princessa: Machiavelli for Women* (New York: Currency Doubleday, 1997), pp. 113–114.

6. G. Gordon Liddy, *Will: The Autobiography of G. Gordon Liddy* (New York: Dell/St. Martin's Press, 1980), p. 263.

7. Philip B. Crosby, *Quality without Tears: The Art of Hassle-Free Management* (New York: Plume, 1985), pp. 34–35.

8. Michael Korda, *Power: How to Get It, How to Use It* (audiotape) (New York: Simon & Schuster Audio & Video, 1986).

9. Ellen Warren, "Where Do You Stand?" *Chicago Tribune*, July 1, 1997, Section 5, pp. 1, 4–5.

Chapter 4

What's Going On Here? Analyzing the Other Players—and the Other Teams

What's good for General Motors is good for the country.
attributed to Charles E. Wilson, president of GM and
later Secretary of Defense, 1953[1]

The political environment in which you operate consists of people, and people do what they do because of their motives and perspectives. Understanding your relationships to the people around you, and the different ways you and they see interests and goals, is critical to effective office politics.

One of the key skills that you can develop is the art of putting yourself in someone else's shoes and seeing the situation as that person sees it. Only when you do that can you understand the motives for the person's behavior, and ultimately predict his or her likely next move.

A few years ago, the business press reported that General Motors was considering eliminating the Oldsmobile division because of poor sales. General Motors at the time denied this, but recently it was confirmed that the Oldsmobile division will be phased out.

GM had been under criticism for some time for lagging sales and perceptions of poor quality, and the Oldsmobile division was considered by elements of the business press as a candidate for closure. There are legitimate arguments to make on either side of the issue. But if you were president of Oldsmobile, what would you have done? Would you have conducted a dispassionate analysis of whether, from the overall corporate perspective, your brand, your division—and your job—should be eliminated?

The natural response for most people would be to fight for your program. You might call in your senior staff and order a study to be conducted of the Oldsmobile brand and its prospects. But it wouldn't really be a "study," because a study carries with it the idea that the outcome is not foreordained. It would be "a study to show why Oldsmobile is still a great brand" as opposed to "a study to determine whether Oldsmobile should be retained." It would be a work of advocacy.

Notice, by the way, that such a strategy, while often the tactic of an unprincipled person, can also, if done correctly, be in accordance with principled behavior. The question is how honestly the basic study is done and what degree of credence it gives to alternatives other than the one you prefer. In other words, different motives can sometimes result in the same (or similar) behavior.

In addition, you might work to build support for the Oldsmobile brand. You might tell your dealers that the brand is at risk and urge them to increase sales efforts, reducing margins temporarily to show that the brand is still viable. You might conduct press outreach, providing information that supports your brand. Again, this can be perfectly appropriate, principled behavior, or it can be unprincipled self-preservation, depending on the motives and the detailed tactics that you use.

You might build allies within the organization. For example, one story in the business press suggested that Oldsmobile might be reinvented as an "upgrade" brand for Saturn and affiliated with that division. Again—and notice that in every case that follows—it's possible to conduct that strategy with a purely principled outlook. Perhaps such a move is truly the right thing for the organization and achieves a win/win outcome for all the participants.

You might also be concerned about other GM divisions. If Oldsmobile were to be eliminated, its resources would be available to be distributed among other brands—Buick or Cadillac or Pontiac or Chevrolet or Saturn. The heads of those divisions might see an advantage to them and their programs in closing Oldsmobile and might therefore conduct "studies" of their own to show that GM resources could be better used elsewhere. (A disadvantage of being an unprincipled person is that other unprincipled people may find that the best way to advance their self-interest is to undercut you. As a principled person, you must be aware that others may find a variety of reasons to justify, at least to themselves, undercutting you or your goals.)

To win support, you might identify any risks that other divisions might have. "If Oldsmobile goes, they might get rid of Pontiac next!" could be an argument that gets the Pontiac division to support your position. If there's truth in that argument, it might be principled and appropriate to use it. The alliance with Saturn, mentioned earlier, is also a strategy you might consider.

You'd use your personal relationships with the chairman of GM and with other top managers to advocate for your position. It's possible that over the years you would have made some enemies, who might use your perceived vulnerability to attack you. You'd need to know who those people are and work out strategies to counter them. There's nothing inherently unprincipled about defense. (Later, we'll look at this problem from the other side—how you would work to get rid of Oldsmobile as a GM division.)

The organizational dynamic that makes office politics your reality is inherently complex and also different in different organizations. You have to understand why some people are allies and others enemies, why certain decisions are made in certain ways, and how numerous outside factors come into play in shaping decisions that are officially supposed to be made only in terms of customer focus and shareholder value. The goal of this chapter is to help you do this.

You and the People You Work With

> We have no eternal allies, and we have no perpetual enemies. Our interests are eternal and perpetual, and those interests it is our duty to follow.
> Henry John Temple, 3rd Viscount Palmerston, British
> Prime Minister, 1848

People, whether they are principled, unprincipled, differently principled, indifferently principled, or extremist, operate on the basis of their interests and principles as they see them. When you are clear about your own interests and your own goals, you can get a picture of how you relate to those around you. When you understand the interests and goals of others, you gain insight into their likely moves and identify countermoves if appropriate. In this book, you'll learn a powerful model for classifying and understanding those relationships and for developing strategies to work better with them.

In this chapter, we'll continue our exploration of the Political Environment model (see Figure 4-1) by seeing how the environment affects the attitudes and behavior of individuals in their relationship with you and others, by looking at the center section of the overall model.

Commonality of Interest

Interests may be shared, conflicting, or compatible. A shared interest in an organizational or project vision may represent two people who agree on substance. A conflicting interest might involve two people who want the same promotion. While the interest is the same, there is no commonality, only competition.

Figure 4-1: The Political Environment/People

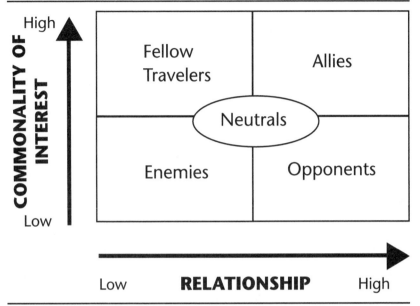

A compatible interest, on the other hand, is a nonidentical interest that supports the same overall plan or strategy. For example, the primary political reason for U.S. support for the Apollo moon program was competition with the Soviet Union. On the other hand, a significant constituency within NASA cared far more about the scientific payoffs and the chance to lay the foundation for eventual human colonization of space than about who got there first. The interests of Congress and the White House on the one hand and the NASA professionals on the other were compatible, but not identical.

WII-FM? Are your goals compatible, or do each of you receive different benefits from achieving the goal? These compatible interests can be negotiated with relative ease, with a win/win outcome quite achievable. Congress and the White House don't lose their vision or goals by accommodating scientific research; NASA achieves far more progress on its mission by accommodating the national competitive need.

It's nice when two or more people share the same vision, but it's not always possible or even necessary. Look for ways that other people can benefit from your objectives, and you'll find yourself with more allies and supporters.

Relationship

Trust is an essential foundation of good relationships, but other factors come into play as well. Personal like and dislike can exist apart from issues of trust, and trust itself can be subdivided into trust in someone's integrity and trust in someone's competence. The shifting alliances in an organization aren't exactly parallel to political parties; they are more like factions, and you often belong—or are perceived to belong—to a faction in your organization, whether you do or not. Whom you have lunch with is a highly significant political act.

Factions form around interests, departments, and programs; they also form around individuals. Because strong individuals often provoke strong reactions, you may find yourself on the receiving end of negative emotions that don't have anything to do with your behavior. That's often the result of your perceived factional alliance. The political biographer Robert Caro observed about New York state politics that there was an expression, "They go way back," used to describe a relationship that is so negative, so toxic, and so apparently immune to reconciliation that the word "hatred" does not quite do it justice.[2]

It's vital to know about such personal rivalries and personal friendships in understanding the relationship terrain.

Classifying the People around You

Take the key players in your organizational environment (the ones identified in the previous section), and classify them using the quadrants in the Political Environment model.

Person	Primary Goals	Quality of Relationship	Commonality of Interest	Quadrant
(SAMPLE) Mary Smith	Career advancement	Good	Frequently in synch	Ally
(SAMPLE) Sandra Jones	Defensive and Project	Poor	Shared interest on project success	Fellow traveler

Understanding and Using the Political Environment Roles

Forgive your enemies, but never forget their names.
John F. Kennedy, President of the United States

Some people inhabit a certain quadrant in the Political Environment model and will never change. Others wander from quadrant to quadrant, depending on the issue at hand, their alliances shifting with their interests. This helps us remember that there are two purposes in using the inner section of the Political Environment model:

1. To identify what tactics are appropriate in dealing with different people
2. To move people from disadvantageous quadrants into more advantageous ones

Both these strategies are possible. Not only can you apply appropriate tactics on the basis of where people are, but you have significant power to move a person's position on the grid. Consider the following principles:

• *Principle #1. Have the courage to make hard decisions, and the empathy to work with people nonetheless.* In business, sometimes you must take stands and make decisions that have a negative impact on others. As a supervisor or manager, you might have to fire people, or you might have to lay people off through no fault of their own. Don't shy away from the deed. Either do it cleanly, firmly, and quickly, or don't do it at all. This is not inconsistent with being a principled person. Having principles does not exempt you from making hard decisions. As one executive observed in a personal conversation with the authors, "You know you're an executive when you realize they don't pay you for making good decisions. They pay you for making decisions when all the alternatives are stinky, dangerous, and unpleasant."

You must do that job, and you must do it cleanly and firmly, even when it may hurt others. But don't neglect relationships even in the worst of circumstances. You can try to help people with outplacement if you must terminate their employment or otherwise work to minimize the human damage, as long as it can be done without compromising organizational principle. If someone isn't going to get a promotion he or she wants, you can still recognize the person's value and empathize with the pain. Obviously, you can't take away all the negativity, but you can usually do something positive.

If you can avoid the need to make a decision that will hurt others, do so. If you cannot, do it cleanly. Is that compatible with being principled? It can be. Consider your objections to the negative behavior: Are they principled or simply squeamish? You can't eat meat and despise the butcher. On the other hand, you might find the sight of blood highly unpleasant. A commitment to a vegan lifestyle, for example, can be principled. A meat-eater's dislike of the sight of blood is simply squeamishness.

Squeamishness is not principle. It is unpleasant to fire someone or lay someone off, but if that is necessary behavior that fits your principled objectives, then you must overcome the emotional reluctance and do the job. Failure to do so would be a betrayal of your principles.

Worse, squeamishness or lack of courage comes back to haunt you in all sorts of negative ways. It opens you up to manipulation, it causes people to think of you as weak and to despise you, even if your cowardice and squeamishness are actually beneficial to them. If someone is behaving in a way that means he or she should be fired, and you don't act, everyone else in your department will recognize your cowardice for what it is, and even the person who escapes being fired will think of you as weak and ineffectual, not as kind and supportive.

• *Principle #2. For long-term success, build good relationships; for short-term success, build commonality of interest.* Your short-term strategies are enhanced by focusing on building commonality of interest rather than on improving relationships. Your long-term strategies, on the other hand, are enhanced by focusing on improving relationships much more than through building commonality of interest. Fortunately, the two are linked. Building on commonality of interest is a good way to improve relationships, and vice versa.

The reason commonality of interest works better in the short run is that people can make tactical decisions that are compatible with yours. But this way does little to build up long-term trust; it's clear everyone is working to achieve his or her self-interest. Relationships based on trust and integrity, in contrast, help you in two critical areas: getting your opponents to respect you and keeping enemies from getting personal.

• *Principle #3. Avoid making enemies.* The worst position for someone to occupy is that of your enemy, because the political fight can get ugly, defense is necessary, and war may be inevitable. The best position is that of ally, because, although people may have different goals, if they can be made compatible in a common direction, everybody can win.

We tend to think of all conflict as rational on some level. That is, the different parties have goals and act in whatever they think is the best way to meet those goals. As Clausewitz's famous dictum has it, "War is the continuation of policy by other means." Clearly, that's sometimes true and valid. But that idea doesn't explain a lot of other human behavior, which is deeply emotional and irrational and often destructive even to the person who is behaving irrationally. Some of the truly negative and horrible aspects of office politics involve people who are willing to damage their own interests if by doing so they can cause pain to others. History demonstrates again and again how irrationality, not rationality, guides conflict and warfare at all levels.[3]

Having opponents is normal, and the tension that results can actually produce positive results in many cases. Having enemies, in contrast, dramatically escalates your risks and produces few, if any, benefits.

Let's look in detail at the five sections people can occupy in your political environment: allies, fellow travelers, opponents, enemies, and four flavors of neutrals.

Allies

> The friendship of nations, built on common interests, cannot survive the mutability of those interests.
> Agnes Repplier, "Allies," *Under Dispute*, 1924

Figure 4-2: Allies

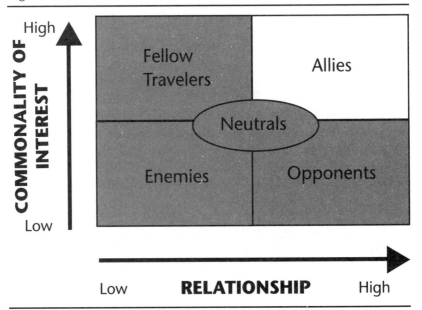

Your allies are people with whom you share a commonality of interest and a good relationship (Figure 4-2). They are the most valuable people in your network, because their actions can advance your interests and you can often share concerns and difficulties with them for constructive purpose.

Your goals in working with allies are:

- To maximize the quality and range of the alliance
- To identify the extent of alliance when people are with you sometimes and not other times
- To increase the number of effective allies in your network

Maximize Quality and Range of the Alliance

In maximizing the quality of your allies and the range of your alliances, consider the following factors:

• ***Permanent and situational allies.*** Allies may be permanent or situational. A permanent ally is someone who sees her or his interests and relationship with you as a key value and can be trusted on a wide range of issues. In the event a permanent ally doesn't see a particular issue the same way as you, he or she may yet decide to go along because of the value of the alliance long term.

A situational ally is someone with whom you have a good relationship and strong commonality of interest on a certain issue or group of issues. A situational ally will sometimes be an ally, sometimes a neutral, and sometimes an opponent, depending on the circumstances. As long as you're aware of the limits to the alliance, this is perfectly okay.

• ***Dominance and relationship issues.*** Whether permanent or situational, an ally likely has interests and long-term goals of her or his own, and understanding those interests is one of the keys to making the relationship work. One possible issue is that of dominance: Does the ally want to be your equal, your protégé, or your mentor? The status relationship of you and your allies can be complex. The communications expert Dr. Deborah Tannen observes that these interpersonal transactions can be both about status and about connection, which are not mutually exclusive, although it might seem that way. The two dynamics can dovetail and even include each other. The same transaction that can bring two people closer can also affect the determination of which one is in control.[4]

One of the reasons for the popularity of *The Godfather*, both as a book and as a film, is that we recognize in the complex world of organized crime echoes of our own environment (without, one hopes, the gunfire). "Every time I try to get out," Michael Corleone says, "they pull me right back in."

In the beginning of Mario Puzo's book (and in the opening of the first film of *The Godfather* trilogy), the relation of friendship and power is made crystal clear in the famous scene in which a man who has spurned Don Corleone's friendship asks for help. Corleone agrees to help him as a friend, observing, "Some day, and that day may never come, I will call upon you to do me a service in return." At that moment, Corleone has no idea whether he will ever want a payback for his favor; it is simply his policy to do favors in the same way another person would save money—it's an investment.

It's generally a bad political strategy to make the quid pro quo that obvious, especially if you're not Don Corleone. But doing favors is a time-honored technique for building and expanding your power and influence—and the act of doing services for others is certainly part of principled behavior. Remember too, that unlike someone who takes a favor from Don Corleone, not everyone for whom you do favors will pay you back if asked. Not all investments pay off.

A related concern, besides the obvious issue of being careful from whom you accept favors, is to make sure you remember clearly that the essential political issue is politics is often primarily about the exchange of favors and support. Friendship matters, but business friendship isn't identical to personal friendship. As the agent who double-crosses Jerry Maguire in the eponymous movie says, "That's why it's called show *business*, not show *friends*."

Don't think it must be that bleak; business friends can have good relationships, even though the level and nature of such a friendship differ from those of social and personal friends. Value all friendships, understanding their range and limitations, and remember that a limited or situational friendship is still better than most available alternatives.

• ***Building alliance relationships.*** The issue of building good alliances is, first, a matter of understanding your own interests and goals and, second, a matter of deep understanding of the interests and goals of your allies.

Understanding others' interests regardless of their relationship to you is a key political skill. The negotiation experts Roger Fisher and William Ury consider that an essential focus is to remember that "the other side" are human beings with values, emotions, backgrounds, and every other aspect of the human context. You must always be careful to keep the human elements in any relationship clear in your mind.[5]

Because interests and goals are seldom identical, you have to be particularly careful in your understanding. The trust you can afford to have in someone is a factor of how well his or her interests are served by your alliance. This doesn't have to be as cynical as it sounds: Savvy people know that long-term friendship is a political asset not to be squandered lightly. Your reputation is of enormous value; once destroyed, especially if it is destroyed by your own betrayal, it is enormously difficult to repair.

In managing your interests with your allies, make sure you maintain honesty and integrity in all your dealings with them. Silence may sometimes be necessary; lying generally is not.

Managing your interests involves seeing your allies' interests and goals as a priority as you decide on your actions and choices. You may not always be able to satisfy all their goals, but you can show your commitment to them in actions and words.

When your allies have interests you don't share but that don't actively conflict with your own, be prepared to show your support for those interests, because in the long run you need your allies to support you the same way. (On the other hand, there are fights that don't affect you at all, so stay out of them.)

Identify the Extent of the Alliance

Whether allies are permanent or situational, they are normally limited to some specific sphere. No matter how loyal you are to your allies, there is probably a limit to the price you're willing to pay in support of your political objectives. You might quit your job over certain matters of principle, but in many other political battles, if you lose you still want to keep your job. When you are asking others to support you, you need to be mindful of the limits in the support you're likely to get.

One of your allies wants your support for a promotion she wants. Of course, you will provide support, but how much, and when does it stop? You likely wouldn't go to your manager and say, "Either she gets the promotion or I quit." That's too high of a price to pay and an ally who would demand it is probably a questionable ally. On the other hand, you might go in and make a pitch for the person, provide background about the job, or give a briefing about the style of the interviewing official.

Similarly, you might expect an ally to support your new product idea in meetings, and let you know about objections and problems privately in advance so you have a chance to modify your proposal or prepare responses to the objections. You wouldn't expect your ally to embrace an idea he or she obviously felt was bad, or to help you preempt discussion by launching it without obtaining approvals.

Consider the following issues:

- *What do they stand to gain?* People will do what you want when doing so benefits them at a reasonable cost with an acceptable level of risk. To work well with allies, you want to maximize their payoff from cooperating and mutual support. To do this, you must first make sure you understand their payoffs, as discussed earlier.

- *What do they stand to lose?* If there is no risk and no potential for conflict, the issue isn't really very political. Be realistic about the risk, cost, and outcome of loss in a political battle. What if your vision for the project turns out not to prevail? What if you don't get the promotion you're after? Consider the losses on your part and on the part of your allies. You can try to reduce that loss or reduce the likelihood of loss.

Perceptions of acceptable loss aren't simply the inverse of perceptions of identical gain. The decision theory expert H. W. Lewis points out that in investment decisions, a dollar isn't always equal to a dollar. If you had a fifty-fifty chance of gaining a thousand dollars or losing five hundred, pure logic might suggest taking the gamble. But for someone on a fixed income, the five hundred dollars might be money needed for survival, compared to a bonus thousand dollars that would be spent on luxuries. The amounts are hardly equal.[6] For you, loss and gain are also not reciprocal. The possible gain of a promotion and raise may be of less value to you than the possibility of losing your job. Such trade-offs are completely rational, as long as you make them thoughtfully.

• *What is their tolerance for risk and conflict?* Tolerance for risk and conflict is a matter of individual style and temperament, affected by what's at stake. When you ask your allies to take risks or engage in conflict above their comfort and payoff level, they retreat into the neutral category. They are still your allies, but not in this fight. Don't be angry or too pushy, or else you'll lose them as long-term allies. If you need them in the fight, you will either have to reduce the risk/conflict or increase the payoff *to them.*

Increase the Number of Effective Allies in Your Network

It may be worthwhile to try to be friendly with just about everybody, but not everyone is worth getting as an ally. To be valuable, an ally must be able to offer something of value to the alliance, making it more likely to achieve its goals. When someone seeks out the opportunity to ally with you, be grateful but careful. People want to be allies with you for *their* reasons, and you must know what they are.

One critically important issue in organizations is that you are often judged and characterized by the people with whom you associate. If a lunchroom group is seen as politically out of touch, or highly disgruntled and negative, having lunch with them on a regular basis will do real damage to how others—especially people at higher levels of management—see you.

You may find that when you start a new job, it's people in the negative or out-of-power groups who are the first to seek you out, the first to offer you inclusion, and that's because they are hungry for new members. While you don't want to reject friendly overtures, you want to wait until you know what's going on and who's who before you become a member of any particular group. (If this sounds a little like high school cliques, that's not surprising. After all, just about everyone you meet went to high school and had experiences parallel to your own. It shouldn't be surprising that such powerful imprinting experiences still affect how people relate in organizations.)

Nevertheless, in general, allies are a source of valuable political power, and your general goal should be to expand your network of allies and supporters. Here are some strategies for achieving this:

• ***Work at moving people from the other quadrants.*** The two most effective methods to make someone an ally are to build a commonality of interest and to build a good relationship. It's often easier to find commonality of interest where mutual trust and respect already exist; you may find it easier to turn members of the opposition into allies than to turn fellow travelers into allies.

The single most effective thing you can do is to be honest and forthright in your dealings, to be someone who is dependable and reliable. People like this attract allies, because they are trustworthy.

The second most effective thing you can do is to work very hard to understand the interests and goals of the people around you. To find a common interest, you have to understand others' interests. Work at putting yourself in others' shoes, seeing situations from different points of view and always providing respectful acknowledgment of others' points of view, even if you disagree with them.

• *Demonstrate that you are an ally worth having.* Not everyone is worth having as an ally because not everyone can contribute to getting the goal accomplished. To have others seek you out as an ally, you want to demonstrate that you have clout, which is the power to get things done. You'll learn more about how to develop power and attract power in Chapter 5.

• *Stand up for your allies.* When the going gets tough, the tough get going—sometimes at full speed in retreat! Be careful about bugging out when the situation becomes more difficult than you had expected. While you want to cut your losses before they become unacceptable to you, you also want to show that you aren't simply a "fair-weather friend." Consider the potential price you may have to pay when considering whether to provide political support or conduct a political action. Be prepared to pay that price and stand up for the people who stand up for you; the alternative may work in the short run but will deprive you of allies in the long run. (Don't turn this into a blank check for your allies, both actual and potential. Is the fight any of your business? Do you really believe that your allies are in the right? What is the level of risk you are running? What level of support is requested, and what do you have to actually do to be useful? It's far easier to lend a sympathetic ear than to resign your job as an act of protest.)

• *Give support to get support.* Not everyone's issue is your issue, but if you value and need the person's support, take on some issues for the sake of the relationship, whether it's building a relationship or nurturing one that already exists. Don't rush around supporting everyone, however; it doesn't work. Instead, focus on being an excellent listener when people come to you for help and support. Make sure you fully understand the issue and what you're being asked to do. Don't make promises lightly, because it's absolutely crucial that you live up to whatever promises you make. Don't be afraid of the quid pro quo: I give you this because I want that. Exchanging favors and support is the primary currency of the political workplace.

WORKING WITH YOUR ALLIES

List your allies and answer the following questions for each:

My allies:

1. _____   4. _____

2. _____   5. _____

3. _____   6. _____

  1. Is this ally permanent or situational?

  _____

  _____

  2. What is the strength of our relationship built on?

  _____

  _____

  3. What are our common interests and goals?

  _____

  _____

  4. How can our relationship be strengthened?

  _____

  _____

  5. Does this ally have specific "hot buttons," either emotional or
     job related?

  _____

  _____

6. What political skills, powers, and influence does this ally possess?

_____

_____

7. What does my ally want from me?

_____

_____

8. How are this ally and this ally's associates perceived in the organization?

_____

_____

9. How can I demonstrate my value as an ally to this person or group?

_____

_____

10. How can I best maximize the value of this alliance relationship?

_____

_____

Using the Exercise in Your Work

To do your very best in an alliance relationship, it helps to understand fully what the relationship is and how it works, who the other person is, and what are the issues and goals that make the alliance strong. By thinking about these questions, you can determine not only how to maximize your current alliance base, but also consider how others might be able to become your allies with some effort on your part.

Fellow Travelers

> Every government is in some respects a problem for every other government, and it will always be this way so long as the sovereign state, with its supremely self-centered rationale, remains the basis of international life.
> George F. Kennan, *Russia and the West Under Lenin and Stalin*, 1961

Fellow travelers are people with whom you share a commonality of interest but with whom you don't have a strong relationship (Figure 4-3). That means you have a limited degree of trust at work and a constant risk that your interests may suddenly diverge. Fellow travelers tend to be with you on some issues and against you on others; their value as allies is limited because you cannot afford to take them too fully into

Figure 4-3: Fellow Travelers

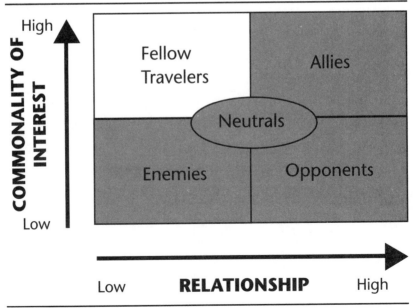

your confidence. The concept of "trust, but verify" is important here; make sure your agreements with them are capable of being measured in objective terms—don't leave very much to doubt and different interpretations.

Some fellow travelers can turn into allies in the long run; others will never move fully into your camp, for reasons ranging from their untrustworthiness to your membership in different power cliques within the organization. Knowing how to work with fellow travelers is an important part of moving within the office political environment. With fellow travelers, your goals are:

- To determine the extent of the common interest
- To adjust tactics and confidence building according to the limits and benefits of the relationship
- To maximize common interest and identify common liability
- To build the relationship

Determine the Extent of the Common Interest

If someone is a fellow traveler on political issues that are of concern to you, yet doesn't qualify as a full ally, then the first thing you need to do is measure the extent of the common interest. In what ways does the person support you or your goals? This is the essence of a lot of political maneuvering.

You can determine the extent of the common interest in several ways. You can make sure communication is honest and complete and that you develop a reputation for clear and candid communication. While this won't solve all your communications or political conflicts, it will help you establish a reputation that will make it easier for you to work with people in all four quadrants. By sharing your goals and plans, you make it easier for others to be candid with you.

Adjust Tactics and Confidence Building

By being realistic about what the relationship and common interest is and is not, you can select a tactical and strategic approach that will work best for both parties. The first strategy is to promote win/win outcomes, those that make both parties to the relationship feel that their essential needs have been recognized and met to the extent possible. Stay aware that these essential needs can be emotional as well as substantive. Roger Fisher and colleagues observe that understanding is not merely about the intellect but also about the emotional level—and often the emotional level is more important.[7] Get in the habit of role reversal, putting yourself in the other party's shoes and seeing the situation from that person's point of view.

Don't push the relationship farther or faster than it will go. If someone is a fellow traveler on a limited issue and you'd like to make her or him an ally on a wider front, you have to start by understanding the current limits of the relationship, the reason for those limits, and the history that already exists that limits change.

Maximize Common Interest and Analyze Liability

As Benjamin Franklin observed at the signing of the Declaration of Independence, "We must all hang together, or assuredly we shall all hang separately." The cooperation of a fellow traveler is a matter of mutual self-interest. You can count on the cooperation as long as the other person believes her or his interests are best supported by cooperation; if that ceases to be the case, you can expect the behavior to change.

Ask yourself (and the fellow traveler) whether there are any ways to increase your common interests and goals. Analyze risk and potential liability should your project fail. Is there a point at which it would be in the other party's best interest to double-cross you or leave you hanging to cut her or his losses? Is there a point at which it would be in your best interest? (This doesn't mean you should double-cross. The double-cross, while sometimes tactically appropriate—although even at best ethically questionable—tends to be strategically inappropriate because the other person remembers it forever. It can come back to haunt you. You can, however, leave an alliance of convenience if necessary; just make sure you are clear and honest in advance of your withdrawal.)

Build the Relationship

Trustworthiness is not the only ingredient in building a relationship, but it is essential.

Building trust takes time, especially with people who have reason to distrust you from past experience or who have reason to distrust the faction or side with which you are affiliated. Patience is highly recommended.

WORKING WITH FELLOW TRAVELERS

List your fellow travelers and answer the following questions for each:

My fellow travelers:

1. ————————————   4. ————————————

2. ————————————   5. ————————————

3. ————————————   6. ————————————

1. What specific interests and goals do I share with this fellow traveler?

————————————————————————————

————————————————————————————

2. What are the limits or problems in our relationship? Can they be overcome, and, if so, how?

————————————————————————————

————————————————————————————

3. What steps can I take to maximize mutual confidence?

————————————————————————————

————————————————————————————

4. What risks and liabilities exist in the relationship?

_____

_____

5. Does this fellow traveler have specific "hot buttons," either emotional or job related?

_____

_____

6. What political skills, powers, and influence does this fellow traveler possess?

_____

_____

7. What does this fellow traveler want from me?

_____

_____

8. How can I best maximize the value of this relationship?

_____

_____

Using the Exercises in Your Work

With all the relationship types in this model, understanding is a source of power. With fellow travelers, pay particular attention to the reasons they aren't full allies. A person can easily be a fellow traveler on one issue and turn on you the next. Use these questions to think about how the relationship is deficient, and what you can do to better it.

Opponents

> Don't oppose forces, use them.
> Buckminster Fuller, futurist

Your opponents are people with whom you share a good relationship but with whom you have little commonality of interest (Figure 4-4). The mutual respect and the strength of the relationship mean that you can often work with them even when your interests are directly opposed.

Like allies (and enemies, for that matter), opponents can be either situational or permanent. A situational opponent on one issue might be neutral or even an ally on another issue, increasing the payoff for preserving the relationship. A permanent opponent is one who sees her or his interests as being in conflict with yours on a more or less regular basis (though

Figure 4-4: Opponents

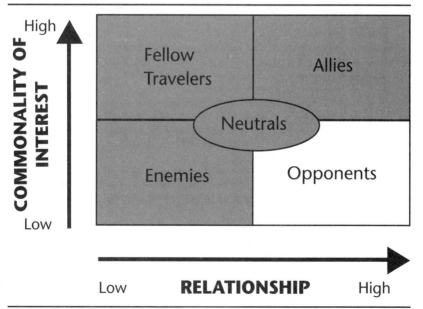

there may be narrow opportunities for collaboration or negotiation) but with whom you enjoy mutual respect and trust.

The great advantage in dealing with opponents (as opposed to enemies) is that they generally don't wish you ill. They want to win, which is different. You may find them more open to discussion and even negotiation, with the goal of finding a way to satisfy both parties.

The following principles apply to dealing with your opponents:

- Preserve and extend the relationship, especially when you have to be in conflict about the issues.
- Identify any common interests and goals that allow you the opportunity to work together.
- Keep lines of communication open at all times.
- Fight fair when you have to fight.

Preserve and Extend the Relationship

Mutual respect, understanding, and empathy are the key ingredients that make your relationships with opponents viable. If someone really is your opponent, then your interests and goals are in conflict. On the other hand, sometimes the perception is that interests and goals are in conflict, but a deeper analysis reveals there is more commonality of interest available than you previously thought. Whichever is the case, empathic listening is an effective strategy.

In the first case, where interests and goals are truly in conflict, the quality of your working relationship is what keeps opposition from deteriorating into enmity. It's much easier to believe the other side is malevolent if you don't know them; similarly, it's easier for them to suspect your motives if you have a poor working relationship. Keeping the conflict from becoming personal helps both parties and keeps your opponents from becoming your enemies.

In the second case, where interests and goals only appear to be in opposition, empathic listening brings you closer to the root problem. Identifying the real underlying issues is often the major element in a negotiation; many problems simply evaporate when they're truly understood. Other times, you may discover that the conflict involves a relatively minor part of your goal, allowing you to compromise or give in on the contested point without cost. Sometimes it's possible to turn an opponent into an ally, and this strategy maximizes the possibility of cooperation.

Identify Common Interests and Goals

Because of the strength of the relationship, even if someone is truly and necessarily an opponent of yours, it's often possible to work together on matters of common interest. Senator Ted Kennedy, a Democrat, and Senator Arlen Specter, a Republican, are at odds on many issues, yet they were able to collaborate on passing a health care plan. Neither senator surrendered his fundamental values; they both were able to find some issues on which they agreed, and both therefore were able to bring their own allies to the table. Probably neither senator got 100 percent of what he wanted, but another principle of politics of all stripes is "Half a loaf is better than no bread."

You'll find an extensive discussion of win/win negotiation techniques in Chapter 8. While negotiation can happen with people in all sections of this model, it is in dealing with your opponents that the maximum opportunity for gain is normally present. The difference between compromise (settling for reduced loss) and consensus (working to satisfy both interests and possibly ending up with 80 percent of what you want) is vital in understanding how to work best in such situations.

Keep Lines of Communication Open

While the strategy of empathic listening is essential, so also is your ability to be candid and exact about your position and your goals. Assertive communication is your ability to be clear, unafraid, and strong in stating what you want and need.

Practice the skill of using nonjudgmental, or descriptive, language. "He hates me" is judgmental language because it is a conclusion. What is the evidence that he hates you? Perhaps there is evidence—he called you names, he told someone else he hated you, he went to your boss to complain—and the description of that evidence is descriptive language. We recommend descriptive over judgmental language for several reasons. First, your conclusion may be wrong. Perhaps he or she doesn't hate you after all; there may be another explanation. Second, judgmental language tends to be resisted and to provoke arguments, especially if someone doesn't like the conclusion you've drawn. It's easier to start and maintain dialogue based on descriptive language.

Avoid "red flag" words and phrases you know that set the other person off. Try to stay away from "should" and "ought" words. Keep your tone of voice even and calm. Maintain good eye contact and relaxed and open body posture. These are the ingredients of effective assertive communication, and, while there are no guarantees, this process tends to support better mutual understanding and eventual solutions.

Fight Fair When You Have to Fight

When it's impossible to find common interest and common ground, then it's time to fight. Fighting is one of the things that happens in the political arena, and occasionally it's appropriate to do so. When you are fighting with your opponents, you certainly try to win, but remember the relationship. Today's fight will end at some point, and one of your goals, win or lose (preferably win), is to finish the fight in a way that the relationship is preserved for the future.

You have the assertive right and need to advocate for your position. To preserve the relationship, fight fairly and with integrity. This includes doing your homework, providing a factual and values-based rationale for your position, confronting openly and honestly, and being assertive, rather than aggressive.

Avoid tactics that either are or seem to be underhanded or sneaky, such as these:

• *Short-circuiting the chain of command.* This involves bypassing your boss and going to higher levels of management to achieve your goals. Whatever short-term gain you may receive from this tactic, it leaves substantial bitterness and distrust in its wake. It also makes you look like someone who isn't aware of the unwritten rules of the organization, or someone who is willing to double-cross or undercut a supervisor.

• ***Undercutting your opponent's position or motives behind his or her back.*** This tactic always presents the risk that your opponent will find out what you've done, which will end up casting a negative aura on virtually everything else you have to say. It's also a guaranteed way to make a fight personal, not professional.

• ***Using anger or negative emotions to influence outcomes.*** Such behavior smacks of childhood temper tantrums, or "I'll take my ball and go home" selfishness. This isn't to say that you must never get angry at work. In fact, anger is a perfectly legitimate emotion and often has a way of adding credibility if kept within bounds. It says that you have passion and that your ideas are important to you, and those are facts that others seriously consider in reaching their decisions. The critical difference is between anger and losing your temper. The first has legitimate uses; the second demonstrates that you're not in control of yourself.

WORKING WITH OPPONENTS

List your opponents and answer the following questions for each:

My opponents:

1. _____   4. _____

2. _____   5. _____

3. _____   6. _____

1. What specific interests and goals are at the root of the conflict with this opponent? Can they be minimized or eliminated?

_____

_____

2. What are the strengths in this relationship? How can they be preserved and enhanced?

_____

_____

3. What steps can I take to maximize mutual confidence?

_____

_____

4. What powers does this opponent have that can be used against me or my interests?

_____

_____

5. Does this opponent have specific "hot buttons," either emotional or job related?

_____

_____

6. What political skills, powers, and influence does this opponent possess?

_____

_____

7. What does this opponent want from me?

_____

_____

8. How can I best minimize the obstacles in this relationship?

_____

_____

Using the Exercises in Your Work

In many ways, opponents, who usually have different goals, can be the most interesting to work with. Sometimes opponents strengthen you and your ideas—so it's best not to take them lightly. Instead, use these questions to improve your understanding of these relationships and to figure out how you can maximize the value that potentially exists.

Enemies

> A man cannot be too careful in the choice of his enemies.
> Oscar Wilde, *The Picture of Dorian Gray*, 1891

Because enemies are people with whom you have little or no commonality of interest and a bad relationship, their opposition can get personal . . . and ugly (Figure 4-5). The first rule of dealing with enemies is not to be too eager to put people into that category, or, as the traditional maxim goes, "Never attribute to malice what can satisfactorily be explained by stupidity."

While making enemies may well be unavoidable in life, the key principle is *never make an enemy by accident*. Most people have broken that rule at some time in their lives. Through a chance remark or clumsy behavior, you may have discovered that you've mortally offended someone without intending to do so.

You may need to make an enemy for good, deliberate reasons. Perhaps the right thing to do for the department or organization is to get someone removed from a position of power and authority. Perhaps you need to bring a mistake or poor judgment to the attention of management. Perhaps someone isn't showing good standards of ethical behavior. Perhaps you need to stand up to a harasser or a bully.

Figure 4-5: Enemies

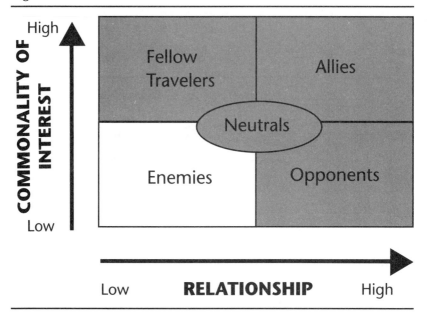

Sometimes you inherit enemies in developing allies. If your manager and another manager "go back a long way," and you feel loyalty toward your manager, you may inherit the enmity. If two departments are rivals, your support of one department may make you the target of another. Sometimes office behavior resembles grammar school: "If you're going to be friends with so-and-so, then I hate you."

It's important to decide whether the value of the ally is worth the liability of the enemy. If it's not your fight, stay on the sidelines and seek neutrality.

In dealing with your enemies, consider the following:

- To what extent you can move them into another quadrant (fellow traveler or opponent)
- Whether the enmity is personal or professional in nature
- How much damage they can do, and how you can minimize it
- What positive and defensive strategies you should adopt in dealing with them

Moving Enemies into Other Quadrants

To turn an enemy into merely a member of your opposition, your goal is to build a positive relationship. Remember that a positive relationship is not the same thing as a friendship, or at least not the same thing as a personal friendship. Here are some specific techniques:

• *Show respect for the enemy's opinions and goals (which is not necessarily the same thing as agreeing with them).* Recognize your enemy's opinions as seriously held beliefs, not merely as cover for some baser motive. Sometimes, of course, they may merely be camouflage for simple selfishness, but it's seldom worth your while to call attention to that fact. Saving face is an important element in determining whether someone will back down from a position under pressure, and you want to provide someone with a graceful way to retreat. It's in everyone's best interest.

• *Act in a trustworthy and honest fashion, even if your enemy doesn't.* In addition to the desirable goal of turning an enemy into someone less dangerous, remember that your actions toward one person, however appropriately motivated, are interpreted by others as evidence of how you might behave toward them in some other context.

• *Listen empathically to your enemy's point of view, and demonstrate that you understand it.* If you cannot understand a point of view, it will not be possible for you to work effectively with it. And good listening always tends to reduce tension and negativity, which allows relationship building to proceed.

• *Take your enemy's objections seriously, and consider them in a thoughtful and appropriate way.* You can always consider carefully what someone says; this does not obligate you to change your mind in any way. From time to time, however, you may discover that taking the time to listen thoroughly and thoughtfully can reveal that there's a deficiency in your own position on an issue and that it may be appropriate for you to back down.

- *Show that you keep your word, and do what you say.*
This applies in both positive and negative situations. Don't
make threats you won't or can't back up; do follow through
on any promises made. While honorable people aren't automatically likable, it's at least somewhat more difficult to hate
them, and that helps move you out of the "enemy" category.

To turn an enemy into a fellow traveler, your goal is to
find and develop commonality of interests. To do that, you
must also practice good listening to get beyond a person's
stated positions to the underlying interests that drive those
positions. Brainstorm creative options—the "third way" approach—to see whether you can discover a win/win outcome
that helps your enemy while helping you.

By practicing these techniques, you can reduce the number of enemies you have and also influence the supporters
of your enemies to think of you in a more positive fashion.
Especially if you've been the victim of bad-mouthing, you can
often turn the tables by being a much nicer, more reasonable,
more honest, and more able person than you've been por-
trayed as being. In that way, someone's gossip or backbiting
attacks on you can actually lead to a more favorable position
for you later on. (This is still another reason to avoid using
such destructive tactics yourself.)

Be patient and don't give up hope. Speaker of the House
Tip O'Neill said, "I ran for the Massachusetts legislature six
times and a total of 118 persons ran against me. The day after
every election, I'd call my opponents, thank them, and ask
them for their support in the general election. When I ran for
Congress in 1952, all 118 signed an ad for me. Always regard
and respect your opponents."[8]

Is the Enmity Personal or Professional?

Enemies are particularly dangerous because they have the
natural incentive to do you harm and in extreme cases will
oppose otherwise good and constructive ideas merely because
you are in favor of them. During the consulship of Julius Caesar in 59 B.C., he had so many enemies in the Roman Senate

that his colleague in the consulship, Marcus Bibulus, who was a member of the opposing party, obstructed everything Caesar proposed.[9] In her novel of the period, Colleen McCullough, drawing from original transcripts of the senate session, reports this dialogue:[10]

> "If you're so against the law, Marcus Bibulus," cried Caesar . . . "then tell me why?" . . .
>
> "I oppose because you're promulgating, Caesar, for no other reason! Whatever you do is cursed, unholy, evil!"

Hatred—even unreasoning hatred—is a powerful weapon, and one you want to avoid giving to your enemies. Where does this kind of hatred come from? Most often, it comes from someone's perception that a personal slight or injury has been done to him or her. If you're on the receiving end of this sort of emotional attack, then you must find out the source of the original injury and repair it if you can. Often, you may find the slight is something you consider minor; perhaps it wasn't deliberate or malicious in intent.

Former senator Bob Dole, the Republican candidate for president in 1996, was interviewed by reporter Bob Woodward for a magazine article. He was informed that President Clinton had some personal dislike for him. Surprised, he asked why. Woodward told Dole that the former senator had called for the appointment of a special prosecutor on the day of Clinton's mother's funeral. "That doesn't sound like me," Dole said, but he checked and discovered that he in fact had done so. As a result, he wrote a letter of apology to the President, who accepted it, and their relationship improved as a result. Both Dole and Clinton well understood the importance of keeping opponents as opponents, not enemies. While their political opposition to each other did not change, this exchange kept the relationship from being one of enmity. If you discover that you've given someone offense, take the high road and apologize immediately and sincerely, even if you think the injury was trivial or imaginary. A simple remark putting someone down at a meeting, or scoring a debating point off someone in the heat of an argument, or even telling a joke that hits too close to home can make someone an enemy. This is how accidental enemies come into being.

Professional hatred can result from things such as getting a promotion or a position deeply desired by the other person, especially if the other person feels that the position was won because of favoritism or by unfair means. Given that people seldom like to think of themselves as incompetent or unable, people are quicker to jump to this conclusion than the facts sometimes warrant. Remember, it's their perception that becomes their reality. While understanding the root cause of this kind of enmity doesn't always allow you the chance to fix it, look for some constructive or positive gesture you can make. Being a good winner is important.

No matter what you do, you can't overcome all enmity that others may feel for you. Remember that the enemy is not the only person you're trying to influence. Your behavior toward your enemies affects the other people in your environment. If you show integrity, honesty, and a desire to make things right, and the other person throws your efforts back in your face, at least you look better to the others in the office, and that's a worthwhile benefit.

Analyzing and Minimizing the Damage They Can Do

In a military sense, the word "threat" is often used synonymously with "capability." In other words, an enemy poses a threat to the extent she or he has the power to do you harm. This is separate from the issue of whether the enemy actually intends to do you harm with that capability. You plan your defense on the basis of what they can do, rather than only what they're likely to do.

So, if you have an enemy, determine what exactly can he or she do to you, either in general or in the specific situation in which you find yourself.

Access to Decision Makers

Does your enemy have the power to go to your boss, your boss's boss, your customer, or other decision makers behind your back to provide information or an opinion that undercuts you before you go in? If so, look for your own ways of access, prepare good facts, and even use your own intelligence network to report on such contacts so you don't get blindsided.

Control of Resources You Need

Does your enemy have the power to decide whether (or when) you get access to the resources you need? This is a particularly pernicious power, especially when used with malice. However, if the person is supposed to give you cooperation, try some of the following ideas: Be respectful, but assertive. The other department or other person often has a responsibility to meet at least some of your needs. Negotiate, compromise, adjust your needs, use any flexibility you have, insist on the basics. Be prepared to seek higher authority if necessary, but go in without emotion, without accusation, and without a chip on your shoulder.

Inappropriate Communications Behaviors

Some enemies are disruptive in meetings, shouting you down like Bibulus did Caesar, using anger and rage as a technique to wear you and your allies down. Because many people are conflict averse, people unafraid of extreme behavior can bully a group into giving them their way. Study "difficult people" books and tapes for a wide range of tactics and strategies you can use to handle others' emotional behaviors.[11]

Appropriate Defensive/Positive Strategies

Here are some general policies and strategies for dealing with your enemies while you're trying to turn them into opponents or fellow travelers:

• *Keep an eye on them.* Make sure you know what they're up to, to whom they're talking, and what their issues are. Spycraft is statecraft, the saying goes; the quality and range of your organizational network is a powerful tool.

• *Keep your emotions in check.* One powerful strategy is to get your enemy to lose her or his temper or become publicly out of control. Don't use that strategy, but keep from becoming its victim.

• *Keep your relationship network expanding.* Don't believe that "the friend of my enemy is my enemy," or necessarily that "the enemy of my enemy is my friend." (At best, this turns someone only into a fellow traveler.) If you can't build a better relationship with your enemy, develop relationships with their friends. Don't use their friends to suborn the other relationship; it seldom works.

• *Keep your eye on your own goals.* As the saying goes, "Living well is the best revenge." Focus on achieving good results with your goals, and your enemies become less and less important in your life.

• *Keep your friends close . . . and your enemies closer.* Although it may be painful at times, refusing to yield to the temptation to just stay away from people who dislike you makes good political sense. You know it's harder to behave badly toward someone if he or she is physically present or is organizationally close enough that word will inevitably get back. It's harder for everyone, including your enemies. Therefore, staying close forces negative behavior to be done in the open, rather than behind your back.

WORKING WITH ENEMIES

List your enemies and answer the following questions for each:

My enemies:

1. _____   4. _____

2. _____   5. _____

3. _____   6. _____

1. What makes me sure this person is actually an enemy? Could something else be going on instead?

_____

_____

2. What events or actions made the relationship bad? Do I owe an apology—or would one help?

_____

_____

3. What steps can I take to maximize mutual confidence and repair the relationship?

_____

_____

4. Is there an organizational reason for this person to be my enemy (e.g., my alliance with others, membership in a faction)?

_____

_____

5. Does this enemy have specific "hot buttons," either emotional or job related?

_____

_____

6. What political skills, powers, and influence does this enemy possess?

_____

_____

7. What does this enemy want from me?

_____

_____

8. How can I best defend myself and protect my interests?

_____

_____

Using the Exercises in Your Work

Because enemies represent such a high level of danger, it's important to deemotionalize the situation and look carefully at what the enmity is about and how it might be modified. Think carefully about these questions to improve your understanding of your enemies and your ability to cope with them.

Neutrals

> We have stood apart, studiously neutral.
> Woodrow Wilson, President of the United States, 1915

Neutrals can have leanings in any of the four quadrants:

1. **Ally neutral:** "Go ahead, I'm behind you 100 percent!"

Figure 4-6: Neutrals

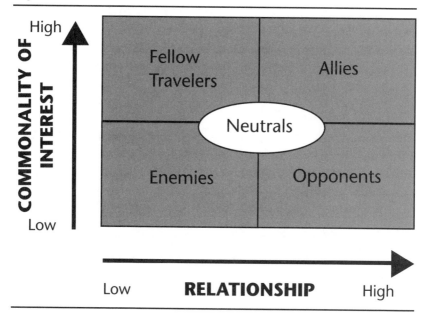

2. *Fellow traveler neutral:* "If you win, let me know."
3. *Opponent neutral:* "I disagree, but I respect you enough to stay out of it."
4. *Enemy neutral:* "I'll let you get into trouble all by yourself."

They all have in common their desire to stay out of the fray, at least in the current situation.

Because neutrals have a toehold in one of the quadrants, the strategies for dealing with neutrals are similar to those for dealing with members of the quadrants (Figure 4-6).

Ally Neutral

The ally neutral is a person who believes that she or he has no personal stake in the fight and quite wisely declines to participate. In other words, the relationship is still there, but the person does not feel there is enough commonality of interest to warrant action or risk.

The first thing you need to do is look at it from her or his point of view. It may be that the person is exactly right, in which case you should consider letting the ally off the hook. Do so clearly and without resentment, because you want to preserve the relationship for another day.

On the other hand, it may be that the person has more of an interest than she or he is aware of. You need to listen closely and understand fully the person's position before starting to sell her or him on participating.

Sometimes, the person has little stake in the fight, but you really need the support. Now it's time to lean on the relationship while still working to preserve it. The art of the "squeeze" is a traditional political act. If the issue is tough but important and there is risk, people want out of the line of fire. That's natural. The ethical squeeze involves not blackmail or threats but rather assertiveness. Make it clear that you need the support, ask for it directly, and also make it clear that you won't forget—either way.

By putting the squeeze on someone to get his or her support, you also create an obligation for yourself. The other party now has a blank check you've signed, and you may have to honor that blank check at some point in the future by going out on a limb when it's important to the other person but not important to you. (By the way, the obligation you've created for yourself doesn't include the obligation to do something ethically inappropriate *unless* the favor you asked of them was also ethically inappropriate. The principled person, of course, won't have let himself or herself get into such a situation in the first place.)

Another of the fundamental political skills is knowing enough about the people in your environment to know their needs and their goals. The more you listen and the more you understand the point of view of others, the more opportunities you'll find to be able to provide favors. Providing support to others on a regular basis creates a network of obligations that gives you power to call on others when you need them. One way to avoid giving people a blank check when you call on them for an important and risky favor is to already have provided so much support that they are already in your debt.

Fellow Traveler Neutral

The fellow traveler neutral ideally would like to coast to victory on your coattails by having you take the risks and do the heavy lifting. Think of the fable of the Little Red Hen, who did all the work herself until it came time for volunteers to help eat the bread.

If you need the support of the fellow traveler neutral, you have to use the WII—FM principle: The two ways to achieve this are (1) to find benefits to the fellow traveler for taking the risks and actions to provide you support, and (2) to offer a trade, or quid pro quo (this for that). In a quid pro quo, you offer support or action on an unrelated issue that has benefits for the other person in exchange for that person's support or action on an issue that has importance for you.

Frequently you'll read condemnation of political figures for engaging in quid pro quo, but there's a fundamental misunderstanding here. "If you scratch my back, I'll scratch yours" ultimately means that two people don't itch—and that's a good thing. All politics, from national to office, runs on the exchange of favors for support. It's the only way to build an alliance network strong enough to get anything done. Quid pro quo behavior slips under the ethical line only when the favors being traded are themselves not ethical.

For example, if you offer to support Mary's budget request, in which you have no personal stake, in exchange for Mary's giving you the resources necessary to complete your project, in which she has no personal stake, both parties and the company benefit from the cooperation. This is ethical and appropriate behavior; sharing and cooperation are part of the kindergarten essentials.

On the other hand, if you offer to approve Mary's fraudulent expense account request in exchange for her not telling on you for stealing office supplies, you've slipped below the ethical line—not because you've traded favors but because the favors traded are themselves unethical. This would also be true if you offered to help Mary's project succeed in exchange for her not telling on you for stealing office supplies. The fact that helping Mary's project succeed is beneficial to the organization doesn't excuse the unethical nature of at least one of the favors being traded.

Also, do favors and provide support to your fellow traveler neutrals without always waiting to be asked so that you create a network of obligations that improves your power. Don't expect to trade on a relationship that doesn't exist; if the relationship isn't good but the commonality of interest is strong, be realistic.

Opponent Neutral

With opponent neutrals, sometimes the wisest thing to do is let them alone. If they want to sit out the battle because they don't have much at stake, this is good for you.

Because people who are generally in an opposing relationship are naturally concerned with their own interests, they can end up feeling threatened without your intent to do so.

For example, imagine that someone really does have a stake in the outcome of a given decision but isn't aware of it. That person is neutral not because she or he doesn't care but because he or she isn't aware. Once the person becomes aware, then she or he turns from opponent neutral into an active opponent. If it's too late to do anything, that person may feel that his or her trust has been abused, and you've taken a step to turn an opponent into an enemy, which is not what you want to do.

Make sure your opponents have good information even if it might make more trouble for you, because the relationship is normally worth preserving even at that cost. If you know an issue will be of concern to someone, make sure she or he knows about it.

Enemy Neutral

The enemy neutral may be like an opposition neutral, content to let this issue alone, or the enemy neutral may be aware that you are likely to fall flat on your face if you pursue your current direction. Allowing your enemy to destroy himself or herself is often very convenient.

Rather than simply being relieved that you don't have an enemy to contend with in a particular situation, take this as a sign that caution is required. Why is your normal enemy not acting in this situation? Does he or she know something you don't? Are you more vulnerable than you think? Does your position have a weakness obvious to others but not to yourself? It's worthwhile discovering answers to these questions before you proceed.

• *Review the situation.* You may have thought you knew what was going on, and you truly may know, but be careful. It's appropriate to review the current situation, looking for any vulnerabilities in your situation. Strive for a balance between sensible caution and paranoia.

• *Watch for nonverbal clues.* Because most people have poor poker faces, watch for nonverbal clues that suggest your enemy knows something you don't, such as the smug smile or the ostentatious silence.

• *Listen to friends of your enemy.* If you've managed to develop good relationships with the friends of your enemy, listen well to find out what your enemy may be thinking. People tend to talk too much about their plans, ideas, and foresight.

• *Consult your allies and advisers.* If you pick up signals that something may be going on that you don't know about, dig deep into the situation to uncover hidden traps. Talk to your allies, your mentors or godfathers, the experts in the area. Knowledge is your best tool to improve your safety in this situation.

• *Consider whether your enemy is working behind the scenes.* Finally, it's possible that the enemy is only pretending to be neutral and has prepared or is in the process of preparing an attack or trap. Again, avoid falling into paranoia, ascribing too much malice or cunning to someone. Few enemies are so implacable, so hateful, and so skilled as to always be plotting against you (though such behavior is not unheard of). Most of your enemies in an organization don't plot; instead, they respond to targets of opportunity that you may provide. In suggesting that you consider these issues, our recommendation is simply that: to consider them. Be aware; be careful—but don't let fear run your life.

WORKING WITH NEUTRALS

List your neutrals and answer the following questions for each:

My neutrals:

1. _____   4. _____

2. _____   5. _____

3. _____   6. _____

1. What type of neutral is this person (ally, opponent, fellow traveler, enemy)?

_____

_____

2. Does the neutral want to avoid the current political issue, or is this neutral someone who generally tries to avoid taking stands on anything controversial?

_____

_____

3. To what extent and in what way do I need this neutral's support or actions?

_____

_____

4. How can I demonstrate a stronger common interest to this person?

_____

_____

5. Are there specific ways I can put appropriate pressure on this person?

_____

_____

6. What political skills, powers, and influence does this neutral possess that I need?

_____

_____

7. What does this neutral want from me?

_____

_____

8. Should I take this neutral's avoidance to be a sign that I haven't looked deeply enough for problems? What might they be?

_____

_____

Using the Exercises in Your Work

Because neutrals are often situational, you'll find that people move in and out of this category at different times.

While thinking about the questions here, also consider the circumstances that might move people who would normally be placed more firmly in one of the quadrants into the center. In the case of positive relationships you don't want this to happen, but in the case of negative relationships, neutralizing them may be quite a benefit.

Notes

1. Although this quotation is cited in *Bartlett's Familiar Quotations* and many other sources, Wilson never actually said these words. In his confirmation hearing, Wilson was asked if he could make a decision that would be good for America but not necessarily good for General Motors. Wilson replied, "Yes sir, I could. I cannot conceive of one because for years I thought what was good for our country was good for General Motors, and vice versa." This was leaked to the press as "What's good for General Motors is good for the country" and held up as an example of corporate arrogance.

Notice that this is an example of a particular type of political hardball, "image equals reality," also known as the strategy of "defining your opponent." The strategy of defining your opponent, because it's necessarily stereotypical and superficial and presents an incomplete and distorted picture of his or her beliefs, is always dishonest and hence always unethical. Paul Kirchner, *Everything You Know Is Wrong* (Los Angeles: General Publishing Group, 1995), pp. 180–181.

2. Robert Caro, *The Power Broker: Robert Moses and the Fall of New York* (New York: Alfred A. Knopf, 1974), p. 283.

3. For an extensive proof of this proposition, see John A. Keegan, *A History of Warfare* (New York: Vintage, 1993).

4. Deborah Tannen, Ph.D., *Talking from 9 to 5: How Women's and Men's Conversational Styles Affect Who Gets Heard, Who Gets Credit, and What Gets Done at Work* (New York: William Morrow, 1994), p. 205.

5. Roger Fisher and William Ury, *Getting to Yes: Negotiating Agreement without Giving In* (Middlesex, England: Penguin Books, 1981), p. 19.

6. H. W. Lewis, *Why Flip a Coin? The Art and Science of Good Decisions* (New York: Wiley, 1997), p. 26.

7. Roger Fisher, Elizabeth Kopelman, and Andrea Kupfer Schneider, *Beyond Machiavelli: Tools for Coping with Conflict* (New York: Penguin, 1994), p. 33.

8. Tip O'Neill with Gary Hymel, *All Politics Is Local (and Other Rules of the Game)* (New York: Random House, 1994), p. 161.

9. Guigliemo Ferrero and Corrado Barbagallo, *A Short History of Rome: The Monarchy and the Republic* (New York: Capricorn Books, 1964), pp. 403–404.

10. Colleen McCullough, *Caesar's Women* (New York: William Morrow, 1996), p. 538.

11. Please consult the bibliography for titles by Bramson, Elgin, Friedman, Pollan and Levine, and Tannen.

Chapter 5

How to Get . . . and How to Use . . . POWER

This is the bitterest pain among men, to have much knowledge but no power.

Herodotus, *The Histories*, ca. 430 B.C.

Power is a relative condition. Our standard ideas of hierarchy suggest that the higher you go, the more power you have, but that's only partially true. It's more like the game of paper-scissors-rock: Scissors cut paper, paper covers rock, rock breaks scissors. Each element has power and sometimes triumphs, but no element reigns supreme. When you think about power—your own and that of other people—you're looking at a complex set of relationships.

You might think that if you became top dog in the organization, you'd have complete power, but that's not true either. Harry Truman said of incoming president Dwight D. Eisenhower, "He'll sit here, and he'll say, 'Do this! Do that!' And nothing will happen. Poor Ike—it won't be a bit like the army. He'll find it very frustrating." Presidents of large organizations aren't more free to do what they want; they're often less free. They can't just fire whomever they please—they have the theoretical power, but not the actual power. Power becomes diversified in an organization, and each member acquires his or her particular brand to use.

To acquire and use your power effectively, you have to respect and be aware of the power of others. You can't take it away from them. You have to understand where it comes from, deal with it, work with it, defend yourself from it, and use it.

Dangers of Power Acquisition

You already know power is necessary; you also know it's dangerous. Not only is there the seductiveness of power—the joy people find in being able to require others to do their bidding—there are more subtle psychological dangers, as well. There has been substantial research on the negative effects of power. When you are successful in wielding power, researchers have found, you see yourself as more powerful and the person you have controlled as less powerful. Evidence shows that petty powers are even more corrupting than major ones: In a study of U.S. Air Force officers, those with the lowest status and the least advancement potential were most authoritarian in dealing with subordinates.[1] You also tend to see your power as a function of who you are and not simply as a function of your position—which can lead to rapid disillusionment when your role changes.

While power is necessary to get things done, your survival—figuratively and sometimes literally—depends on learning the proper relationship between you and power.

Melburn McBroom was known as a domineering and temperamental boss, who also happened to be an airline pilot. In 1978, his plane was approaching Portland, Oregon, when he noticed a problem with his landing gear. He went into a holding pattern while trying to correct the mechanism. As he worked, the fuel gauges moved toward empty, but his copilots were so afraid of his temper they said nothing. The plane crashed, killing ten people.[2] In that situation, fear was at work.

In other environments, don't forget that a traditional way to revenge oneself on one's boss is a behavior known as "malicious obedience to orders," or obeying an order with stupefying literalness while perfectly aware that this behavior will lead to disaster. This maneuver is one of the most common forms of sabotage[3] in the modern organization. People who practice it wear the "stupid look" when confronted, and say, "But that's what you told me to do." They often escape the consequences of their actions or, better yet, put the consequences on their bosses.

You need to recognize the potential for a corrupting psychological effect within yourself when you seek to acquire power. (People don't normally have trouble seeing the corrupting effect in others.) As a principled person, you know that you must strive to know yourself as well as others, maintain your commitment to good character and good relationships, and respect the dignity and worth of others. But, you may ask, does this really work?

In a study of star performers at Bell Labs, researchers discovered that there was little innate difference in the intellectual abilities of the star performers and the average to below-average performers. The difference was their command of interpersonal and emotional strategies to work with others and to recognize their emotions. One of the most important skills turned out to be the ability to develop rapport with a network of key people.[4] In other words, feelings and emotions—those of yourself as well as others—are not, as often supposed, simply a distraction from the Serious Business of work. Quite often, they *are* the business of work.

Aware of the dangers and pitfalls, you must nevertheless move ahead with the acquisition of power, because you need that power to get anything accomplished.

Ethical and Unethical Power

Remember that power by itself is ethically neutral. The key questions are how you get it and what you do with it. In the discussion that follows, you'll see that for each type of power, there are ways to get it and use it that you will find appropriate and acceptable and other ways that you will likely find ethically unacceptable. That's good. You need to understand how different people can use these techniques, even if you disapprove of them, because success in the political environment depends first and foremost on being completely realistic about the way things are. If you don't like the way things are, you can work toward changing them—but if you start with the assumption that things are other than what they are, you'll get into trouble in a hurry.

Sometimes the dividing line between ethical and unethical political behavior is clear and obvious; sometimes not so obvious. The Watergate figure John Dean explored his own trip across the line:

> I began my role in the cover-up as a fact-finder and worked my way up to idea man, and finally to desk officer. At the outset . . . I took considerable satisfaction from knowing that I had no criminal liability, and I consistently sought to keep it that way. . . . On such half-truths I sustained the image of myself as a 'counsel' rather than an active participant for as long as I could, but the line blurred and finally vanished. . . . I am still not sure when I crossed the line into criminal culpability.[5]

Expediency provides a temptation to cut political and ethical corners, to shave a little bit close to the line. In the short run, it solves problems and get things done. But there is a risk, and a profound one. Most of the people who get into serious trouble playing politics didn't start out to be unethical and never made a conscious choice to go in that direction. They just made decisions one day at a time. Playing with power is playing with fire—but fire can be very useful as well as dangerous.

To be successful over the long term as an office politician, it's important to establish your core principles and live by them, even when your short-range objectives might benefit by compromising them. You'll find that your choice of tactics, your use of power, and your goals fall into place, and you will avoid the pitfalls more readily. Principles and integrity are a large part of your defense against the pitfalls of power.

Earlier, you learned about the Political Power Model (see Figure 1-1), and we discussed the center element, Reason Power. Now, we'll learn how you can use the other power sources in formulating your own power strategies.

Role Power

> There is no worse heresy than that the office sanctifies
> the holder of it.
>
> Lord Acton, *Letters*, 1887

Your role in the organization consists of your job title, your hierarchical position, your special assignments (project manager, team leader), and the organizational norms and behaviors that accompany those roles (Figure 5-1).

Role power and resource power are the only two sources of power that are often or primarily given to you by outside forces. If you're an assistant director, an executive vice president, or a junior clerk, that role was assigned to you by your employer. To get a promotion and a better, more powerful role, you must persuade those in charge to assign it to you.

Figure 5-1: Role Power

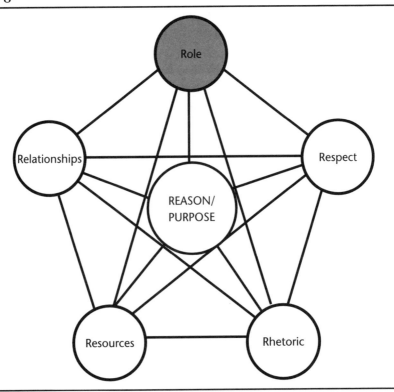

A certain basic grant of authority and power comes with a given role. When most people think about organizational power, that's all they think of. This is dangerous as well as incorrect, for three reasons:

1. You may not really have all the authority and power that is in the official grant. For example, while you normally have the official power to fire an insubordinate or incompetent staff member, in reality you might not be able to fire a specific person because of his or her relationships or history in the job.

2. Some job titles are given as part of the phenomenon of being "kicked upstairs," or promoted to a position that has no responsibility or power. All jobs at the same hierarchical level are not created equal. Among vice presidents, one has the power to command millions of dollars, while another can barely order a role of toilet paper on his or her own initiative.

3. Within a given job, your actions and strategies have an enormous impact on how much of the official power you are able to use or exploit. Combining role power with the other forms of power gives you a synergistic effect, in which the whole can be greater than the sum of the parts.

Strategies for Maximizing the Power of Your Position

Start with your job title. Does it describe what you do? If your title is marketing services coordinator, for example, your job might be writing copy for catalogs or it might be managing millions of dollars in direct mail contracts. In the first case, the title sounds better than the job. Leave it alone. In the second case, you might consider asking for a more descriptive title, such as direct marketing contract coordinator. When people don't know what you do, they're less likely to assume you to be powerful.

Does your job title sound powerful? Vice president is better than director, manager better than coordinator. But before you ask for a higher title, check your organizational norms. In some organizations it matters very much whether you're a "manager" or a "director," because those terms have very specific hierarchical meanings; don't let yourself be embarrassed by not knowing this information. In other fields—banking, notably—vice president is often not a particularly powerful or significant position. If possible, enhance your job title to improve the perception others have of your role.

Look at your job description. Does it accurately describe the range of work you actually do, particularly at the higher levels? Try to have it rewritten to bring it more in line with your real responsibilities. Then, if your organization is large enough and you think you'll come out better, ask to have your human resources department regrade the position.

The vice president of one major hotel corporation hired a consultant (one of the authors of this book) to rewrite the job descriptions of all his staff members in response to an organizationwide reorganization initiative. His stated goal was to use the job descriptions as a way to grab more power for his department.

Don't overlook the power inherent in temporary roles. These include acting assignments, in which you temporarily occupy a position of higher rank, using its authority, while the normal incumbent is on vacation, on travel, or being replaced. These situations are often unofficial auditions for your later advancement. Don't abuse temporary authority, by the way, because once it's taken away you're vulnerable to revenge.

In addition to acting assignments, project assignments are a source of role power. Project roles can help you build networks at senior management levels, give you increased visibility, and set you up for further growth. (They can also set you up for failure, so look carefully for hidden traps in major project assignments.)

Committee and task force roles provide temporary additions to your role power. If there's a hot new management initiative, volunteer for it. To be a player, you have to ask to get into the game.

Strategies for Maximizing Your Power in the Hierarchy

You don't exist in a vacuum. Your role power is related to the roles and powers of those above and below you in the organizational structure.

Study the organizational chart. Where are you? Who is at your level? Who is above you? Who is below you? Independent of your title and actual job, you have a hierarchical rank, and that, too, is a source and indicator of your power. That's often the reason some organizations, as noted, are sensitive about who calls herself or himself a "manager" or "director." Those words represent hierarchical position and are jealously guarded.

Where you are in hierarchical rank often determines what meetings you can attend and which decisions you can participate in. Even people of unequal job title and job description power have roughly equal hierarchical power if they are on the same level of the organizational chart.

As you learned from our discussion of office perks, hierarchical power is often demonstrated in the size and position of offices. Make sure you notice the subtle as well as the obvious signs—the high-floor corner office with windows may in fact be less prestigious and represent less power than a smaller office that's next door to the division vice president. If you're given a choice of office placement, go for proximity to power over any other element. A great office that's isolated can keep you out of important decisions.

In addition to proximity to people of high power, being in the traffic flow of the office can convey advantages. Seeing the comings and goings of others as well as being available and accessible can aid in networking and relationship building laterally through the organization. Some people maintain candy jars simply as bait for passing staff members; it's a good way to keep in the informal information flow and to stay visible and connected.

Strategies for Using Titles and Honors

A college history professor who didn't have his Ph.D. nevertheless insisted his students refer to him as "Doctor," a term he felt he needed as a show of respect. With students, it worked, because his position power included the ability to assign grades, a significant portion of the process being quite subjective. With his colleagues, it backfired. While people gave him respect to his face, he was laughed at and patronized behind his back. The suicide a few years ago of the U.S. Chief of Naval Operations was attributed in part to challenges as to whether he was entitled to wear some of the medals that he did. This is a testament both to the power of titles and other badges of honor and the need to claim only titles you earned and possess.

The ideal situation is to downplay your titles and honors and have others carry the news. However, this is not always possible. You do deserve the credit and power that come with what you have earned, but all displays must be in line with organizational culture. Benchmark appropriate methods of displaying any awards and honors you have by monitoring what others do. Here are some general guidelines:

• *Don't frame and display any educational achievement at the bachelor's degree level or below.* Frame and display master's or higher degrees if (1) most others at and above your level do so, (2) they are equal to or above the attainments of most others in your peer group, (3), they are relevant to your position, (4) your position requires lots of customer contact (generally, impressing customers is considered more appropriate than seeming to try to impress peers and superiors).

• *Frame and display any certificates or degrees that entitle you to do something (e.g., medical or bar license, certified financial planner, CPA), if you regularly see customers in your office and if others in the organization also display such licenses.* Watch out for certifications that, while arguably useful, aren't actually required for people to do a certain job; they may antagonize people who do the job, believe they do it well, but don't possess the particular certificate.

• *If others do so as well, display significant honors and awards that are job related; leave golf trophies at home unless the organization's top management is wild about golf.*

• *Beware of mail-order honors.* Some of the "Who's Who" type volumes are actually "sucker books"—they list anyone who's willing to buy a few copies. If someone knows, you look silly.

• *Consider your organizational environment, personal status, and political goals when thinking about hanging photographs of you with well-known people or letters of commendation and praise.* While in some circumstances (especially when dealing with the outside world) they can add to your credibility, they can all too easily identify you as a braggart.

• *Avoid showing off.* If you have a lot, display only a few highlights; underplay rather than overplay your credentials.

• *Avoid displaying jokes and cartoons with an anti-management edge, even if others do so.* Display only jokes that are jokes on yourself, such as "last place" awards at the company picnic games.

Strategies for Managing Organizational Norms Using Role Power

When the Clinton administration nominated Massachusetts governor William Weld to be ambassador to Mexico, U.S. Senate Foreign Relations Committee chairman Jesse Helms, who was opposed to Weld, refused to hold confirmation hearings for Weld, effectively blocking his nomination even though Weld had the votes to achieve confirmation. How could one person block the will of the majority? The technique used here is called "managing organizational norms," or using the rules (written and unwritten) and customs of the organization as a power tool to achieve goals.

The power to decide when or whether to hold a meeting is a significant power. So is the power to decide who will attend and who will not. So is the power to write a job description. Politically savvy people often seek the opportunity to draft a policy statement or a contract, even knowing that the final product will have to be approved by a senior manager or committee, because the power to write the draft is effectively the power to set the agenda and to decide what will or will not be discussed.

The manipulation of organizational norms can be done in two basic ways: by putting something on the table and by taking something off the table. The first use is relatively benign and is less likely to backfire. The second use creates enemies, because when you deprive people of even the opportunity to make their case, they resent it terribly. You already have opposing interests (otherwise you wouldn't keep their point of view off the table), and now you have a poor relationship, as well.

What do you do when others manipulate the norms to keep your issues off the table?

1. Learn to recognize the techniques they use to see whether you can manipulate the norms in the reverse direction.
2. Expand your intelligence network to get advance warning of such moves. If you know about them in advance (that an item won't be on the agenda), you're in a better position to fight.
3. Find alternative channels to promote your goals.
4. Remember that someone who uses this technique is choosing to be your enemy. Use the techniques discussed in Chapter 4 for dealing with your enemies, including those that focus on improving the relationship and finding a commonality of interest.

MAXIMIZING YOUR ROLE POWER

Consider role power issues involving yourself and the others in your network.

1. *Position power.* Is your job title both correct and powerful? Can it be changed to increase your power? Does your job description accurately reflect the power you have—or the power you want?

_____

_____

2. *Hierarchical rank power.* What is your relative position on the organizational chart? What perks and privileges come with it? If

a reorganization is imminent, can you change your hierarchical rank for the better—or preserve your current status?

_____

_____

3. *Titles and honors.* What titles and honors do you possess that can benefit your role power? How can you display and use them effectively?

_____

_____

4. *Organizational norms.* What organizational norms and systems do you control, especially in meetings and agendas? How can you use those norms to advance your positions?

_____

_____

5. *The people around you.* Consider your allies, opponents, fellow travelers, and enemies. What role power do they possess? Review the first four questions in this worksheet for each significant power player in your network. What role power do they have, and how can they use it? What defensive strategies can you use in return?

_____

_____

_____

_____

Using the Exercise in Your Work

Because your organizational role is a fundamental source of power, it's important to consider all the ways it can be maximized. By thinking about these questions, you may discover that you already possess more power and influence than you thought, or may discover directions that allow you to maximize such sources. Don't forget to think about these questions with respect to others as well.

Respect Power

Full twenty times was Peter feared,
For once that Peter was respected.
                    William Wordsworth, *Peter Bell*, 1798

The opinion that others hold of you has an enormous impact on whether they will follow you. Respect (and fear) is an enormous source of power that you can use (Figure 5-2).

You can be respected for many things: your reputation, both professional and personal; the level of knowledge you possess; your experience; your longevity in the organization or profession; your special skills; your age; your special status or group membership; physical characteristics; and the fear you can engender in others.

You can lose respect, fairly and unfairly, in these categories as well. There are two general rules of respect: The first rule is that you must give it to get it. There's nothing more obnoxious than someone who preens around demanding your respect while looking down at you; it's even worse when you must give the person respect because of his or her talent or accomplishments. This kind of respect, though, is given grudgingly, and people look for an opportunity to withdraw it. Give respect to others generously to make it easier for them to respect you.

The second rule is that others must know of your merits to respect you for them. If they don't know about your knowl-

Figure 5-2: Respect Power

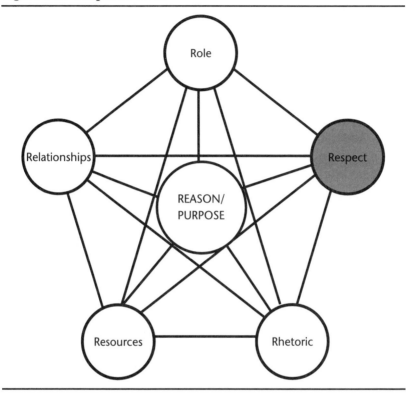

edge, wisdom, and track record, they can't very well respect you for them. On the other hand, becoming known as a braggart and self-promoter gets you into trouble, as well. Adults in the workplace must master the difficult tightrope act of promoting their accomplishments without being seen to be bragging. Be calm, be factual, underplay it slightly, and (most important) get other people to praise you.

Strategies for Developing a Powerful Reputation

You can't help but acquire a reputation, because everything you do that people notice goes into it. What kind of reputation do you want? Here are some key words:

- effective
- smart
- principled

- honest
- creative
- ethical

- reliable
- successful
- knowledgeable

You can acquire a negative reputation. Do others associate any of these words with you?

- dishonest
- boring
- unprincipled

- unreliable
- stupid
- greedy

- clueless
- ineffective
- self-centered

Plan the reputation that you want to acquire, and make sure your behavior and actions reflect it. If your goal is to change your reputation, remember that it is harder to change an opinion already formed than to build an opinion from scratch. It can be done, and it's done all the time, but you will have to be patient. If you've earned a negative reputation, then you'll have to counteract it. If you've acquired a negative reputation unfairly, you still have to counteract it, but you may be able to use publicity about the good things you've already done.

People react to you professionally (and personally) on the basis of your reputation, so it's a big source of power.

Knowledge

Experts on success are virtually unanimous in their commitment to "lifelong learning," or ensuring that you make knowledge development a key part of your career development. Knowledge is power, after all, and improving and broadening the scope and depth of your knowledge will translate into improved respect power.

There are practically no problems you have or will ever have that haven't been faced or solved by someone else. Management is an exhaustively studied topic, and this book is only one example. Read, listen to tapes, watch videos to learn more about the art of management. As you develop your skills, you will advance in your career.

There are certain collateral skills you will need in your

career, in addition to the core technical and management knowledge you will need to do your job.

Technical and Subject Matter Knowledge

In a technically driven business world, technical knowledge matters. But it doesn't matter as much as people generally think, especially if you're in a managerial or leadership role. Exactly what you need to know depends on what you need to do. As a manager, you normally need enough to know what's going on with the work, to converse about technical issues, to evaluate the information that technical specialists bring to your attention, and to understand how technical issues affect your business.

Because quite a few of us enter management from the technical ranks, it may be that technical expertise has previously been the foundation of your organizational influence. And, if you're currently a technical whiz, you probably already know that the depth of your knowledge—and how good others perceive it to be—is a core element of your power.

However, it frequently happens that a technical person will deliver you a technical judgment only to have it dismissed out of hand by someone without technical skills: "I don't care. I want it done this way." This situation arises most often when the technical judgment is negative: We can't do this, it will take longer, it will cost more, it won't deliver these features. Managers tend to discover that negative technical opinions yield to pressure. "It can't be done" often turns into a successful project in the end. As a result, "can't do" technical opinions tend to be valued less than "can do" ones, and you can easily see why that's the case.

If you're a manager, and your subordinates have greater technological or subject matter knowledge than you have, it doesn't have to stop you, but you do need to know how to use power effectively. Make it clear that you have a limited interest in hearing why something can't be done, but rather your interest is in hearing how it *can* be done. Stay firm on your goals, but be more flexible in how they can be achieved. This opens the door for brainstorming and other techniques of creativity. Focus your attention on those who have a positive attitude about the process; pay less attention to negativists, who often thrive on attention and who will therefore feel pressure to change their tune.

The reason this works in the majority of cases is, of course, that most goals are achievable, even if they are difficult. The second reason this normally works is that the savvy manager puts the pressure on toward the desired goal but is willing to accept less, as long as it's the very best that can be done under the circumstances. If shooting for the moon ends up putting you in low Earth orbit, that's still a lot higher than you might have gotten without a lofty goal.

Management and Supervision

Basic concepts of management and supervision are part of every organization. You must understand these key concepts. It's a good idea to learn about the key thinkers and names in management and supervision. One reason you see so many references in this book is to help you know other places to look. Also take the time to learn about management thinkers such as Ken Blanchard (author of *The One Minute Manager*), Peter F. Drucker, Warren Bennis, and Frederick Herzberg.

Managers quickly discover that a key to advancing in the organization is the support and action of your subordinates. Many top managers realize and readily admit the truth: They were promoted more by the actions of their subordinates than by the actions of managers senior to them. It's been suggested that if you are faced with the choice of being personally incompetent with a great staff or personally brilliant with a poor staff, the first alternative will get better results.

There's a substantial gap between the minimum acceptable performance level and the best performance of which people are capable. Anybody can get people to do the minimum; effective leaders and managers get people to do much more than that. The application of good fundamental supervisory skills—effective delegation, clear goal setting, regular and positive feedback, skill development, motivation, and the like—also have a political element.

Politics, as we've learned, is the informal and sometimes emotion-driven process of allocating limited resources and working out goals, decisions, and actions in an environment of people with different and competing interests and personalities. This clearly describes the relationship between supervisor and staff every bit as much as between that between a manager/professional and his or her peers and superiors in the organization.

Improve your supervisory and managerial effectiveness by applying the principles of enlightened office politics to your relationship with your subordinates. Here are some tips:

• *Identify personal goals and objectives for each member of your team.* There are three basic strategies. First, ask them what their goals and objectives are. Second, observe them to see in what circumstances and under what conditions they tend to do better work. Third, experiment with different motivational techniques to see what works and what doesn't.

• *Show personal loyalty toward your staff.* Go to bat for them when they get into trouble; take responsibility for mistakes made by your team, and don't apportion blame. This not only increases your respect and credibility among team members but aids your reputation with senior management as well.

• *Remember that negotiating goals and outcomes with team members isn't a sign of supervisory weakness; instead, it's often a sign of strength and self-confidence.* People don't work for money—they show up at the office for money, but work is an entirely different concept. People work because they choose to work, and your mission is to help people make that choice in a positive manner.

• *Assist your staff in professional and career development.* Recommend them for promotions. Help them find opportunities in other departments. It may seem counterproductive to give your best employees to other departments and other organizations, but in fact it's a way to build your strength and power. The people you help place in other positions tend to be grateful, and their support and the information and access they can provide can be a major element in your strength (for more, see the discussion of Relationship Power later in this chapter).

Finance and Accounting

Finance is the language of senior management. Even if your job isn't primarily oriented toward finance, it's essential to understand it. If you don't, you're at the mercy of the information and interpretation of all those who do.

Basic accounting concepts such as assets and liabilities, debits and credits are part of the normal dialog within the organization. Learn what the key financial statements are: balance sheet, income statement, sources and uses of cash statement. Learn how to read them. The organization's financial condition may be stated in terms of financial ratios, such as return on investment, return on assets, and return on equity. These aren't synonyms. Depreciation and inventory costing can completely turn the financial picture of the organization upside down. Concepts such as "earnings before interest, taxes, depreciation, and amortization" and economic earnings are benchmarks that enable performance and accomplishments to be measured more clearly.

Consider signing up for seminars, arranging for coaching through groups of retired executives (also a good source of career and strategic advice), reading books, and listening to tapes on the topic. Many carry a generic title, on the order of "Finance and Accounting for Nonfinancial Managers."

Once you've got a basic handle on these concepts, start reading the business section of the paper regularly, and consider subscribing to one or more of the standard business magazines or newspapers. You'll get the executive perspective about what's going on, which will always translate into greater power, reach, and influence.

Project Management

Project management is also part of every job, sooner or later. While you may not need to understand the intricacies of calculating uncertainty on the critical path, you need at least the basics of Gantt charting and project organization.[6]

Project management has become in many organizations the current management theme, in the same manner as TQM in the 1980s. The concept of "enterprise project management," which involves thinking of the organization as a collection of projects and managing accordingly, is quite popular. The political ramification of this is that you should be familiar and supportive of the newest concepts, because this brings you into contact with powerful people at all levels.

Political skills are also part of the realm of project management on a day-to-day basis. Projects, pretty much by definition, are things outside the normal routine of work. They tend to have an ad hoc management structure, one that works in parallel to the traditional organization. Project managers tend not to have fully developed and articulated statements of authority, at least in part because significant elements of projects can't be defined in advance, so working with the informal organization—the political side—becomes crucial. A great project manager is usually a great office politician.

Knowledge develops your power and influence. Study not just what you need to get today's job done; study what will get you where you want to be tomorrow.

Experience

Experience in a job gives you credibility, a source of respect power. Experience is something you obtain almost without conscious effort merely by being in a job, but there are two important qualifiers.

The first is that you can improve the quality of your experience by working to get good job assignments and volunteering for projects. One of the rules of getting promoted is that you normally get jobs you've already done, so look for projects and task forces and special assignments that prepare you for the job you want next.

With that in mind, you should take a second look at a common event in organizations that is often very frustrating: being asked to take on substantial additional responsibilities without getting the title and pay that go along with it. It's more useful to look at such a situation as an audition for promotion, because quite often the title (and pay) will come along sometime later—normally after you've proven yourself in your new responsibilities.

The second is that experience is surprisingly easy to dismiss and challenge, and people do it all the time. One way people dismiss experience is by questioning its relevance: "Sure, the Smith Project last year involved building a database, but this problem is totally different." Another way is for others to claim equivalent or different experience that led to a different conclusion. "Well, the Jones Project, which I managed, solved the problem even better by going a different way." A third way is for others to act as if experience has contaminated your creativity. "Sure, you've done it the old way several times, but we're looking at a new paradigm here." Don't expect that you'll be listened to simply by advancing your experience.

How, then, do you get your experience validated? First, as we discussed in the section on technical and subject matter knowledge, "can do" statements are heard more positively than "can't do." Statements that confirm and support the person advancing the idea gain credibility. You can often use a form of "verbal judo" by starting with strong support for the other person's idea, using your experience as a validation for them. Once your experience has been accepted as relevant (because it's supportive), you can then introduce areas of challenge or difficulty, using the same experience to support your discussion of problems.

By staying resolutely positive (even if you have strong doubts about the idea in question) and framing all your statements as ways to help the other person achieve his or her goal, you stand the best chance of getting the other person to recognize any potential flaws or dangers and to take corrective action.

Longevity and the Rule of Slack

Simple longevity in a job is, surprisingly, a source of power, and we're putting it under "respect" because it's more similar to that quality than to other categories. It is, however, a power source on its own. It's best when combined with experience, ability, and knowledge, but, depending on the organizational culture, it's more powerful than you might think all by itself. Longevity is a special case of the Rule of Slack, as in "cut me some slack," an important concept in understanding the dynamics of the unofficial organization.

In your career, depending on your actions and attitudes, you acquire a certain amount of slack, which is the organization's willingness to excuse a certain degree of failure, misconduct, or bad behavior. Different employees have different amounts of slack, and the amount of slack you have may differ depending on the current manager you have.

Earning and Losing Slack

If you fail on a project, turn in a bad job, or make a mistake, the consequences you suffer depend on the amount of slack you have: "She's always been a top performer; let's cut her some slack on this one," or "This is the fifth failure in a row. We've had it with him." The respect you've earned through your track record stands you in good stead in those moments where your performance has not been what it needs to be.

Organizational Slack

Slack can be earned (or lost) by your performance, but it's also a function of the administrative and emotional difficulties involved in getting rid of you. It's often said that it's impossible to fire a government worker or a union member, but of course that's not true. What is true is that there is a significant burden of effort placed on a supervisor or manager who wishes to do so. A number of supervisors decide that it's simply too much trouble to fire someone or to learn how to fire someone, with the result that all employees are cut extra slack.

Inertia and Slack

Some supervisors have experienced the problem of trying to fire someone who's been with the organization a long time but who has never been a very good performer. It may seem that a person like that would have no remaining slack. The reality is, however, that longevity alone produces slack, because there's just too much inertia associated with both the person and the organization.

Here's the scenario: John has always been a mediocre performer, so supervisors have tried to shuffle him off onto other departments. If they gave him a truly honest performance appraisal, they couldn't very well get anyone else to take him. So he gets good appraisals. Now, twenty years later, his work is still mediocre, and you decide it's time to get rid of him. You'd think you'd get support, but instead you get resistance from your management, and you may not be able to fire him at all. His accumulated slack account is very large, and you must be realistic in dealing with that as a source of power.

Getting Rid of Someone with Slack

The basic way to fire someone with a lot of slack is to take advantage of his or her ego. People often overestimate the amount of slack they have. Accordingly, the technique is to give the person enough rope to hang himself or herself.

Company Mascots

Another special slack situation occurs when certain people become, in effect, company mascots. We feel enormous sympathy for some people, even if their competence and ability are marginal. In some organizations, such a person can become completely unfireable, no matter how well you document any performance difficulties. Oddly, your staff will resist the attempt to fire the mascot even if others are having to shoulder the burden of his or her performance failures. No one will officially acknowledge the company mascot's special role, but you should beware if you find people frequently griping about a poor employee but then getting defensive if you make moves to discipline or terminate the person. Generally, it's not worth the cost to your political status to take action; leave the person alone. Of course, note that in cases of layoffs, managers take the opportunity of the no-fault basis to get rid of people who would be difficult to terminate otherwise.

Special Skills

Specialized expertise is often a source of respect, although it tends to be focused on relatively narrow areas of the organization. Remember that a single person can have more or less power depending on the area and topic under discussion. A person's input and opinions can be dismissed across a wide range, but in a narrow area he or she may call the shots. One way to increase your respect power is to find those occasional skills and master them.

If you possess (or gain) such skills, make sure you promote your knowledge and ability; you'll find that the organization doesn't as a rule go look for special skills you possess. You may even find the company hiring outside experts—at great cost—to do what you can do yourself.

This kind of respect power is substantially more effective when you combine it with skills in communication and people influencing. Otherwise, you will find yourself relegated to support roles for managers with lower degrees of technical expertise. Note also that it's important whether you tend to be positive or negative about the projects and topics involving your special skill area.

Age

Your age relative to that of your peers and managers is a potential source of power. Being older can carry a presumption of experience and wisdom; it can also type you as being out of touch. Being younger can brand you as naive or innocent or as creative and in touch with the newest fads and fashions.

Among the reasons age has been historically venerated is that the experience that accompanied age was of great value. However, in technological fields, the experience of age is frequently obsolete and irrelevant when it comes to the work. (Management and other human disciplines profit enormously from this kind of experience, however.) The technical workforce becomes younger and younger, and even if you're not actually very old, you may suddenly find yourself stroking your imaginary gray beard while some young stripling demonstrates technical wizardry on equipment that didn't exist in your youth. And there may only be five years of age difference between you.

To improve the value of your age as a source of respect power, make sure you're seen as a lifelong learner, someone who works to expand and keep current his or her critical technical skills. Again, be known as someone who tends to be positive, and you'll find that your age-generated wisdom is better respected.

If you are very young, make sure you present your ideas and directions as particularly well thought out, and consider trying to enlist people older than you as allies and supporters. Often, your willingness to make essentially cosmetic changes in your ideas at the request of people who are seen as more organizationally mature than you will gain you substantial credibility.

Special Status

Special status can include gender or membership in a given racial, ethnic, religious, cultural, or socioeconomic group. This status can increase or decrease your respect power, depending on the stereotypes and beliefs others in the organization hold about the group(s) of which you are a member. In the real world, it's an advantage to be a member of the dominant group, but it's not necessarily fatal not to be.

The first political rule is to accept the reality of your situation, including the stereotypes and ideas that others hold about you, regardless of how incorrect, prejudicial, or just plain wrong they happen to be. The second political rule is to practice a kind of judo—to use the mental pictures others have of you as your tool, not theirs. The third political rule is to leverage your strengths to compensate for areas in which your power is limited or restricted.

First, make sure you don't confuse general mistreatment, aimed at everybody, with discriminatory treatment aimed at you as a member of a specific group. This is not to suggest that there isn't real discrimination—clearly, there is—but that there's lots of mistreatment that is distributed on an equal-opportunity basis.

Second, develop mentoring relationships across groups to make sure you have the benefit of different perspectives, both on problem situations in which you may find yourself and on the likely effect of different coping strategies.

While it may take extra initiative and extra effort for you to find and develop the critical contacts and relationships if you belong to a less-represented group, you can do it. Virtually everyone who succeeds professionally, regardless of category, does it that way.

Diagnose the underlying motives and issues that produce any negative or apparently discriminatory behavior. Besides bona fide racism or sexism, other reasons include general misanthropy, class consciousness, and xenophobia.[7]

People who are actually racist or sexist believe that it is a fact that members of a designated group possess certain characteristics or deficiencies. While you're unlikely to change the belief directly, it's interesting how often such people make individual exceptions. Play against type; be aware of the stereotype, and either mock it gently or act the opposite.

Misanthropes hate everybody and often lash out at others. Often, they have a radar-like sense of where you're vulnerable and attack at that point. A racist or sexist attack may be made not so much because the person believes it but rather because he or she knows it will hurt. To the extent that you don't react, the attacks will lessen.

Attitudes based on social class are far more common than most of us suppose and can be extremely damaging. Much of what we label as racist or sexist is actually based on class consciousness. The advantage is that the signs of class membership can be simulated. In this case, the appearance *is* the reality. Pay attention to class signals and cues, and make sure that in dress, grooming, and other external signs, you look like part of the group to which you wish to belong.

Xenophobia, or fear of strangers, is another problem. Most people have some degree of xenophobia, which can be expressed both in negative terms and in an exaggerated and phony friendliness. It's unfortunate but true that you tend to carry the burden of change, to break the ice and open communication.

Physical Characteristics

Another source of stereotyping comes from physical characteristics: tall or short, strong or weak, slim or stout. Body language constitutes the majority of the impression you make on someone else. Some parts of body language you control, such as hand gestures or facial expression. But your body type and shape all by themselves end up communicating their own message. Following the general principle that you have to play the hand you're dealt, look for the body language that plays to the strengths you possess and that minimizes the weaknesses. The stereotype says, for example, that tall is stronger than short . . . but check with Napoleon Bonaparte before you decide that if you're short, it's all over.

Observe the physical characteristics of the senior level of the organization. Some organizations put an inordinate emphasis on physical fitness and athleticism—the organization as a football team—and if you're not working out at the gym or playing the right sports, you may find yourself not on the fast track to promotion.

Some aspects of your physical characteristics are fully under your control; others are not. Some characteristics you may wish to change anyway—another excuse to get to the gym may be quite productive—but others are closer to your core identity and you may choose not to compromise them.

If a physical characteristic is under your control and you're willing to change it to move ahead, do so. If it's not under your control or you're not willing to change it, look for other ways to link with the power group. It's seldom the case that there is only one way to be part of the team.

Fear

Some people are more feared than respected, and while there are obvious problems with deliberately seeking to be feared, you probably know some people who use fear as a method of achieving and wielding power. Machiavelli answers his own famous question—is it better to be feared or loved?—with the idea that while one would prefer both, it's safer to choose fear.[8]

But are there any ethical, principled ways to use fear as a source of power? Oddly, the answer is yes.

One way to use fear as a principled person is to earn a reputation for doing exactly what you say you will do. Never bluff or make a threat that you will not or cannot carry out. If something must be done that is painful, do it. For example, if you promise that there will be disciplinary consequences for repeated misbehavior, deliver on your promise. This not only affects the person who receives the discipline, but also tends to serve as an example to others. One advantage of this is that the people who fear you are likely to be your enemies, not your allies, and they will respect you as they fear you. Keeping your word, after all, is good policy.

Another way to use fear is the well-placed temper tantrum. Make them few and far between, make them over matters of important principle, and don't blow up and lose control. Anger is a powerful weapon, and legitimate when properly—and rarely—used.

MAXIMIZING YOUR RESPECT POWER

Consider respect power issues involving yourself and the others in your network.

1. *Your current reputation.* How do people see you right now? Is their evaluation fair? Are you getting credit for what you deserve? Are you getting blame for things you do not deserve? What could you do to improve your reputation?

_____

_____

2. *Knowledge.* What knowledge goals are you setting for yourself? How can you maximize your value? To get to the next step in

your career, what knowledge to you need to get? How can you build allies at the same time you're getting the knowledge?

_____

_____

3. *Experience.* What experience value do you possess? How relevant is that experience? How could you get more powerful experience?

_____

_____

4. *Slack.* How much slack have you accumulated? How much do you have left? Why do you have it? How have you used it? What has happened to others with similar amounts of slack?

_____

_____

5. *Special skills.* What special skills do you possess that can up your respect value?

_____

_____

6. *Age.* Are you younger or older than your peer group? What are the advantages and disadvantages? How can you maximize the value of your age?

_____

_____

7. **Special status.** Are you part of a group that is stereotyped by the majority power players in the organization? How can you leverage your position for greater achievement?

_____

_____

8. **Physical characteristics.** What physical characteristics affect others' perceptions of you? How can you maximize the value of what you've got? What changes can you make and are you willing to make them? If not, what other approaches can take you where you want to go?

_____

_____

9. **Fear.** How can you use fear as an appropriate power tool?

_____

_____

10. **The people around you.** Consider your allies, opponents, fellow travelers, and enemies. What respect power do they possess? Review the first nine questions in this worksheet for each significant power player in your network. What respect power do they have, and how can they use it? What defensive strategies can you use in return?

_____

_____

_____

_____

_____

_____

_____

_____

_____

Using the Exercise in Your Work

Respect Power is almost infinitely expandable, and it's worth your while to think carefully about these questions, not only to determine the current level of your respect, but also identify ways in which you might grow it over time. You need to be aware equally of the respect others have earned, remembering that if others respect someone, that person has power, even if you don't have a lot of respect for him or her.

Rhetoric Power

> So you're the lady who wrote that little book that started this great big war.
> Abraham Lincoln to Harriet Beecher Stowe
> (attributed)

Command of persuasive language—speaking and writing—is an enormous source of power, and one largely independent of position or status. Everything else being equal, the better communicator is the more powerful person in a given exchange (Figure 5-3).

Speaking Ability

From one-on-one communication to small-group presentation to major public speaking, your ability to communicate clearly and powerfully using the spoken word is an essential ingredient in political success. You'll notice that a large number of the great leaders in world history were and are also persuasive speakers: Winston Churchill, John F. Kennedy,

Figure 5-3: Rhetoric Power

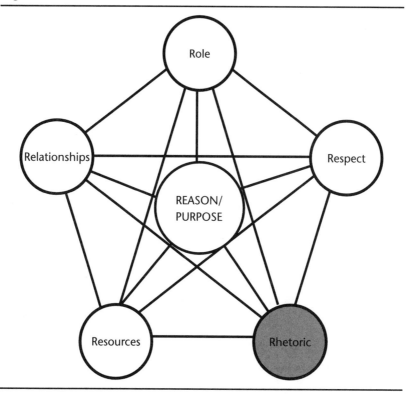

Martin Luther King Jr., Gandhi, Susan B. Anthony, and hundreds of others.

Evaluate your communications effectiveness and consider working on some of the following areas:

• *Clarity.* Nothing else matters if your message isn't heard and understood by the recipient. Do you use the right, powerful word in each case? Can you paint word pictures to get your message across?

• *Understanding.* Getting your message accepted by the listener requires that you have some understanding of the listener and his or her own agenda. Don't forget WII—FM!

• *Correctness.* Proper grammar doesn't help only with clarity, it's essential for your professional image. People judge your social class, education, and credibility by your grammar.

• *Listening.* All good talkers must also be good listeners. Picking up nonverbal cues by your observation of your audience helps you adjust your message to make sure it is understood and accepted.

• *Nonverbal communication.* Tone of voice and nonverbal communication (body language, dress and grooming) make up the majority of the message received by others. Are you showing the right image as well as saying the right words?

Public speakers frequently videotape or audiotape themselves so that they can see themselves as others see them. Only by getting an outside perspective on yourself can you truly see how you can change to become more effective.

Writing

A recent survey revealed that lack of crucial communication skills accounts for 80 percent of the reason that people don't get promoted. Many people actually turn down job promotions because they are afraid their writing and speaking skills won't measure up to those required in higher level positions.[9]

In addition to obvious categories like major reports and proposals, even the simple memo and e-mail have political implications. In a large organization, your memos are often the only thing senior management sees of yours. Consider each to be an audition showing your ability to be concise and effective. Follow the KISS rule: Keep it short and simple. Don't ever use e-mail to vent your frustration or send private messages that are derogatory about anyone in the organization or the organization itself. A growing number of companies have an official e-mail snooping policy. Even if yours does not, all companies have the legal right to read your e-mail anytime they want. Your office computer is your company's property—the company can download and inspect and monitor it any way it chooses. In cases where you have no reasonable expectation of privacy, don't expect privacy.

It's surprising to realize that you can quickly and easily improve your writing skills if you remember the essential rule for writing as effective communication: Write in your own voice. You do this by writing as closely as possible to the way you talk, and you'll discover that your writing voice becomes more lively, powerful, and engaging. People regularly speak in simple, clear, easy-to-understand sentences, and when you write in the same way, your writing becomes much easier to understand and to accept. Your grammar becomes better, too. It's much more difficult to get it wrong in a short sentence; it's nearly impossible not to get it wrong in a very long one.

Don't shy away from the opportunity to write; the more you do it, the easier it will get. One practical tip is to listen to yourself speak what you are planning to write, then just write it down—that's the easiest way to get a good conversational tone.

Personal Persuasiveness

All communication is purposeful: You want to achieve something—for someone to learn something, to feel a certain way, or to do something. If nothing happens as a result of your communication, you might as well be writing or talking to yourself.

One way to look at it is to understand that there are a few "universal" professions—careers you have whether you recognize them or not. One universal profession is sales: Every day, you must sell your ideas, your ability, your program, your goals to people around you. Whether or not you're in "official" sales, it's worth your while to learn the techniques that make some salespeople great. These include the following:

- Effective salespeople know what they want to achieve.
- Effective salespeople know the benefits to the other party.
- Effective salespeople know how to listen well.
- Effective salespeople have empathy for the other person's point of view.
- Effective salespeople look for objections, listen carefully, and know how to overcome them.
- Effective salespeople ask for the sale.

- Effective salespeople don't take rejection personally, and they try again . . . and again.
- Effective salespeople know when—and how—to close.

Promises

Keeping your word is part of your personal integrity, and one of the hallmarks of the principled person. It may surprise you to know that promises—keeping your word—are the currency of politics. It's one of Tip O'Neill's core principles: "A politician's word is his bond."[10] In spite of conventional opinion about politicians and promises, if you think about it you'll realize that this really must be so. When you're looking for support from allies and especially from fellow travelers, you will need to make some pledges to them to obtain the support you need. What if you don't keep your word? In the short run, you may win a victory. The next time you have to go to these people for support, however, good luck. Why should they believe you? You've already proven yourself to be unreliable.

Similarly, if someone makes you a promise and fails to deliver, you aren't likely to forget. What about the next time someone wants you to take a risk on her or his behalf?

You have to keep negative promises, too. "If you keep coming in late, I'm going to fire you." If the person keeps coming in late and you don't fire him or her, not only will that person no longer take you seriously; the rest of the people in your department will know that they don't need to take you seriously either.

Withholding

The absence of speaking and writing can also be communication. When you don't give people information they could use in ways you don't want, you're practicing the technique of withholding.

There are legitimate as well as improper ways to use withholding as a technique. It's not appropriate to keep job-related information from someone to set him or her up for failure. While you may get away with it, you will have created an enemy, and you'd better have a pretty good reason for your action. In addition, if you get caught withholding job-essential information from someone, you end up looking pretty scummy.

It is certainly appropriate—sometimes legally necessary—to withhold confidential information from people who aren't entitled to it. It is also perfectly legitimate to withhold information about your own strategies and plans, but you need to be concerned about what that does to the potential for better relationships in the future. When you gain a reputation for operating in secret and using manipulative strategies, those who know you start to question whether there is something hidden in your treatment of them.

Humor

Skillful and appropriate use of humor is a valuable political and communications skill.

The appropriate part of office humor is most crucial. Is the joke relevant to the office situation? Does it put people at ease or break the tension? Avoid risky humor, ranging from group stereotypes (unless you're making fun of your own group), to sarcasm, "playful" insults, practical jokes, and "off-color" humor.

People who are concerned about "political correctness" sometimes complain that "you can't even make a joke any more." It may be helpful to realize that wit and humor are frequently—perhaps always, according to some psychiatrists—disguised aggression. Only when the disguise is deep enough do we find it really funny; when the underlying aggression or hostility can be seen, it's not surprising that it gives offense. It isn't "just a joke." It's poorly disguised hostility and aggressive behavior.[11]

Above all, if you don't know how to tell a joke, don't tell a joke.

Meetings

It's obvious that there are a lot of bad meetings, and they are wasteful and unproductive, but why are there so many? The reason, of course, comes back to office politics:

- Meetings are the "common ground" of office communication. How you behave and deal has a strong impact on your overall reputation and acceptance.
- Meetings are where major decisions are made or ratified. To be a "player," you have to be part of the right meetings with the right point of view.
- Meetings, regardless of their other purposes, are also about relationship building, and those relationships impact every other element of your work.

Being an effective office politician means mastering the art of meetings. The trick is that most of us already know how to have a good meeting, yet we do not. For example, there's no one in the world of business today who hasn't heard— repeatedly—that one should never have a meeting without an agenda, yet most meetings are still held without agendas. Why? Frankly, sometimes because the underlying political purpose has trumped the official one. Being a good meeting participant can have a surprisingly disproportional impact on your organizational reputation. Make a personal commitment to worthwhile meetings rather than complain; prepare yourself for the official agenda and the unofficial one (by checking around and making educated guesses about it); be on time (not too early, though); and don't sit in the same place with the same people every time.

One simple way to improve your reputation, effectiveness, and relationships in an organization is to be one of the people who knows how to run top-notch meetings . . . and does so. Among the fringe benefits is that when you are a participant in a meeting, the meeting leader is likely to behave better than he or she might if you're not there.

If you're not the meeting leader, you can still subtly interject some good meeting techniques without taking over the meeting. Suggest that nonagenda items be put in a parking lot for the next meeting. Identify and paraphrase action items, and query to make sure responsibility is assigned. Time the topics discussed, and provide gentle feedback on how much time has been spent when it's becoming excessive.

Finally, if the meeting topic is critical, try to determine beforehand whether consensus exists on an issue. In many cases, all the decisions are really made before the meeting gets started. Don't get caught short.

MAXIMIZING YOUR RHETORIC POWER

Consider rhetoric power issues involving yourself and the others in your network.

1. *Speaking ability.* How effective is my speaking ability in one-on-one, small group, and large group situations? What are the areas on which I need to work? What steps can I take to improve my skills?

_____

_____

2. *Writing skills.* How effective is my writing ability? What are the areas on which I need to work? What steps can I take to improve my skills?

_____

_____

3. *Personal persuasiveness.* How persuasive am I? What are my sales strengths? My sales weaknesses? How can I improve my ability to persuasively communicate my message and my goals?

_____

_____

4. *Promises.* How trustworthy am I? Do I have an absolute reputation for keeping every promise I make? Do I make promises too lightly?

_____

_____

5. ***Withholding.*** What information should I withhold from others? What is my job-related rationale for this withholding? What information should I share with people other than allies?

_____

_____

6. ***Humor.*** How am I at the appropriate business use of humor? How do my professional humor skills need to be improved?

_____

_____

7. ***Meetings.*** How well do I manage the political agenda of the meetings I attend? How can I improve?

_____

_____

8. ***The people around you.*** Consider your allies, opponents, fellow travelers, and enemies. What rhetoric power do they possess? Review the first seven questions for each significant power player in your network. What rhetoric power do they have, and how can they use it? What defensive strategies can you use in return?

_____

_____

_____

_____

_____

_____

_____

_____

_____

Using the Exercises in Your Work

Like Respect Power, Rhetoric Power is something that can be grown and developed. In thinking about these questions, consider both where you are now and how you might add to your power. In considering the rhetoric power of others, think not only about your opinion of them, but about general or more widely held opinions. Both Bill Clinton and Ronald Reagan were considered great communicators in their presidencies, but it's the case for both men that some Americans were deaf to their charms. In analyzing influence and power, you need to consider how *others* react, not just yourself.

Resource Power

> Every man will by thy friend
> Whilst thou has wherewith to spend:
> But, if store of crowns be scant,
> No man will supply thy want.
> Richard Barnfield, "Address to the
Nightingale," 1598

Everything you want is owned or controlled by somebody else. Otherwise, of course, you'd already have it. Because you want it, you are normally willing to pay some price for it. Not any price; there is a point beyond which it isn't worth it to you. But up to that point, the person who owns it has power

Figure 5-4: Resource Power

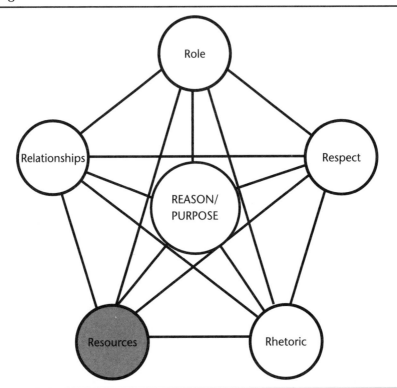

over you, because you will do certain things in exchange for what you want. This, of course, is a political situation.

What is most interesting is that it doesn't matter whether you own the resource someone wants as long as you control it. In an organization, you normally possess control over certain resources of value. Those resources are limited in quantity and must be distributed in a way that helps productivity. Within those boundaries, you have the power to provide support to some and less or none to others. This is known as resource power (Figure 5-4).

Controlling Assets

Earlier, we mentioned the concept of quid pro quo, or trading for value. The ethical issue is not about the fact of the trade, but rather about what is traded. By adopting the principle-centered philosophy for your political agenda, you can evaluate your opportunities to use your asset control to advance your political agenda within the scope of good ethical and professional behavior.

Determining What You Have

First, make a comprehensive list of the assets you control professionally. These may include budgets, work assignments (good ones and not-so-good ones), opportunities for advancement, access to equipment, tools, and others.

Second, determine what you are obligated to do for the productivity of the organization. You cannot, even if you want to, use those assets to harm your enemies if doing so harms the organization. There is normally a minimum amount of support and cooperation you must give everyone, regardless of feelings or goals. Give this level cheerfully and without resistance.

Third, determine the maximum you can do for any one person or group. There is normally a limit to what you can legitimately provide, regardless of the politics that may be involved. Make it clear what the limits are.

Fourth, armed with this information, determine the legitimate amount of discretion you have in employing those assets. This is part of your political capital. Now you must determine how you will use it.

Figuring Out How to Use It

As with manipulation of organizational norms, you can use this power in positive or negative ways. Positive use is using resource power to benefit your objectives and your allies and supporters. Negative use is withholding assets to punish opponents and enemies. Generally, positive use is much better for your long-term interests. It's appropriate to use your discretionary assets to advance your organizational goals. Nevertheless, both uses of this type of power can be principled.

To use this power in a principled way, you must be clear

about your principles and goals. It may be perfectly appropriate for you to withhold resources for agendas you believe are contrary to organizational vision, mission, and values. That's one of the purposes of having this kind of power in the first place.

Make sure you focus on principles more than people in using your discretionary assets. Seeming to play personal favorites—even with positive use for your allies—harms your reputation and makes you seem petty and vindictive. On the other hand, when you use your assets to help achieve goals you've been very clear about, that's very legitimate. After all, an organization makes decisions by how it chooses to allocate its resources, and that's what you're doing.

Controlling Information Flow

Earlier, we looked at the communications technique of withholding. Controlling information flow is a wider application of withholding and carries with it the same concerns—positive use tends to be stronger than negative use, and appearing vindictive and petty tends to work against your long-term interests.

Controlling Time

Delay and time management can be political techniques of great effectiveness, although normally they are on the ethically questionable list. Giving people inadequate time to do a job assignment, giving insufficient notice of an important change to stifle protest, setting a meeting at a time when key opponents cannot attend—these are ways to use time as a political weapon. Like many resource weapons, it is more dangerous, as well as more ethically risky, to use this power in negative ways than in positive ways.

When this technique is used on you, one traditional countermove is to get it in writing. If a person is using power in a petty way, he or she often hates to leave a paper trail and may change the time requirements previously imposed. This often works if the attack is an active one. If it's passive (e.g., use of regulations or lack of support from a person who doesn't have an official obligation to go out of his or her way to help you), then the best you can usually do is learn to avoid the problem next time. If your ability to do your job can be hampered by someone's negative use of rules and regulations (see our discussion earlier in the chapter of the manipulation of organizational norms as a function of your role power) then you must become an expert on those rules and regulations. It's an overlooked source of power.

A positive and principled way you can use this type of power is to give extra time or deadline extensions, schedule a meeting to help someone attend who might otherwise not be present, and give ample notice of change to those who may have other ideas. It's often powerful (as well as principled) to provide that extra time to enemies and opponents so that they have the perception that at all times they have been treated fairly.

Controlling Access

Among Lemuel Gulliver's travels was his visit to the floating island known as Laputa. No person of importance on that island ever listened or spoke without the help of a servant, known as a *climenole* in Laputian. This servant's only duty was to flap the mouth and ears of his master with a dried bladder whenever (in the servant's opinion) it was desirable for the master to speak or listen.

Climenoles are everywhere in the world of work. They are called executive secretaries, gatekeepers, administrative assistants, and chiefs of staff: "You'll need to speak to my boss about that . . . but my boss isn't available." Climenoles acquire enormous effective power by their control of access.

As with all resource powers, the climenole power isn't absolute. The climenole must allow certain access, because the boss does need to hear certain information and speak to certain people. Some people are powerful enough to impose their will on the climenole.

If you need to deal with a climenole, befriend him or her. Share information. Treat climenoles with respect—they have power, and they deserve respect. Don't try end runs or manipulative behavior, you'll regret it.

If you are a climenole, or at least perform the functions of one, build your relationships with those who require access. This expands your network and your knowledge. Don't abuse your power. Remember, this power is situational, delegated by the person who wants gatekeeping service, and disappears when the person changes her or his mind.

Dealing with Others Who Control

It's important to use resource power in an appropriate manner, remembering that the power is seldom owned by you but rather is delegated to you. It can be taken away. Many powerful people are shocked when their position changes, the resources they control vanish, and others' respect for them melts away.

Never rely exclusively on resource power for your own base; use it gently and positively.

When others don't follow this advice, try some of these techniques:

• *Respect them.* People who abuse resource power are often personally insecure. Build their confidence and they are less likely to use the power against you.

• *Identify their needs and try to meet them.* Trade what you have to offer for what they have. Help them meet their goals.

• *Insist on what you're entitled to in a firm, friendly way—and make sure you are really entitled.*

• *Go over their heads if necessary and only as a last resort.* Have good documentation, know the rules, and phrase your position in terms of the organization's interests, not your own. Try to remain anonymous, seek and accept no personal reward or increased power as a result, and don't tell anyone about it.

MAXIMIZING YOUR RESOURCE POWER

Consider resource power issues involving yourself and the others in your network.

1. *Assets.* What assets do I control that others will find valuable? In what ways must I distribute them to benefit the organization, and in what ways do I have discretion? What is the minimum and maximum I must provide?

   _____

   _____

2. *Information.* What information do I control that others will find valuable? In what ways must I share this information, and in what ways do I have discretion? What is the minimum and maximum I must provide?

   _____

   _____

3. *Time.* How do I control timing issues? What are the limits of that control? What discretion do I have?

   _____

   _____

4. *Access.* To whom do I control or limit access? What is my obligation to that person? What is my obligation to others? What discretion do I have in shaping access?

   _____

   _____

5. *The people around you.* Consider your allies, opponents, fellow travelers, and enemies. What resource power do they possess? Review the first four questions for each significant power player

in your network. What resource power do they have, and how can they use it? What defensive strategies can you use in return?

_____

_____

_____

_____

_____

_____

_____

_____

Using the Exercise in Your Work

A resource is a resource if it's of value to someone, even if it isn't of value to you. Think carefully about these questions to determine the resources available to you, and be aware of the resources controlled by others, especially those you may need.

Relationship Power

> He who has a thousand friends has not a friend to spare,
> And he who has one enemy will meet him everywhere.
> Ali Ibn-Abu-Talib, *A Hundred Sayings*, A.D. 661

There are many sayings and slogans about relationships and power: "It ain't what you know, it's who you know"; "How to win friends and influence people"; "The 'old boy' network."

The idea that your relationships with others is a key in-

Figure 5-5: Relationship Power

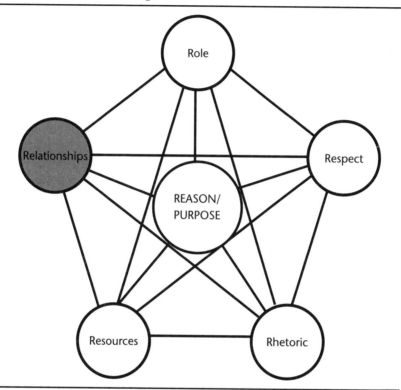

gredient in your personal power is well known. What is less well known is that relationships tend to be powerful only when combined with the other forms of power we've been discussing (Figure 5-5).

Some people just try to sleaze by on their relationship skills—they don't do the work, they don't gain the knowledge, they only use their people skills. That often works . . . for a while. And that's the problem. A recurrent theme in this book has been the importance of separating tactics that produce short-term gains from those that are of long-term value. Short-term tactics should be resorted to only in emergencies and with full awareness of the damage they can cause to your long-term success. Often, you have to clean up after yourself, rebuild trust you've lost, reearn relationships. Sometimes, you can never get back completely to where you were before.

The other reason to study short-term tactics is that others often use them. You need to know what they're doing, why they're doing it, and how to counter it. As you study the issues of Relationship Power, consider both what you should do and what others do for their immediate perceived advantage.

Relationships matter on every level, from self-development to achieving your political aim. We've focused on techniques for dealing with all the different types of people in your environment: allies, fellow travelers, opponents, enemies, and neutrals. Here are some additional insights.

Associating with Powerful People

Power rubs off on you. When you associate with powerful people, you acquire, as if by osmosis, some of their power. If you are perceived as speaking for them, carrying their messages, representing their interests, then you become, in a practical sense, more personally powerful.

Perception and Relationships

The key is perception. You know people who suck up to anyone in power, pretend to an intimacy that may well not exist, then come out to lord it over everybody else, using the perception of the relationship as their source of power. That behavior often gets its comeuppance, and people are delighted when that happens.

Another person may be afraid to trade on the relationship, and even when that person is supposed to be a representative or advocate for the powerful person's interest, she or he may not state forcefully and clearly what is to be done. Unfortunately, that behavior gets punished, too.

Make sure that you don't get in the habit of overstating the relationship or pushing it beyond its limits. You'll be better off erring on the side of modesty.

It's perfectly okay to seek relationships with powerful people for the sake of acquiring political power for yourself, as long as you go about it in the right way and for the right motives, and as long as you use this power wisely and fairly.

Why They Want to Associate with You

Why should a powerful person wish to be friends or allies with you? There are a number of reasons:

- It's flattering to be admired, respected, and thought of as a role model.
- One's personal power and influence increases by developing other people (*The Godfather* once again).
- The people in a powerful person's network can provide support and work toward that person's goals.
- The powerful person gains access to wider information and different points of view.
- The powerful person acquires sources of intelligence— the spy network.

Avoiding Being a "Brownnoser"

If you've ever been brownnosed by someone, you discovered two things: You immediately knew what it was, and you found it wasn't entirely pleasant or unpleasant. Brownnosing is flattering to the person being flattered. But beware of temptation. Machiavelli warns that the only defense against flattery is to let people know that they don't offend you by telling you the truth. But when pretty much anybody can tell you the truth, you can lose their respect. When you are in a leadership role, limit the number of people who can speak to you with total candor; others need to ask permission.[12] In other words, the wise powerful person recognizes flattery and uses flatterers but does not take them into her or his inner circle.

The problem with brownnosing is that it makes you weak, not strong. Certain office bullies are caught in this trap: They grovel for the recognition of people in power, then make up for it by abusing others. Instead, seek to become one of the select few who are valued for honest and good advice.

How do you do this? Choose the truths you tell and the battles you fight carefully. Tell your boss when and why you're pushing back or resisting a change or direction. Have your facts straight. Always have the information and background or a perspective the other person doesn't have. Style is often crucial; be positive and make sure you're never seen as acting out of self-interest.

People Who Outrank Your Boss

One area of opportunity—and danger—is to develop organizational relationships with people who outrank your boss. This is acceptable as long as you don't use those relationships to reverse your boss's decisions, get job assignments without your boss's approval, or keep your boss in the dark about those relationships.

You can use relationships with higher-ups to advance your boss's agenda and keep him or her in the know. Always pay attention to the relationship that exists between your boss and his or her superiors. Be aware how such relationships are seen in terms of the overall corporate culture: rewarded or unrewarded? Seen as self-promotion or a way to advance organizational goals?

You *are* violating the chain of command—and can get into trouble—if you are approached by someone higher in management who gives you a job assignment or decision and don't either ask the manager to clear it with your boss or, at an absolute minimum, personally clear it with your boss at the earliest practical moment. That doesn't mean you should refuse the assignment or be uncooperative with the senior person. He or she is also violating the chain of command, and it's still negative behavior even though he or she has the power to do so. Don't compound the mistake by keeping your boss out of the loop.

Notice that if your boss feels bypassed by his or her own boss, feelings of paranoia and persecution may result. It is obviously more difficult for your boss to confront or change the behavior of his or her own superior, so you may find yourself bearing the brunt of your boss's resentment. Depending on your relationship with the senior person, asking him or her to check with your boss may be a supportive and practical thing to do.

Networking Inside and Outside

The terms "mentoring" and "networking" have been so over-used—and abused—that they are in danger of becoming clichés. Still, it's important to understand and use the fundamental ideas for you to be successful and effective as a principled office politician.

Mentoring

Mentors are people who give you help and advice on the basis of their own position, experience, knowledge, and accomplishments. Mentors can be role models, trainers, and coaches. Perhaps most important, mentors are people with political clout and power who are well disposed toward you and willing to help, advise, and support you in the development of your own power. You need to develop effective, mutually beneficial relationships with people outside your own department and outside your own chain of command.

While your boss is and must be an essential element in your success within the organization, you must expand your reach and relationships to truly succeed. The trick, of course, is how to develop these relationships without (1) threatening your boss and (2) appearing to be a brownnoser.

The first issue may be the most difficult, depending on how threatened or vulnerable your boss may feel. In order not to generate feelings of paranoia in your boss, which would certainly be counterproductive, you need to make sure that your boss knows that you are personally loyal to him or her and that nothing in the outside relationships will be used to undercut that relationship. Your boss should always be at least unofficially aware of such relationships.

In addition, try to make sure that the value you get from mentoring relationships also provides direct benefit and support to your boss. For example, if you discover useful information and insight, pass it on—respecting confidentiality, of course. Remember that there is not a lot of benefit in "hogging" a mentoring relationship. If your boss is not well connected in the organization, share your connections. It won't hurt you, and it will benefit your boss.

Try to avoid using the word "mentor," and, in particular, don't ask someone to be your "mentor." Instead, approach people for help and advice; build the relationship over time.

Listen to your mentors. Even if not all their advice is 100 percent situationally appropriate, it's still always valuable. Extract lessons you can learn in all cases.

Support your mentors. You owe people for the help and support they provide to you; make sure you're there for them when they need support. One of the reasons people in management provide mentoring is to build a base of loyalty and support for later in their careers. While no one will necessarily say anything to you, you'll find that if you don't support those who support you, there will be a lot fewer people who support you.

Networking

As with the word "mentoring," try to avoid actually using the word "networking" to describe what you do, because the word has picked up a negative connotation for many people, suggesting something manipulative. Think of networking as relationship building, talking to people, getting to know the people in your organization, learning about the work of different departments.

You don't want to make networking about "using" other people. Offer information, support, and help to others in the process. Here are some tips for building an effective network in a principled fashion:

- Go to lunch with different people on a regular basis.
- Ask questions to get to know the person as an individual as well as questions to understand his or her role in the organization.
- Participate in office parties, picnics, sports teams, and other informal groups. This is work, not just fun.
- Make sure you use proper business and communications etiquette.

- Absolutely respect any and all confidences shared with you.
- Follow through on any promises you make. If you can't keep your promise, at a minimum go back to the person and explain the situation.
- Listen and consider the advice you get, whether or not you eventually follow it.
- Join associations, trade groups, and professional societies in your field to expand your relationships in other organizations.
- Volunteer for committees and project groups that give you cross-departmental contacts.

Make networking and relationship building a habit. Set yourself a personal goal of at least one new contact each week. Set aside regular time to call and follow up on your relationships—but don't pester them.

As in the case of mentoring, make sure you use the information and support to help achieve your boss's goals; don't let your networking appear to be a threat, actual or even potential.

Outside the Organization

If there is a professional or trade group in your industry you can join, join it. Go to meetings; get involved. At trade shows, set a goal of getting to know people in your industry. Not only is this valuable to your career; it's a valuable resource within your company. There are three key benefits:

1. Contacts throughout the industry cause you to be listened to more readily in your own organization, they increase your status—and they might come in very handy when it comes time to change situations.

2. Whether they want to or not, organizations tend to breed a little bit of "tunnel vision" about their methods and processes. Getting to know your industry helps bring a breath of fresh air into your own company, and everyone benefits.

3. Listen carefully, read widely, and follow the trades, and you'll discover that you can learn a lot about what's

really going on. Without spying or other ethically question-able behavior, you'll automatically learn valuable informa-tion.

Obligating Others

Even if you don't particularly care about a concession or re-quests that someone else makes of you, it may still be worth your while to call attention to the favor, just so you're in a better position to ask for a return favor later on. Phrases like, "Oh, it's nothing," are dangerous because there's always the chance someone will believe you. And there are few things as maddening as finding that other people have dismissed the value of the favors you've done.

We noted in Chapter 4 that the political world operates on a quid pro quo basis, and that this is not necessarily a bad thing. The currency of politics is often the favors you owe and are owed. As a result, a good strategy is to cheerfully provide support to others so that you can later request it in turn.

You don't always have to be blunt, and often it's better not to be. Sometimes, the fact that you do favors for others makes them reciprocate without being asked. But sometimes you do have to be blunt. In Chapter 4 we talked about putting the squeeze on a neutral. When you've done favors in the past, you can make it clear that now is the time you want to be paid back.

The goal in asking for payback is to be proportional in your request. If people come to feel that, by doing you a favor, they're leaving themselves vulnerable to a form of emotional blackmail, they'll stop accepting your favors. Don't expect someone to lie for you, to behave in an unethical manner, or to risk her or his career prospects, regardless of the favors you've done in the past.

Identifying with Significant People and/or Organizations

In the military, it is said that you salute the uniform, not the person in it. The uniform is a symbol, and the person wearing the uniform gains a form of delegated power. Some of the most powerful people are not so much powerful in their own right; rather, they are the representatives of their organization or group.

When you identify with your organization or your department, you gain some of that power, but the trick is that you really to have to identify with the organization and make its goals your goals.

Name Dropping

There is an art to effective name dropping. Poorly done, name dropping makes you look weak and grasping; properly done it adds to your credentials and respect power.

Strong name dropping has the following elements:

- The name dropping is appropriate to the level of the relationship; you don't pretend to be someone's intimate friend when you are a casual acquaintance.
- The name dropping isn't forced; it is natural and appropriate to the conversation. If it isn't, you don't do it.
- The name dropping is relevant to the issue at hand; it helps in decision making to know that someone supports or opposes a particular course of action.
- The name dropping is done in an offhand manner; it doesn't seem calculated, egotistical, or planned.
- The name dropping doesn't involve the same name (or the same story) over and over again; once or twice is plenty, unless there is a strong, relevant, ongoing relationship.

A subspecies of name dropping is quoting. Having a collection of pithy, appropriate quotes for the situation can make you appear more educated and more intelligent (if not over done). Besides, the great writers and speakers of history often say it better than the rest.

Unofficial Relationships and Involvements

Every resource on career management recommends against romantic or personal entanglements at work; nevertheless, it's a very common phenomenon—if for no other reason than for many people, the office is the largest social circle to which they belong![13]

There are two aspects to this situation: your own relationships and relationships among others in the organization that can affect you.

Your Relationships

First, take for granted that any such relationship will be discovered and broadcast on the office grapevine. People find this kind of news titillating and broadcast it widely and rapidly.

Second, organizations have different official and *unofficial* policies about such relationships, and the unofficial policies should be of just as great concern to you as the official ones. One or both of the parties may end up shut out of consideration for a promotion or advancement, cut out of some information networks on the assumption that whatever one knows, the other will soon know, and possibly the subject of moral disapproval, warranted or not.

Find out what the policies are, and live by them. If you can't live by them, you'll need to go elsewhere. You can sometimes negotiate with management and human resources, depending on your organizational position, political leverage, and slack. Notify your supervisor of the relationship, at least unofficially, if it could be construed as politically sensitive even if it's not covered by policy. Learn about the organizational history surrounding such relationships; this will often suggest the precedents that will apply to you.

Third, remember that where there's smoke, there's not necessarily fire. Be aware that, if you work in close contact with a member of the opposite sex and you get along personally, quite a few people may be eager to jump to conclusions. Even if there is a complete absence of a romantic or sexual relationship, a rumor can still start and you and the other person can suffer the consequences, even though nothing whatsoever is going on. You can find yourself in trouble, accused of violating policy, even if nothing has actually taken place. Be sensitive to appearances as well as reality.

If a relationship does take place, make sure your own behavior doesn't add fuel to the fire. Keep appropriate professional distance at work, regardless of the nature of the relationship outside work. Don't allow yourself to be seen as playing favorites; this may mean that you must under some circumstances be harder on your partner than on someone with whom there is no relationship.

Finally, should a relationship come to an end, you still have to work together in a professional manner. Regardless of the circumstances, unless one of you plans to leave, you need to negotiate how you will behave at the office. Sexual harassment policies apply, and apply strongly in these circumstances. Make sure that your conduct doesn't lend itself to an accusation of harassment, and realize that you may be looked at more strictly as a result of the relationship than might otherwise have been the case.

Others' Relationships

Because others may or may not follow this advice, you actually have a need separate from any personal enjoyment of gossip to be aware of any major romantic entanglements in the workplace. You need to know if an alliance is threatened because the partner is on the other side. You might need to tread carefully if you have to bring bad news about one partner to the other. This is particularly difficult when one partner is higher on the hierarchical ladder than the other one.

In addition, there is the question of whether you are supposed to know. If a relationship is officially secret, you must act as if you know nothing about it, even when everyone in the office is gossiping about nothing else.

Don't take for granted that others will behave rationally in this situation. Be careful.

MAXIMIZING YOUR RELATIONSHIP POWER

Consider relationship power issues involving yourself and the others in your network.

1. ***Powerful people.*** What powerful people do I know? What is my relationship with them? In what ways do I represent their interests? How can their power add to my power?

    _____

    _____

2. ***Mentors.*** Whom do I have as mentors currently? What can I do to attract the right new mentors and associates in powerful positions? What do my mentors need from me?

    _____

    _____

3. ***Brownnosing.*** Am I perceived as an empty flatterer? How can I provide valuable support to those whose support I need?

    _____

    _____

4. ***People who outrank my boss.*** Do I have associations with people who outrank my boss? How can I avoid having those relationships threaten my relationship with my boss? How can I use these relationships to benefit my boss?

    _____

    _____

5. ***Networking.*** Whom do I go to lunch with? What questions do I ask, and how well do I listen? What office social events can I use as a vehicle for better networking? How can I expand my network of relationships, both inside and outside the organization?

    _____

    _____

6. **Obligations.** Whom can I do favors for? Whom can I support? What level of obligation can I legitimately put on other people?

_____

_____

7. **Identifying with the organization.** To what extent can I identify with the organization and its institutions in an honest and legitimate way? In what ways can this identification give me greater leverage to achieve organizational goals?

_____

_____

8. **Name dropping.** Whose names can I drop, and how can I drop them in an appropriate and powerful way? What good quotes and expressions can I use to improve my communication?

_____

_____

9. **Involvements.** Am I involved in a romantic relationship at work? Is it within policy guidelines, both official and unofficial? Have I notified the right people or groups? How well known is the relationship? How can I manage it to minimize problems? What will happen if it breaks off? How can I preserve the relationship? Am I behaving tactfully in the office? Could I be perceived as being involved in a relationship when it's really not the case?

_____

_____

10. **The people around you.** Consider your allies, opponents, fellow travelers, and enemies. What resource power do they possess? Review the first nine questions for each significant power

player in your network. What resource power do they have, and how can they use it? What defensive strategies can you use in return?

_____

_____

_____

_____

_____

_____

_____

_____

Using the Exercise in Your Work

Relationships can be a great source of power, but in some cases they can be heavy liabilities. If your analysis of these questions identifies specific relationship problems, conduct a more thorough political analysis of all your circumstances to figure out its effect on your total power as well as what strategies you might apply to correct or minimize the problems.

Notes

1. Watts S. Humphrey, *Managing Technical People: Innovation, Teamwork, and the Software Process* (Reading, Mass.: Addison-Wesley, 1997), pp. 234–247.

2. Daniel Goleman, *Emotional Intelligence* (New York: Bantam Books, 1995), p. 148.

3. "Sabotage," by the way, is commonly supposed to be a military term. It is a business term, derived from the word

sabot, a wooden shoe worn by the French peasantry. In the early days of the Industrial Revolution in France, when factory owners pushed their workers too hard, the workers would throw their wooden shoes into the machinery, bringing the factory to a halt; hence *sabotage.*

4. Goleman, op. cit., pp. 161–162.

5. John W. Dean III, *Blind Ambition* (New York: Pocket Books, 1976), pp. 117–118.

6. Michael S. Dobson, *Practical Project Management* (Mission, Kans.: SkillPath Publications, 1996), and *The Juggler's Guide to Managing Multiple Projects* (Newtown Square, Pa.: Project Management Institute, 1999).

7. Michael Singer Dobson and Deborah Singer Dobson, *Managing UP!* (New York: AMACOM, 1999), pp. 214–221.

8. Machiavelli, op. cit., p. 93.

9. Barbara Pachter and Marjorie Brody, *Climbing the Corporate Ladder: What You Need to Know and Do to Be a Promotable Person* (Mission, Kans.: SkillPath Publications, 1995), p. 63.

10. O'Neill, op. cit., p. 129.

11. Martin, Grotjahn, M.D., *Beyond Laughter: Humor and the Subconscious* (New York: McGraw-Hill, 1966), pp. 10–16.

12. Machiavelli, op. cit., p. 117.

13. *Truth-in-advertising disclosure:* The authors of this book met at work and eventually married and didn't consider the political issues at all.

Chapter 6

The Search for Role Models—Leadership and Office Politics

Everyone is always and everywhere, more or less consciously, playing a role. . . . It is in these roles that we know each other; it is in these roles that we know ourselves.

Robert E. Park, *Behind Our Masks*, 1926

Outstanding office politicians are always and necessarily outstanding leaders, whether for positive or negative ends. After all, the purpose of playing office politics is to get others to do what you want them to do, whether it's to pursue a common goal, follow your lead, or simply leave you alone. And getting other people to follow your lead is what leadership is.

Leadership is the apotheosis of playing politics. Your goal is to influence the organization as a whole and people as individuals in the direction you wish, even if that direction is simply that they leave you alone to do your work. While definitions of what constitutes leadership vary, they all contain some sense of getting others to do your bidding (or, as Dwight D. Eisenhower put it, "[Leadership is the] art of getting someone else to do something you want done because he (or she) wants to do it.").

Reading biographies of people who became great leaders, or indeed became highly successful in any area you value, teaches one key lesson: their ultimate success was hardly ever foreordained or inevitable. They had setbacks, they had deficiencies, and they had to learn. Most fundamental competencies can be learned, and that is especially true in the area of leadership. That doesn't mean it's easy; if it were easy, everyone would do it. But what distinguishes the highly successful from the rest of the world is often the degree of grit, determination, and work. The ability to suffer setbacks and get back on one's feet helps a lot, too—as does a sense of humor. Read about successful people to discover your own ideas and your own methods for success.

The various methods of analyzing the landscape and the other players, of gaining and developing power, are also simultaneously methods to increase your leadership skills, because the skills of office politics are at a minimum a subset of the skills of leadership.

We've studied and analyzed people in our organization so far with the goal of improving our ability to manage them effectively. But there's another reason to expand our study of others: the search for role models.

Role models are at the core of your ability to expand and extend your political skills, because they serve as living examples you can use. Role models may include mentors, supervisors, and managers and others with whom you have a relationship. However, you can also learn from people without having a relationship with them. In leadership research, people mention outside role models, including historical figures and well-known contemporary leaders, as sources of inspiration, self-development—and sometimes as a warning of what not to do—every bit as often as they mention internal figures.[1]

In this chapter, you'll work to identify a series of role models both inside and outside the organization, to determine how they reached their goals, to see the obstacles against which they struggled and the barriers they broke down, to understand how their principles supported them and in some cases limited them, to recognize where they failed to live up to their own ideals and where they succeeded, and to see how all this broke down into specific strategies for action. There's practically no problem you've ever experienced that someone, somewhere, hasn't met and overcome. If you can find out who that person is and do the same thing, you'll find that's often very helpful.

Because office politics never takes place in a vacuum but occurs in an organizational context, certain tactics and behaviors that have demonstrably worked brilliantly elsewhere don't necessarily translate—or translate without modification—to the present environment. Even if you've been successful elsewhere, it's important to follow the advice given beside any railroad track—stop, look, listen—before putting your own political campaign into operation.

That's why, in addition to external role models, you need to identify some role models within the organization. As part of your search for and development of mentors, key elements in your path to political (and leadership) success, you need to identify those people whose specific orientation and style make them particularly suitable for you.

Who is successful in your organization? What characteristics make those people successful? Do they fit into the power models you've learned in this book, or are they successful in spite of flouting the official rules? Are they lopsided, so strong in a single characteristic that they counterbalance flaws and weaknesses elsewhere? Of the people who are successful and effective, which ones would you want to emulate?

Admiring admirable people is a good idea, but learning from them is an even better one.

Identifying and Using External Role Models

The following worksheet can be adapted to almost any area of personal growth you might want to explore, now or in the future. The purpose of the exercise is to identify role models in history, fiction, or current events that can serve as inspirations and problem-solving models for you as you face a wide variety of challenges.

IDENTIFICATION OF EXTERNAL ROLE MODELS

Role Model	Leadership Characteristics	Political Characteristics	Weaknesses/ Failures	How Does This Fit Me?	Notes/ Comments

1. Using the grid provided here, or a separate piece of paper if you prefer, write down the first names that come to your mind when you think of great leaders. You may list people from history, current figures, or even fictional figures.

   _____

   _____

2. Now, write down the first names that come to your mind when you think of highly effective politicians, using the same criteria as in question 1.

   _____

   _____

3. If there are any names common to both lists, make a special note of them.

   _____

   _____

4. Take the twenty (or fewer if there are overlaps) names, and for each person write down one or more specific characteristics about that person that make him or her a good leader.

_____

_____

5. Now identify the characteristics of each of the twenty individuals that make him or her an effective politician.

_____

_____

6. If there are any characteristics that make someone *both* an effective leader and a politician, note them in both columns.

_____

_____

7. Take the list of characteristics you've developed, and put a star or check beside each characteristic you believe you possess.

_____

_____

8. From your list of twenty people, identify those for whom you listed the same characteristics.

_____

_____

9. Using the reduced list of people, which of them are similar to you in terms of gender, age, or other personal characteristics?

_____

_____

10. Select and star two or three names and key characteristics that form the best fit for who you are. By the way, if additional names and characteristics occur to you at any time during the exercise, feel free to add them. Don't let an arbitrary number count constrain your thinking.

_____

_____

11. Make a commitment with yourself to find biographical information on each of the people on your final list. Read about their journey and struggles. Read about the methods they used to overcome the obstacles in their path, and the personal characteristics that helped them triumph, paying particular attention to the characteristics that you also have.

_____

_____

12. Pay particular attention to any situations in which the person demonstrated weakness or failed. Note such cases on the grid. What led to the failure? Was it part of the characteristic that made the person strong, or something different? Was it a lapse in behavior or a personal tragic flaw?

_____

_____

13. As you read, keep a notepad handy. Every time you find something of relevance to you, write it down.

_____

_____

14. As you review your list, consider what long-term strategies you ought to pursue to make you stronger in the same way as the role models you've chosen? How can you learn from their mistakes and struggles? What developmental areas should you focus upon?

_____

_____

15. When you're faced with a political or leadership dilemma that you're trying to solve, stop and think how the people on your role model list would have handled it. What can you learn from them? How can you adapt a solution one or more of them employed to the present circumstances?

_____

_____

16. Continue your research into role models by looking for cases in history, fiction, and current events that fit your character and that offer ideas you might be able to use.

_____

_____

Using the Exercise in Your Work

This is a powerful technique, and we highly recommend that you take the time to do this exercise thoroughly. Many of us are less successful than we might be because of barriers in our self-image or self-esteem. By identifying ourselves with people who have overcome such barriers, we can open some new doors within ourselves. A substantial amount of real power comes from within, from your own vision and from your sense of possibility. Maximize this insight not only in the political arena, but in other areas of your life as well.

Identifying and Using Internal Role Models

In several of the worksheets in this book, you identified various "players" in the political arena, both positive and negative. People inside the organization can be role models, too, and, because they have been successful in the same arena, the lessons they have to teach you are often very powerful.

IDENTIFICATION OF INTERNAL ROLE MODELS

Person	Quadrant/ Shared Goals	Ways More Successful	Ways Less Successful	Role of Character	Role Model Behavior	Notes

1. Go through the worksheets in Chapter 4, in which you listed people in your own office or organizational environment. Copy all the names onto a single list. Keep the answers to the previous exercises handy; copy the information when it's appropriate, but

also think about any additional answers that might apply to the questions in this exercise, and write them down as well.

_____

_____

2. Identify the players with whom you share goals in the office political process. Where does each person fit in the Political Environment model (e.g., ally, fellow traveler, opponent)?

_____

_____

3. In what ways are they more successful than you? What characteristics have provided them their success?

_____

_____

4. In what ways are they less successful than you? What characteristics or behavior have interfered with their achieving their goals? Remember, as in the previous worksheet, to learn both from successes and from failures. Negative lessons are as useful as positive ones from your role models.

_____

_____

5. Whom on your list do you consider to have high principles and good character? In what ways have those principles and character contributed to those people's success? In what ways have those principles and character interfered?

_____

_____

6. What types of behavior can you find that you would like to emulate? What types of behavior should serve as negative role models for your conduct?

_____

_____

7. Armed with this knowledge, what would you like to do differently as a long-range plan?

_____

_____

8. When you're in a difficult situation, ask yourself how some of the others on your list would handle it. Would those behaviors work for you?

_____

_____

9. As in the previous worksheet, come back to this work from time to time to see whether your answers have changed or developed.

_____

_____

Using the Exercises in Your Work

People have much to teach you, if you're willing to learn. Sometimes, your best lessons come from surprising people. By thinking of the people around you as potential role models, you not only have the ability to profit from some of their insights, but also gain a better, more detailed understanding of them.

Both positive and negative role models are useful as examples of behavior to emulate and behavior to avoid, and you can (and should) keep a variety of role models active in your mind at all times.

A role model need not be someone who is better than you across the board—there are very few who would qualify. To be useful, a role model must exhibit some specific quality that is relevant to who you are or would like to be, and that quality must have some elements from which you can learn. For example, if you have neither the talent nor the desire to play the violin, Yehudi Menuhin might be someone you admire tremendously, but he'd be pretty irrelevant as a role model, although some of his personal characteristics might be adaptable to your circumstances. Think creatively.

In order for you to be successful in implementing the ideas in this book in your own organization and in your own career, you will have to take personal responsibility for fine-tuning the tactics and advice. And there's no better way to leverage your own strengths than by learning from others. There are, after all, two different ways to learn from experience: Have the experience and learn from it, or find others who have had the experience and learn from them. The second way puts a lot less wear and tear on your system.

Note

1. James M. Kouzes and Barry Z. Posner, *The Leadership Challenge: How to Keep Getting Extraordinary Things Done in Organizations* (San Francisco: Jossey-Bass, 1995), p. 331.

Chapter 7

Political Communication— From Lying to Spin Doctoring

If dogs could talk, we wouldn't get along with them, either.

Fred Pryor, seminar leader, 1993

The act of communication is at the heart of office politics. In fact, that's what you—and others—do when practicing it. The majority of political acts are communications acts. You persuade people to your point of view, you figure out what their goals are by effective listening, you shape the flow of information and how it is perceived in speeches and memos—all this is politics in action. Therefore, your effectiveness as an office politician is significantly proportional to your effectiveness as a communicator.

Earlier, we talked about Rhetoric Power—the part of your power base that results from your communications skills. As we showed, that's an essential element of your power base. But there's more. How you express and use the other elements of your power ties back to the concept of effective communications.

Communication takes many forms, from talking to listening, from memos to wall graphics, from nonverbal cues to strategic silences, from hearing the words people say to reading between the lines. When we communicate, we influence, we describe, we inform. Sometimes we withhold, we mislead, we even lie.

Probably the biggest single step you can take to improve your communication is to increase your awareness of it. You can't help communicating; you communicate even without opening your mouth. Therefore, a lot of your communication ends up purposeless and works against your goals rather than in support of them.

Especially in business, and to a great extent in every aspect of your life, when you communicate, you want to achieve something. There is a purpose, or at least some sort of underlying intent. When your communication works against your intent, you're in trouble. By keeping your purpose firmly and constantly in mind, you will almost instantly see a real improvement in the quality and effectiveness of your communications behavior.

Purposefulness

Why are we communicating? We communicate because we are trying to get something. You may want someone to *act*, you may want someone to *believe*, you may want someone to *know*. By knowing your purpose, you'll automatically find it easier to select the right styles and approaches to get what you want. Notice that Reason Power—knowing who you are and what you want—is a critical part of your overall power, and applying that concept to effective communications strategies leverages Rhetoric Power, as well. Let's look at the various goals of communication and show how knowing your purpose and keeping it clearly in mind helps you get the results you seek.

Act

When you want someone to take an action, to do something, your communication must include a clear statement of what you want the person to do. If you don't tell the person, then there's a significant chance he or she won't know. Because most normal people don't do the Vulcan Mind Meld like Mr. Spock on *Star Trek*, it's an unwise strategy to expect them to read your mind about what you want. That's pretty obvious, but it is amazing how often you hear people say some variant of "You should have known." "How could you not know that?" "I thought it was perfectly clear what I wanted!" In most of these cases, the communicator seems to believe his or her brain waves transmitted the message and that no speech was necessary.

You've heard it said, "If you don't ask, you don't get." That doesn't mean people aren't interested in helping you or being supportive. It means that if you don't ask, it's a good idea not to assume that people magically know. In assertiveness training courses, people often discover that their effectiveness in getting what they want goes up tremendously once they learn they have to actually state what they want. They often don't have to use special tactics or methods; they simply find that others are often (though admittedly not always) willing to help.

Believe

Getting people to believe or feel something is the core of persuasive communication. From putting the right "spin" on a particular situation to conveying your position on controversial issues in a way that moves people on your side, persuasiveness is one of the cardinal skills of the effective office politician.

Wrong ways to accomplish this abound. When most people try to be persuasive, they treat their point of view as if it were merely knowledge to be shared. "The fact is . . ." they begin and then state their point of view in a tone that does not allow for disagreement. This tactic is often successful in shutting other people up, but it does nothing to change an opinion. Another technique you'll often see employed is insulting someone's intelligence or values, especially by employing emotionally loaded words. "That's just typical liberal/ right-wing/mushy/heartless nonsense." Again, just having the skill necessary to get someone to shut up is no evidence that you've been persuasive. You may even have created an enemy.

The initial step in actually persuading others to your point of view is to understand their point of view. If someone doesn't agree with you, there is a gap between the way that person sees the situation and the way you see it. By understanding the position from which the person starts, you can begin to develop a strategy for achieving some change. As we've said earlier, there is no single skill as critical to your effectiveness in the political arena.

Why doesn't the person believe what you believe? One reason may be that the person doesn't have the knowledge you have, in which case, by sharing the knowledge, you may be able to change the belief. That's fairly straightforward, but unfortunately there are other potential problems as well.

Another reason is that the person's interests may be opposed to yours. Believing what you believe may be in your best interest but not in the other person's. This calls for listening to WII—FM and looking for some way that sharing your belief can be beneficial to the other person on his or her own terms.

A third, and quite common, problem is that the other person sees the world differently, operates from different values, proceeds from a different fundamental assumption. Such differences are frequently intractable, and you have to know when continuing an argument or an attempt to persuade is likely to do you more harm than good.

In such cases especially, you'll find that listening is often more effective than talking when you want to make progress in changing the other person.

Know

Conveying knowledge or information, although not necessarily carrying the persuasive burden of getting people to act or believe, is often tougher than it looks. Remember that your audience, not wanting to appear stupid in your eyes, tends to reply, "Yes, I understand," even when it's not the case. Use the following rules and ideas to get your information across more effectively:

• *Measure the knowledge gap.* It's hard to convey your information without having a good idea of your audience's current level of understanding. If you underestimate their knowledge, you bore them through repetition. If you overestimate their knowledge, you lose them. Look for ways to discover this in advance. Techniques include surveys (written or oral), advance visits, and checking with others. Ways to discover their knowledge on the spot include asking questions, watching for body language or facial expressions that suggest either boredom or confusion, and precalling (providing advance warning, for example, "Please forgive me if I repeat information you already know").

• *Simplify your message.* The well-known rule KISS ("Keep it short and simple") is a good way to convey most messages. Avoid unnecessarily long words and phrases that dance around the truth ("eliminate human resource redundancies" as opposed to "fire" or "lay off"), use the active voice ("We decided" as opposed to "It was decided"), and get your main point in at the beginning of your statement.

• *Use metaphors to increase understanding.* In explaining the theory of relativity, Albert Einstein asked physicists to imagine an elevator moving at high speeds through empty space. By imagining what the person inside and outside the elevator would see, the reader could develop a much better understanding of Einstein's radically new ideas. How can you paint a picture of your great idea? How can you create a model, an example, or a picture with which others can identify? Target your metaphor toward your audience, emphasizing the kinds of things in their ordinary experience.

• *Use feedback to verify understanding.* When you communicate, you must overcome hurdles. The first hurdle is, Was your message received? Second, Was your message understood? And third, Was your message accepted? Asking for feedback by requesting that the other person repeat his or her understanding of the message, by asking the person to explain it to you, or by asking the person to answer questions that require an understanding of the message all help you be certain the message got through. If it didn't get through, always take the responsibility yourself, rather than criticize the listener, or else you'll find increasing resistance to your communication. Ask for questions, but always be prepared by knowing more than you need to know so that you won't be caught short when asked to explain. (This is particularly important when you're a technical person explaining to a nontechnical audience.)

Nonverbal Channels

You communicate even when your mouth is tightly shut. In fact, you can't help communicating all day, every day, because nonverbal communication is much more powerful and far-reaching than the words you actually use. It's easy to demonstrate this in practice. If you're hunched over with downcast eyes and someone asks how you are feeling, and you reply, "Fine," the person will instantly—and quite reasonably—doubt you're telling the truth. Most people automatically assume that when there's a conflict between body language and spoken language, the body language conveys the real message.

That isn't always true, of course. If someone is fidgeting and crossing and uncrossing his or her legs, it may be that the person is bored with your conversation and wants to escape your company, or it may be that the person must urgently answer a call of nature. It's dangerous to overread someone's nonverbal communication, though of course we do it all the time.

Similarly, the sound of your voice has an impact on your communication far above the words you speak. There's a world of difference between "OH-kay," which signifies strong agreement and compliance, and "Oh-KAA-AY," which means, "I'll do what you said, but I think you're making a big mistake." We make reference to this all the time. Someone has a "whiny tone," or a "dead voice," or "sounds cheerful." Some accents grate; others enhance the message. Some voices sound educated, others low class. It's important for you to remember two things: First, you may be wrong in the conclusions you draw. Second, other people draw such conclusions—whether right or wrong—about you all the time.

Telephone customer service and telemarketing professionals are taught the "mirror trick": keep a mirror on your desk, and when you talk on the telephone, look in the mirror and smile. Although the person on the other end can't see you, the physical smile on your face changes the sound of your voice. They can *hear* the smile, and it affects how they perceive and react toward you.

Professional speakers are told over and over again that they should video- and audiotape their speeches from time to time and watch them first with the sound off, second without looking at the picture, and third with picture and sound together. It's an amazing experience; the sound-only and picture-only views often come across dramatically different. If you're not being perceived the way you want, it's likely that aspects of your personal presentation, whether body language or sound, are getting in your way.

The good news is that if you're finding your political presence and effectiveness hampered by the sound of your voice and your body language, it's quite possible to change. From a Toastmasters group to home study courses, from personal coaching to workshops, there are a wide number of tools available. If you need them, get them.

Dress and grooming are inextricably part of your nonverbal communication. Dress and grooming reflect your social status, your adherence to corporate culture, the seriousness with which you take a given situation, and your sense of appropriateness. The savvy office politician never forgets that he or she is always communicating and stays conscious and in control of the messages he or she transmits, from dress to tone.

Dishonesty

The lies people tell are often as significant as their truths— sometimes more so, because we choose our lies. One of the best and most useful of political skills is the ability to listen so well that even others' lies come across as clear communication. Train yourself to look for the truth—no matter how deeply buried—in everything everybody says. It's always there.

Let's look as some categories of common lying to determine ways to extract a useful message:

• ***Self-aggrandizement.*** A very common form of significant lying is the exaggeration of one's credentials or accomplishments. Earlier, we discussed the tragic suicide of the Chief of Naval Operations, which was widely attributed to his mortification over accusations that he wore medals to which he was not entitled.

Politicians are no more susceptible to this disease than anyone else, but of course if one's enemies catch you in the act, they like to harp on it, as many politicians in public life have learned to their eternal embarrassment. Most of us fall into this trap from time to time, but when such claims become habitual, it's often a tip-off that the person is insecure in the area in which he or she claims the extra accomplishments.

To build a better relationship with that person, find truthful ways to praise him or her in the same area as the inflated personal claims. There is a temptation to challenge a claim in the same setting it's made—in public. But please know that if you do puncture someone's claim in a public setting, that will provide a public humiliation that will never be forgiven or forgotten. It's a sure recipe for making an enemy, and for both practical and ethical reasons you want to avoid that outcome.

• ***"Little white lies."*** Whether "little white lies" are principled behavior continues to be debated. The etiquette authority Judith Martin ("Miss Manners") believes hypocrisy to be an unappreciated virtue. "[People must] forgo the honest expression of their true feelings and adjust—not to say dissemble—their behavior in order to cater to the feelings of others."[1]

In our study of nonverbal communication, we realized that a lot of communication takes place outside the confines of literal speech. Similarly, the entire area of etiquette—including business etiquette—is a method of communication, one that shows your social class and degree of consideration for others. People skilled in etiquette can convey all kinds of information, including negativity, in a way that is subtle and relationship preserving, which is clearly a cardinal political virtue.

If it helps, you may think of this kind of dissembling and hypocrisy not as lying but as a special form of nonverbal communication, in which the true message is conveyed even though it appears to contradict the literal meaning of the words being said.

Remember as well that a literal truth can result in a terrible misperception of your real message. People are likely to hear a statement such as, "You can be completely honest with me, and I promise there will be no negative consequences," especially when it comes from someone who outranks you or who has power over you, as meaning virtually the opposite: There *will* be negative consequences, and being honest can only get you into trouble.

• **The agreeable but undependable person.** The character Eddie Haskell from the television show *Leave It to Beaver* is an archetype for a certain kind of office politician—ever polite, beloved by grown-ups everywhere, but secretly a scoundrel. People with an excessively great desire (or even need) to be liked by everyone will tend to say whatever they have to say to get that approval, but it doesn't necessarily translate into a commitment to action or to behavioral change.

Because for some people the idea of being disliked is so threatening, you need to remove the threat in order to do business with them. That doesn't mean you're really being threatening in any objective sense, but it does mean that they perceive a threat in the possibility that you might become angry or disappointed. They prefer the short-term value of sending you away happy over the long-term possibility that you'll be *really* angry when you discover the truth.

As a principled office politician—or simply as a manager or team member—it's hard to trust and work with these people unless you learn how to listen to what they are actually saying underneath the pleasant words. Perhaps it's really their responsibility to change, but the reality is often that they will not; therefore, if you are to work successfully with them, you must change your attitude and approach.

The basic rule for dealing with the agreeable but unreliable person is to remove the potential threat that the person perceives. First, listen very actively for the small cues that reveal that the person has a problem with your request. A subtle joke, a change of subject, silence in the face of an idea, all should be a trigger for you to probe more deeply, to ask questions, to bring any problems out in the open. Second, validate that you still like and value the person even in the face of a disagreement. Emphasize that you like the person *better* as a result of the increased honesty. Third, when the person makes an unrealistic commitment, propose a more realistic one in its place. After all, the commitment someone follows through on is better than the one simply promised.

• **Problem avoidance.** A military cadet in Robert Heinlein's novel *Space Cadet* gets drunk while on leave. An officer spots his friend in the same bar, and then summons him over. The lieutenant says, "Go back and tell Jarman to quiet down before I have to come over there and ask him what his name is."[2]

This is an example of another common type of untruth—pretending not to see what you saw or not to hear what you heard. As the example shows, there are many situations in which that can be the best move. If you're forced to notice something "officially," then you must often act much more severely, sometimes producing a result that is not in your interest or the organization's interest. Better in such cases to pretend you didn't see or hear it if in doing so you can still send the necessary message and achieve the desired change.

The same technique is used in less positive ways as part of excusing one's bad behavior, on the grounds that ignorance is better than malice. In Chapter 5, we talked about the technique of "malicious obedience to orders." There's a similar game people play when given a job assignment they don't like, or when the manager micromanages or overcontrols them. They "go limp," putting on the stupid look we described earlier, slow down their performance, shift their brains into neutral, and wait until the manager becomes so frustrated he or she gives up and finds someone else to do the work.

In a recent real-life encounter, after a year of not answering repeated letters or returning numerous telephone calls, a business executive said with utter innocence, "I thought that matter was taken care of months ago! I never heard anything to the contrary." It's obvious to everyone concerned that this is untrue, but it's to the party's interest to pretend that it is true in order to close the deal and get the matter successfully resolved.

There are two underlying strategies at work here. The first is "ignore it and hope it will go away," and the second is to "act in a manner that frustrates the other person enough that he or she will settle for less just to get the matter resolved." Both techniques have a track record of success in the political environment, as you already know. A strategy of direct confrontation will likely make the situation worse, not better.

Spin Doctoring

The concept of "spinning" is well known to anyone who follows national politics. Politicians and political parties have "spin doctors," people who go on talk shows to present the events of the day in a way that makes their own side look best. Of course, we put it differently. The other side has spin doctors; our own side simply has honest communicators. Spin, you see, is often in the eye of the beholder.

Spinning has a role to play in the game of office politics, and, like many of the other techniques, it is capable of being employed in both principled and unprincipled fashions.

It's perfectly legitimate, even positive, to put the best face on a bad situation, to accentuate the positive (and eliminate the negative), as long as you don't actively cross the line into outright dishonesty. The problem is that the line can be somewhat fuzzy, so you have to be careful.

We all face the situation from time to time in our careers of going on an employment interview. We know—and the interviewer knows—that we have a goal to present ourselves in a positive manner and to turn any deficiencies, weaknesses, or problems in our background into positives, or at least into neutrals. Under the normal and accepted rules of the game, we aren't expected to volunteer problems in our background, but we must answer questions truthfully. We are allowed—even expected—to spin our answers. The interviewer knows the rules as well and wants to probe as deeply as possible to find out whether we are a good fit. What's interesting is that our skill in playing the interview game is one of the real and legitimate qualifications for the job—it shows something about our communication and presentation skills, our attitude, and our social class appropriateness.

No one thinks it's unethical to wear a "power suit" and make a special trip to the hairstylist in advance of an important presentation. You probably don't look as good day in and day out as you do when you're expected to present or defend an important proposal before a skeptical audience. You are presenting yourself at your best. The audience, accordingly, tends to discount your current appearance in figuring out who you really are. The audience may even give you a pass on some nervousness or uncertainty, because of the inherent stress of the situation.

But what's particularly important to remember is that taking extra care with your appearance isn't dishonesty; it's showing respect. By dressing up, by presenting your ideas or material in an assertive and positive way, even by showing some degree of nervousness, you are stating in nonverbal language that you value the material you're presenting, that you care about making a good impression, that you possess certain skills of communication and presentation, that you can fit in—all of which are true, but stating it in mere words would have little impact. The action is the message.

"Being yourself"—which would mean more casualness in dress and demeanor, treating the meeting like any other encounter—would, paradoxically, send a message that you didn't particularly care or value the opportunity. If you want the presentation to succeed, "being yourself" would communicate the opposite message. It would, strangely enough, in effect be a lie.

As a result of your presentation, the audience may ask tough questions. It's good strategy to prepare by having others ask you the questions you expect so that you'll be prepared and articulate. Role playing and practicing in such cases is exactly what a political "spin doctor" does. Spin doctors discuss the likely tough questions of the day and strategize (sometimes even script) a positive response. This is essentially a sales process, in which you come up with the key selling points and look for opportunities to slip them into the conversation.

Don't make the inexperienced spin doctor's mistake of relentless optimism in the face of disaster. Spin is a special case of sales, and the skills of a good sales professional are part of the arsenal of the effective office politician. Like many of the other skills we've covered, these techniques can be employed in both principled and unprincipled fashions, but there's nothing intrinsically unethical about salesmanship.

Salespeople work at the art of meeting and overcoming objections. In fact, they know that getting the prospect to state objections is a necessary and desirable part of the sales cycle: People who have no objections most often don't buy. If you don't take objections seriously and validate the person making the objection, that person feels attacked and implicitly criticized and usually doesn't buy. If you aren't willing to grant that some problems are real, even if they are outweighed by advantages, you don't have credibility, and, again, the person usually won't buy. The art of the spin requires a commitment to honesty, because there often are multiple ways to present the truth, each completely legitimate, and some more helpful to you than others.

Don't oversell your position. Trying to do so often betrays inner weakness and can result in serious problems. Follow KISS once again, focus on your strongest points, tell the truth in a positive way, and you'll get the best outcomes.

Political Correctness

There are few quicker ways to start an argument or get people into a shouting mood than to introduce the concept of "political correctness." Whether you approve or disapprove of political correctness, it's a very serious matter, and dismissing it out of hand or ignoring it is a tactical and strategic mistake.

What's interesting is that nobody considers himself or herself "politically correct," in the same way that no one would admit to being a "yuppie" or any one of a number of words that have a negative public meaning. People whom others might consider politically correct might say they avoid "hate speech" or try to show respect for others or that they're just being natural.

This is an important communications issue related to the concepts of *denotation* and *connotation*—what words mean literally and what they signify in practice.

Let's look at the phrase "politically correct" itself. Notice that the word "correct" is normally considered to be a positive term. We would generally prefer to be correct rather than incorrect. But the phrase "politically correct" has a negative meaning—in fact, it means just about the opposite of the literal meaning of the words. It suggests an oversensitivity to using exact and ever-shifting phrases to describe various groups in society, the tendency to follow a (usually politically liberal) party line. It's parodied more than practiced.

How can a phrase have a real meaning that is opposite to its literal meaning? Words and phrases possess both denotation (what they literally mean) and connotation (the associations they evoke). Because connotative meanings can be unintentional (such as the experience of offending someone with a word or phrase you didn't intend to have negative meanings) or self-revelatory (betraying feelings and attitudes you would rather have stayed hidden, such as dislike, distrust, or concerns about the ability of a team member to do the work), the connotative meanings are normally much more emotionally powerful than the denotative meanings.[3]

The question of whether a word or phrase is politically correct or incorrect has to do most often with its connotative meaning. The words "employee," "team member," "associate," "worker bee," "rank-and-file," and "cubicle dwellers" all refer to the same people—that is, their denotative meaning is the same—but the emotional image—the connotative meaning—conjured up by the various terms is quite different. To call someone an "associate" or "team member" is an expression of value; to call someone a "worker bee" is somewhat degrading. Similarly, many inappropriate terms for minorities and ethnic groups have the same denotative meaning but radically different connotative ones. Being aware of connotative meaning is important, because the connotative meaning shapes the likely emotional reaction of the other party.

Sometimes, however, the issue is in the denotative meaning. For example, the objection to such terms as "handicapped" and "disabled" is that the denotative meaning is not true. A "disabled" person is not necessarily unable to do a wide range of jobs. It is not the person who is disabled; the person is able to do a great many things but has specific limitations. You may or may not feel this is an important distinction, but in general we know that words matter. We know that "sticks and stones may break my bones but words will never hurt me" is a lie from our own experience; we have all been hurt by either careless or sometimes deliberate words.

Probably the most controversial element of political correctness is the common concept that the rest of the world has become humor impaired. All kinds of jokes that once were considered funny aren't funny any more. That's true, of course—but it doesn't necessarily mean others don't have a sense of humor. As we discussed in Chapter 5 (Rhetoric Power), humor is a way in which we disguise negative emotions. When we find a joke funny, it's because it serves as a relatively safe way of expressing our socially unacceptable feelings, our fears, our frustrations, and our anger. The problem is that the fear, frustration, and anger are still there, and others can see them. Listen closely at the next joke you hear, and you'll find it's easy to spot the underlying negative emotion. Others—especially those who are the targets, directly or indirectly—of such jokes will understand a truth that we sometimes conceal from ourselves: that there is a real negative emotion underneath.

It takes enormous skill as a humorist to make the joke funny enough to overcome our awareness of the underlying hostility; few of us possess the necessary skill. That's why the same joke told on yourself, or on a group of which you are a member, may be found acceptable, whereas if someone else tells it, it's offensive.

Regardless of your political orientation or your feelings on the matter, it's important for you to realize this is a real issue, and one that can have significant consequences for your career potential. It is not usually necessary to be oversensitive or hypersensitive to the nuances of your language, but you should be aware that your words have connotative and denotative meanings that can hurt others and make them into your enemies, sometimes without you being aware of it. And enemies, sooner or later, take revenge.

The Sound of Silence

Probably the best, yet often most overlooked, communications technique is knowing both when and how to keep your mouth shut. Silence and good listening skills carry enormous power. In one study, participants were asked to have a conversation with two different people in two different rooms. One of them was instructed to show the participants just how smart and talented he was, to share his accomplishments and strengths. The other was told to listen and to ask about the participants. At the conclusion, participants filled out a questionnaire. One question was, "Which person did you like best?" Not surprisingly, the answer was the listener. Another question was, "Which person was smarter?" Somewhat more surprisingly, the answer was also the listener. We not only like good listeners; we tend to imbue them with other virtues, from intelligence to wisdom—not to mention the good taste to recognize how witty and entertaining we happen to be.

The effective office politician is always a good listener, respectful of others and interested in them. It's important not only to listen in reality but also to appear to listen, using the various body language cues (from head nodding to leaning forward) that show listening behavior.

The effective office politician keeps confidences. You want people to share with you, to disclose information and perspectives that help you know what's going on, so that you can better plan and prepare yourself. To do that, people must trust you absolutely, knowing that what they tell you will not go further.

Because business communication is designed to achieve your goals, the effective office politician doesn't speak until he or she knows what the situation is and what other people think and feel. That knowledge is what gives you the ability to shape your message for maximum impact.

Notes

1. Judith Martin, *Miss Manners' Guide to Excruciatingly Correct Behavior* (New York: Warner Books, 1982), p. 679.

2. Robert Heinlein, *Space Cadet* (New York: Ace Books, 1948), p. 96.

3. An excellent discussion of connotation and denotation can be found in Wilfred Stone and J. G. Bell, *Prose Style: A Handbook for Writers*, 2nd ed. (New York: McGraw-Hill, 1972), pp. 98–101.

Chapter 8

The Art of Negotiation

He never wants anything but what's right and fair; only when you come to settle what's right and fair, it's everything that he wants and nothing that you want. And that's his idea of a compromise.

Thomas Hughes, *Tom Brown's School-days*, 1857

Politicians know how to negotiate, and they understand that negotiation normally takes place inside relationships. There's the issue on the table, and then there are the people involved. Even after the issue is resolved, the people remain—and remember.

At the same time, the point of being an effective office politician is to get your goals accomplished, and that means conflict is often inevitable. How to get what you want without throwing the relationship away is the key to effective negotiation.

The Art of Negotiation

We are all—and always will be—somewhere on the line between utterly helpless and all-powerful. In an organization, or in any environment, there will automatically and naturally be conflicts between your goals and the goals of others. You may triumph over others sometimes; they will triumph over you other times. But the issue frequently comes down to the negotiating table, in which your skill at that vital art often determines your outcomes. Like communications in general, negotiation is what office politicians do—persuade others, often of different opinions, to accomplish their goals without creating long-term problems for themselves.

The "Used Car" Model

Most discussions of negotiation at some level revolve around the "used car" model, at least in part because it's a common negotiation situation with which most of us can easily identify. A successful negotiation strategy, according to this model, must ultimately revolve around the idea, if you're the buyer, of getting the very best price. You don't really care if the dealer makes a profit; every dollar cut from the price is a dollar in your pocket. Similarly, the dealer wants to get as much as possible for the car; every extra dollar you spend is a dollar more in the dealer's pocket. Neither party cares about a long-term relationship; the likelihood is that you will never see each other again.

There are a variety of tactics suitable for this sort of negotiation. First is research: What is the dealer's cost for the car?; what other prices are being offered for that car? Second is approach: Don't betray eagerness or focus immediately on the car you really want; look around; don't show any urgency. Third is tactics: the "flinch" ("Ouch! You mean that car costs $35,000? You're kidding, right?"), the "walk-away" ("Well, I'm afraid that's the best I can do, so I don't want to waste any more of your time. I'll just go to the next dealer," and "I've got to take this offer to my manager"). Fourth is closing: the "urgency close" ("I'm afraid this offer is only good for the next hour"), the "forced-choice close" ("Did you want that SUV with or without the leather seats?"), and the "puppy dog close" ("Why don't you take it home for the weekend, and, if you don't like it, you can bring it right back").

This approach tends to be adversarial, not collaborative, and you walk away in most cases wondering whether you really did prevail, or whether the salesperson's "Wow, you really aren't leaving me with anything on this sale!" is sincere or just a way to camouflage how badly you've been rooked. (Playing down any successes in a negotiation is a way to lessen "buyer's remorse," or the regret you feel after you've spent the money. It's a good general technique for reducing the negativity in the situation.)

The hidden problem in this negotiation model from a political perspective is that it assumes there won't be a relationship after the negotiation is complete and that therefore it doesn't matter what kinds of feelings are left over.

Relationship Negotiating

But that's not the reality of organizational life. You have to negotiate every day, with supervisors and managers, employees, coworkers, people in other departments, customers—not to mention all the negotiation that takes place in your personal life. In the majority of cases, you have to preserve the relationship while still getting enough of what you want and what you need, which means that a number of used car–negotiating techniques simply aren't appropriate. They may well help you win this battle—but they'll surely lose the war.

As a successful and principled office politician, how can you negotiate, win, and still keep the relationship on steady ground?

Win/Win Negotiation

The concept of win/win negotiation, at first blush, seems suspiciously optimistic, at least in part because of the prevalence of the "used car" thinking we're used to. We can easily understand "lose/win," in which the other person takes advantage of us, because we've experienced that too often. We can understand "win/lose," even though we may feel some ethical discomfort with the idea that we have beaten someone or taken advantage of them. But it's hard to imagine what win/win would really look like.

Let's imagine that you have had a disaster in your manufacturing operations and that you will be physically unable to meet your contractual obligations to a particular customer, one with whom you've had a good relationship and one with whom you have hopes of continuing to do business.

"Listen," you say, "we've had a disaster, and I promise you we're doing everything we can, but I just am not going to be able to get the widgets to you by the end of the month. I can do it by the fifteenth, but there's no way I can do it any earlier."

"That's just not good enough," replies the customer. "I understand you've got problems, but so do I. I've made promises based on the deal we had, and my customers are expecting me to deliver on time. I don't have any flexibility here. If you can't meet my deadline, I'm afraid I'll have to sue for damages under the contract."

Now, notice that everybody is being friendly and understanding each other, but it's not solving the problem. You can't deliver on time; your customer can't accept late delivery; there are a lot of dollars at stake. Neither party wants to end up in court, but it looks like that's where this is heading. The negotiation will end up being about allocating damages, not about creating solutions.

Asking Questions

We've stated that the most important political skill is being able to put yourself in the other person's shoes. One of the easiest, and often most powerful, ways to do that is simply to ask questions. "Tell me," you say, "what exactly will happen if you get the goods on time, as opposed to what will be different if you don't. I understand your customers will be upset, but what exactly is the process?"

"Well," replies your customer, "I have to receive the widgets from you; they come in caseloads, and that's too many for each of my customers. I have to break the caseloads down into smaller lots for the customers and reship them, and all that takes two weeks. I could handle your being a day or two late, but I can't make up two weeks of delay—my customers won't get their goods for a month!"

It's a good idea at this point to paraphrase. "Let me see if I understand the process," you say, and you lay it out step-by-step, preferably in the customer's own words and concepts. If there's any confusion, keep at it until you get it right. Once you do, it's time to brainstorm options.

"We both want to meet the needs of your customers," you might say. "What if, instead of us shipping to you, then you repacking and reshipping, we drop-ship the individual orders directly to the customers? It would be a little extra work for us, but not very much, and they'll end up with their orders, all individually sized, by their original deadline. You can invoice them directly, and we'll invoice you as usual. Would that solve your problem?"

You always want to finish any proposal you make with words like "Would that solve your problem?" You're suggesting an idea, not setting it in concrete. Notice that you're focusing on solving the other person's problem within the parameters of your manufacturing disaster.

"I don't know. It might. I wouldn't want to pay extra for nonstandard packaging, and I'd like my name, not yours, on the boxes."

From Conflict to Problem Solving

Whether or not you can accept those terms depends on your situation. There will be some extra cost involved in this custom shipping proposal. But this adversarial conflict that was headed for a lawsuit is now a discussion about problem-solving methods. Even if you have to pay the additional costs, it's certain to be a lot less than the cost of litigation, and, on top of that, you preserve the relationship and the opportunity for future profits.

Win/win outcomes are often possible because people don't necessarily want the identical thing from a negotiation. Even in the used car model, one person wants a car and the other person wants money. Where needs are not identical, which is most of the time, it's at least theoretically possible to achieve a win/win outcome if you can look at the situation creatively enough.

Clearly, win/win is the goal of a principled person. What's interesting is that it's also the goal of a practical person, because preserving the relationship and making all participants feel their needs are at least acceptably met is not only ethical; it's advantageous.

Preparing for Negotiation

A big reason people lose in negotiation is that they don't prepare. There's a lot you can do to place yourself in a deservedly strong power position before you ever sit down at the negotiating table. If you negotiate with someone who is unprepared, you start at a tremendous advantage. If you negotiate with someone who's also well prepared, you both are likely to benefit. As people who negotiate frequently will tell you, two skilled and prepared negotiators often reach an outcome that is better for both parties than a solution that could have been achieved by less prepared negotiators.

Determining Your Goals

Oddly, many people don't really think about their own goals and objectives in a thorough way before they negotiate. In such a case, as in other situations in which you don't know what it is you want, you're at a tremendous disadvantage. You tend to preclude win/win outcomes this way, because you don't give the other person a lot to work with. The other side can still win, but it's hard to see how you can. The issue is not that you don't have a general idea what you want; of course you do. But a deeper analysis can help you discover better ways to get it.

Try this seven-step goal-setting process:

SETTING GOALS THAT WORK

1. Write down a goal you currently have.

_____

_____

2. Why do you want to achieve this goal? (Write down as many reasons as you can; the more the better. If some reasons seem silly or petty or not appropriate, write them down as well—sometimes they can be great motivators.)

_____

_____

3. What obstacles stand in your way? (There are always obstacles between you and any goal you have; otherwise, you would have already achieved it. As in question 2, write down as many obstacles as you can, including those that seem silly, petty, and unworthy of you. Sometimes such psychological barriers are the most potent of obstacles.)

_____

_____

4. For each obstacle, what steps could you take to overcome it or at least weaken its power?

Obstacle	Strategies for Overcoming or Weakening It	Who Can Help?
1.		
2.		
3.		

5. Who can help? (This includes friends, allies, fellow travelers, and colleagues, obviously, but also can include other resources, such as training courses and professional assistance. Support can be actual work on your behalf or simply encouragement.)

6. Take a deep look at the benefits of achieving the goal, as well as the cost of achieving it. Is it worth it? (This is a serious question, because not all goals are worth the price you have to pay to achieve them. If the goal isn't worth your while, then don't pro-crastinate—drop it altogether.)

7. If you decide to pursue the goal, list the specific action steps you need to take, or at least the first few steps. (If it's a goal about which you've been procrastinating, make the initial steps as small as possible; it makes it far more likely you'll get started.)

Using the Exercises in Your Work

This is a powerful goal-setting model, and you'll find that it works on almost any type of goal, not merely political or organizational. If you're not sure how to get started, try mak-ing your next New Year's resolutions using this process as a template. You'll be surprised at the impact it has.

In preparing for negotiation, take a deep look at the "why" part of this process. What are all the different ways you might achieve the underlying purpose or reason?

The "Why" of Asking for a Raise

Let's say you want to get a raise. Do you want one because you actually need those extra dollars right now, or is it more because you want a title and compensation that more accurately reflect the quality and level of the work you do? Is it a matter of earning a salary comparable with those earned by others at the same level in the same organization or the same industry? Is it about getting validation and respect for your hard work and achievement? Is it less about the current situation and more about setting yourself up for the next level of advancement, where the rewards will start?

Your reason might well be all of these, but by identifying your primary reasons for wanting a raise, you can look at other alternatives. If the issue is a need for extra cash, there may be multiple ways to achieve the goal. If you want a title to set yourself up for further advancement (here or elsewhere), you may find it easier to negotiate for a title than for currency. And so forth. The more you know why you want what you want, the more creatively you can seek out a variety of ways to get it.

Determining Your Walk-Away Alternative

Assume for a moment that the person with whom you are going to negotiate turns out to be utterly unreasonable and refuses to cooperate in a negotiation, even if it's in his or her best interest. The key question to ask yourself is, what then? What can you do without the cooperation of the other person? Your walk-away alternative (also often called the BATNA, or "best alternative to a negotiated agreement"[1]) is one of the critical pieces of information you need to know before you negotiate. Obviously, if you can achieve a certain level of outcome without negotiating, there's no point in accepting any less than that when you do negotiate. It's your "walk-away" alternative because if you can't do any better than that, you should get up and walk away from the negotiation.

It's smart negotiating strategy to work on ways to maximize your walk-away alternative, or BATNA, before the negotiating begins. The person who has the best alternative is normally the person with the most power in the negotiation.

In terms of the raise example, what will you do if you can't get any extra money at all? Perhaps there simply isn't any money in the budget for raises in your department. Perhaps you've topped out at your current grade level. Perhaps your boss perceives a problem with your performance, or even a problem with you.

Now what? Will you quit? Will you get a job somewhere else? Will you appeal over your boss's head or seek a transfer? Will you simply knuckle under and slink helplessly back to your desk to stew in frustration? Will you propose that your bonus incentives be adjusted in lieu of cash in your paycheck right now? Would a new title be helpful even if there aren't dollars attached to it? What is your best alternative?

Your ability to quit, for example, probably depends on the state of your current finances. If you've got enough in your 401(k), you might decide to chuck it all and become a beachcomber in Tahiti. Now that you think of it, is that your real goal? Is it achievable? Is going after a raise the best way to end up in Tahiti, or should you be negotiating for a transfer to the Papeete branch office? If quitting, again as an example, is a realistic choice for you, consider how much stronger you'll be in the negotiation with your boss.

Can you get another job for the money or opportunity you want? Perhaps you might want to sound out a few headhunters or do a little networking to find out whether you're marketable at the level you want. If you've got a firm offer in hand, you'll likely be very powerful in the negotiation, and if your organization doesn't want to stretch itself to keep you, so be it. You'll discover, however, that your attractiveness and value go up substantially once it's clear others want you too.

In considering your walk-away alternative, you might discover that, rather than begin to negotiate right now, you would do well to explore some other alternatives and try to maximize them.

Your walk-away alternative doesn't just make you really stronger in the negotiation; it makes you feel stronger as well. Your self-confidence and your ability to be assertive will naturally increase the more you know you have an alternative to fall back upon. You won't be tempted to take any crumbs you're offered; if the best you can do is less than your BATNA, take the BATNA. If it's better, then you know that you've increased your position through negotiation.

If your walk-away alternative is very poor, you need to know that going in. Perhaps pounding your fist on the table and demanding some extra money is too risky a strategy for you to follow. You can be more mindful of the risks you're running. You'll behave smarter.

Determining the Other Side's Positions, Interests, and Walk-Away Alternatives

"Know thyself" is the first great lesson; the second is like unto it: Know thy opponent. We've emphasized repeatedly the vital importance of looking at the situation from the other person's perspective.

What do they want, and why do they want it? In the same way you looked deeply at your own position and underlying interests, think about the other side's. The goal is to maximize the ways the other side can meet your needs. When you can give it alternatives that meet its objectives, it is more likely to accept those alternatives and help you win. If you want a raise, but your boss doesn't have the power to give you one right now, are there things your boss can give you instead? Examples might be a high-visibility project assignment, a title increase, or some training opportunities that might make you eligible for a promotion and raise in the future.

What are the obstacles faced by the other side, and what are its fears? People have a strong tendency to feel their position to be weaker than it really is, but our fears are often so great that we don't see that the other person may well be as frightened as we are. How does the other side see its own weaknesses and vulnerabilities? How does your boss look at the possibility of your leaving for other employment (or Tahiti)?

What is the other side's BATNA? What is the best it can do if it can't reach agreement with you? Are your job functions easily reassigned, or not? Do you have special knowledge that is not easy to replace? Do you possess particularly valuable skills or information? Would your organization be particularly concerned if you went to a competitor?

Research Methods

Once you know what's in the minds of the people with whom you negotiate, you can quickly determine whether or not there's a zone of mutually possible agreement and, if so, reach agreement pretty quickly. But, of course, it's not quite that simple. You don't always or necessarily know what the other side is thinking and feeling, and part of negotiation posturing is presenting your side as stronger than it really is. For example, you might choose to bluff that you have a firm job offer elsewhere. If your boss believes you, you might win. Of course, if your bluff is called, you might be in serious trouble. On the other hand, you might have a firm job offer but exaggerate its virtues in the negotiation, which is a less dangerous bluff because you have the job to fall back on if necessary. People in negotiation frequently exaggerate and sometimes flat out lie about their needs, goals, and alternatives in order to pressure others into a deal that is more advantageous to them and less so to the other party.

You can't always know with certainty where the other person stands, but the more you can find out and the better you determine what the probabilities are like, the more effective your negotiation strategy will be.

In Chapter 2 (Defensive Goals), we talked about building a personal spy network in the organization. One of the reasons you need it is to prepare for negotiations. What can you find out about the perceptions and situation of the other side?

The first source of information you have comes from empathy: the ability to put yourself in the position of the other person and to see the world as he or she sees it. The act is akin to playing chess with yourself—when you are the other player, you think as he or she thinks and try to strategize the best possible move he or she can make. It's possible in reality that the other side in the negotiation will be less efficient and less prepared, but it's almost always better to assume that it will be fully prepared. You can always revise your expectation downward in the actual negotiation.

The second source of information is the rumor mill, although, as in all uses of the rumor mill, you have to discount the value of the information received. In the case of the raise negotiation, you want to get information on the overall financial state of the company, who is getting raises (and who isn't), what the promotion patterns are, and so on. Rumor mill information tends to be general, not specific, but it helps you set an overall context.

Is there published or reported information that will help you in your negotiation? Everything from memos and reports to news magazine coverage and information from the Internet can be useful. You'll pick up a detail here and a detail there, and with some intuitiveness you can make some educated guesses about the overall environment.

Next, investigate the possibility of having some preliminary discussions with the other side before the negotiation formally begins. Consider that, in the case of the raise, the other side doesn't necessarily know that a negotiation is in the works. Careful probing in advance can often reveal a lot about the intentions and positioning of the other side.

What does the other side value or want? In the used car model, there's only one variable: money. The amount paid for the car can be more or less. But in most real-world negotiations, it's possible to extend the number of issues, which makes finding a win/win trade-off much easier.

Spend some time on preparation whenever possible. Careful and thorough preparation makes a tremendous difference. Write down what you learn to help you understand the overall picture. If you have to make educated guesses, that's normal and acceptable. If you're left with a few specific unknown elements, you know that in the actual negotiation you'll have to work to fill in those blanks, sometimes by means as blunt as a direct question, other times through more indirect communication.

Negotiation Culture and Personality Styles

How do you usually negotiate? Is your style aggressive and pushy, or is it oriented more toward listening and problem solving? As you can imagine, the style you use in negotiation can have a significant effect on your outcomes. And the right strategies and tactics are affected by the types of tactics and maneuvers you expect from the other person.

In our raise example, is your boss the kind of person who tends to react with hostility to your attempt to get a raise? Is that hostility real, or is it an act designed to help him or her get the desired outcomes?

To answer that, think about the negotiating culture you're a part of. Most of us are familiar with certain stereotypes about the negotiation styles of different cultures. Less familiar, but equally real, is the idea that within our culture, different people and different organizations have different negotiation norms. Is it allowable to exaggerate or even lie about your underlying objective in order to push the other person? Is negotiation generally hostile in tone, or are overt displays of hostility frowned upon? Notice that when you move from an organization with which you're familiar into new territory, the norms you're used to may not apply.

Your own negotiation approach has to fit within the boundaries of the negotiation norms, and you have to be familiar with those norms to discount certain kinds of misleading behavior—obviously outrageous demands or shouting on the one hand, deceptively mild statements and questions that turn out to have great significance on the other hand.

What are the personality characteristics of the person or persons with whom you are negotiating? In addition to norms of an organization, individuals have standard approaches to negotiating, "hard" or "soft." Knowing what to expect in terms of a stylistic approach can help you select your own style and also help you avoid falling into traps that others lay for you. You may find it useful to modify your own approach or personality style depending on the person you're negotiating with. This is often a situation that calls for some talent as an actor.

One of the pitfalls in the issue of negotiating style is that if there is a significant style mismatch between the parties, the negotiation can fail even if it is in both parties' best interest to reach an agreement. If we actively dislike or distrust someone, any deal looks fishy.

Distrust

Of course, there's also real distrust. The deal on the table may be advantageous, but perhaps there's reason to distrust the other party. "I can only give you a $5,000 raise right now," the boss says, "but when bonus time comes around, I can give you an extra $15,000 instead. Which do you want?" The answer depends on the trust you have for your boss. If your boss is very trustworthy, clearly the $15,000 is a better deal. But if you have reason to suspect the boss may renege or be unable to fulfill his or her commitment, then you have to look at the probability. If you think the chances are about 50-50 you'll get the promised bonus, then $5,000 < ($15,000 × .5), so take the bonus offer. But if you think it's 75 percent against, then $5,000 > ($15,000 × .25); it's not an advantageous deal. (It's legitimate to also adjust the payoff on the basis of your personal tolerance for risk and the resentment you would feel if you didn't get the bonus after all; so if you decide not to take the bonus even in the first instance, that's a personally defensible decision.)

Tactics and Behavior during Negotiation

Effective negotiation planning doesn't so much write a script for you as prepare you to handle the surprises and uncertainties that are part of the negotiation process. Planning not only gives you more and better tools; it also increases your self-confidence, which turns into an additional asset.

Let's take an actual negotiation example and discuss some of the steps and methods involved.

Case Study: Negotiation for a License

Michael was a department manager for a game and toy company, and in that role he wanted to acquire a license to adapt a media property as a board game. He had a narrow range of negotiating authority and a firm maximum he could pay as an advance against royalties.

In the first round of negotiation, the agent for the property informed him that there was already a bid on the table. The bid included an advance payment that was significantly more than Michael's allowable maximum. (While there was no specific reason to doubt this claim was true, neither was there firm evidence that it was true.)

Because he couldn't increase the advance payment, he tried to show other benefits for the license: wider distribution, promotional opportunities, quality of design. The agent listened politely and seemed interested in continuing the discussion, but there was no movement.

Because the tone of the negotiation was friendly—among other reasons, there was always the possibility that the two would work together on other properties—they chatted about other issues. Michael wanted to learn more about the agent's side of the business and began asking questions. One question was, "What's the biggest trap you ever fell into?"

There was a long pause on the other end of the telephone. "Funny you should ask that," the agent said, "because it's the reason I'm not going to license this property to you. You see, I once did a license with someone who promised me the same sorts of things you're promising—distribution, marketing, and so on—but with a small advance. I took the deal and then discovered that the company was planning to put out a competitive product. They wanted the license only to tie up my property so that it couldn't compete with theirs. I got the advance, all right, but they never released the product, and, by the time the rights reverted, my client's property was worthless."

"Well, I'm definitely going to publish this product," Michael replied. "To prove it, what if we put in a contract clause guaranteeing you a large extra payment if we don't put it out on time—a kill fee, in other words? Would that make you more comfortable?"

In negotiating backward with his boss, Michael was able to argue that the extra contract clause really wasn't spending any money, because the intent was to publish. With that addition, the deal was successful.

Negotiation Process and Issues

Relationships

Especially in the sphere of office politics, your negotiating space is often affected by the need to keep the door open to long-term relationships. If there were no possibility of future business relationships, the negotiation just described would probably have shut down after the first round or two, when it became clear that there was no direct or obvious place where a deal was possible. Because neither party wanted to foreclose the possibility of future business, there was substantial pressure to keep the negotiation on friendly terms and to build a relationship over several rounds of telephone calls, regardless of the outcome of the specific matter on the table. In the general game of office politics, the quality and range of your relationships is a key ingredient in your personal power, and it is almost always worth the investment of your time and energy.

But consider as well that there were multiple relationships involved in this seemingly straightforward encounter. In our example, there was the relationship between Michael and his vice president, as well as with others in the organization, some of whom had "get the license" as the main goal and others who had "don't spend much money" as their primary goal. We are seldom the sole source of decision power on the negotiations in which we take place. That complicates the situation.

Lack of Decision Power

Most managers and staff in an organization have more "no" power than "yes" power. When you are negotiating with someone who has only the power to say "no" and does not have the power to say "yes," it's irrelevant how persuasive your arguments, how good your negotiating skills; the person *can't* say "yes." The only hope you have of success is to negotiate with the person who possesses "yes" power. The first part of your strategy is to probe to determine what decision power the person with whom you are negotiating actually possesses. The problem with that is the person often doesn't want to tell you the truth; it's embarrassing to admit you can't make a "yes" decision.

You often have to probe around the truth with leading questions, such as, "You've raised X issue. If I could solve that problem completely, would you then be willing to accept the deal?" It's irrelevant for now whether you can actually solve the problem; your goal is to discover whether the problem on the table is what is really standing between you and a settlement. If it is, the person has some power (actual or delegated) to say "yes"; if not, stop trying to solve that problem and start asking questions to find out the real objection or real issue.

If you find out (or at least are able to make an educated guess) that the person doesn't actually have the power to say "yes," that doesn't automatically mean you can—or should— bypass that person and move to the actual decision maker. First, you may not be able to. People with "no" power often are gatekeepers—climenoles—people with the responsibility to protect the actual decision maker from the outside world. Second, you may make an unnecessary enemy. People who are bypassed may well resent it, especially if they are later called on the carpet for not handling the situation well.

Negotiating through Intermediaries

In fact, it's often recommended in negotiation books and other resources that front-line negotiators should not have final authority, because it's too easy sometimes to be pressured into a hasty and disadvantageous decision.[2] Better to be able to say, "That sounds good; let me check with my people and get back to you." (When you are on the other side, don't take that as an automatic cue that the person doesn't have "yes" power. It's a common stall to give someone time to think, and it is a face-saving way for them to back out of agreements that turn out not to be advantageous on later reflection.) Whether it's a formal negotiation with people outside the organization or a sensitive mediation role to solve an internal political dilemma, this is a very common situation for negotiators.

Validate the other person's role as a negotiator, and continue to probe with questions about the position of the other side, not only the position of the negotiator. Offer to be of help in presenting a position or structuring a proposal, but don't be surprised if your offer is turned down. Keep in mind that it's not enough to persuade your opposite number; you have to help that person persuade others.

Trust issues come into play here, as well. It's almost axiomatic for some managers to believe that when you send someone to negotiate with the other side, that person becomes their ally against you. As a negotiator, you must be aware of this. Regardless of what you really say or feel, your utterances become suspect and your loyalty is questioned—and that's something else requiring a political response. The usual answer is to "sell" the concessions you've wrung from the other side, to appear tough and aggressive, to gloat—but only to managers on your own side. A labor relations negotiator for the company comes back to the office with a contract with the union and says, "I really beat them down to nearly nothing this time." The reality might be that the negotiations were quite collaborative and win/win, but saying that might make management suspicious that it didn't get the best deal. This posture is part of the office politics of negotiation, and it can be as important to your career and even to the success of the negotiation as the work you do with the other side.

Linkage

The concept of linkage is central to many negotiations and often applies to negotiations in the political world. Buying a used car is a "one-off" deal—while you'll buy another at some point, you usually don't actively seek out the same salesperson; you look for the car you want and get it wherever it seems convenient. Many negotiations, on the other hand, have linked outcomes. Imagine our used car salesperson is negotiating a fleet purchase for a company that buys forty cars a year and trades them in every two years. It might be very profitable to lose money on a few cars (say, by upgrading the cars for the president/CEO and the purchasing director at no extra charge) if necessary to get the relationship and linkage to future sales.

There is an inherent but not specific linkage in the deal between the publisher and the literary agent, but the biggest linkage is between Michael and his own management. If Michael can persuade his management to sweeten the pot for this deal, he loses some degree of flexibility on future deals and future negotiations—the problem of "going to the well once too often." There is a price to pay for winning concessions, and that price is sometimes exacted in the future on other, ostensibly unrelated deals. We've emphasized that you want political power and political clout to enable you to accomplish things. There's only so much power to go around, however, so when you use your clout to get something done, you weaken your ability to go back to get something else done. (Of course, if the first deal is astoundingly successful, you'll get back more clout than you spent, but that doesn't mean you didn't spend it in the first place.) Go to the well often enough without replenishing it, and it runs dry.

Searching for Solutions

For there to be a win/win outcome, the participants in a negotiation must each walk away from the table with at least their minimum requirements met. But if you have to have at least $1 million and all the other person is willing to pay is $500,000, then it looks like no deal is possible. And, of course, no deal may be possible. It isn't always in the cards to achieve a win/win outcome under every circumstance.

Real negotiations, however, are frequently about multiple issues or can be extended to cover multiple issues. It's certainly the case that, in our example, the agent wanted all he could get for his client's property, and that's completely legitimate. The size of the advance, though, is not the only thing of value. Almost by accident, the negotiators stumbled on an additional issue: the agent's fear (based on experience) that the product would never come out, which certainly would not advance his client's interest. Suddenly there were two issues of value on the table. While Michael couldn't compromise on the advance issue, he knew that the company intended to produce the licensed product. Therefore, providing a substantial penalty clause for nonperformance was a cost-free alternative for him and provided the agent with significant contractual protection for his client. This is clearly a win/win outcome for both participants, and it was possible only because they explored additional issues that turned out to be of disproportionate value to the participants.

What these participants happened on by accident is what

you should make part of your planning for effective negotiation. If you know you will be negotiating, put yourself in the other person's shoes and try to think of as many concerns and issues that side might have as possible. The more problems the other side has, the greater the opportunity is for joint victories. Think of low-cost and no-cost ways you can satisfy the other side's concerns; these become bargaining chips that have a higher value to the other person than to you.

Similarly, look at your own position. Besides the main issue you are negotiating about, what other concerns or problems do you have? You may be able to discover ways the other side can help you at low or no cost to it, providing a wider avenue in which bargaining can take place.

Your ability to find these things in advance is necessarily limited. When you sit down to negotiate, don't assume you understand the situation fully. Ask questions, probe into the other side's issues, and demonstrate your concern for those issues. It's appropriate in a tactical sense to avoid laying out all your potential solutions on the table from the first moment. Take your time. Because negotiations frequently rise and fall on the issue of the personal relationship of the negotiators, patience and relationship-building skills will frequently get you a better outcome.

Trust

In serious poker, if you fold, you don't have to show your cards. If you don't, and everyone else folds, you take the pot and you don't have to show your cards. No one will ever know whether you were bluffing.

Two key representations were made at the beginning of the negotiation in our example. The first was the agent's representation that there was another offer for more money; the second was Michael's representation that he had an absolute limit on the amount he could offer. We've stated as one of the givens that Michael's representation was true (although he did try to get some additional money). However, the agent had no way of knowing whether the representation was true or false.

Because the cards were not shown at the end of the deal, we do not know whether the agent's representation was true, false, or exaggerated (as in, there was a deal, but not for the amount claimed). In negotiations, it's common for one or both sides to make strategic misrepresentations[3] about its situation during the process of negotiation. You need to remember in any negotiation or discussion that not everything claimed to be true is true.

It's a mistake both to accept the other person's word unquestioned and to assume that every statement is a manipulative lie. The truth normally lies somewhere in between—it's an acceptable part of negotiation. There are cultural and organizational norms that we use to help us, but it doesn't follow that everybody is playing by the same rules.

On your own part, if you're willing to pay up to $20,000 for that used car, you know perfectly well that you don't want to start with that offer. We assume that both sides will start at an extreme and work toward a midpoint. (Sharp negotiators often use that to their advantage, starting even further away to tilt the balance to their inevitable favor.) Is it a lie to misrepresent what you're willing to pay? Have you crossed an ethical boundary? There are no hard-and-fast answers available. One way to look at it is that if all sides know there is a game of misrepresentation, it's not really lying. If you told the truth exactly, people would assume it was a lie and act accordingly. The lie ends up communicating something about your real goals, and in that sense it's informative. Of course, that is at least somewhat a rationalization, but everyone in the world of office politics has to somehow come to grips with the difficult ethical challenges they face and draw a communications line that works for them.

If you shun any sort of game playing, you will end up at a severe disadvantage in negotiating, but if you become an aggressive champion of the "anything goes" method, you'll acquire a long-term disadvantage as someone who can't be trusted to bargain honestly. The best advice we can give, knowing it's far from exact, is that you need to think in advance about your strategy and how it fits in with your principles, rather than decide on the ethical line "on the fly."

Threats

There is one implicit threat in every negotiation, which is that you might say "no deal," get up, and walk away. And that kind of threat clearly falls into the realm of the fully principled person. Walking away from the deal if it doesn't meet your needs is your right. However, there are many other threats possible in a negotiation, some ethically appropriate, some less so. You need to know both how to make threats and how to deal with them.

Making Threats

There are two elements of a threat: actuality and delivery. It's important as a communications strategy to separate the two. The delivery often produces a stronger emotional impact than the threat itself, and that's something that can result in all kinds of negative consequences. When personal face is at issue, a threat is just as likely to harden opposition as it is to weaken it; even when it's perfectly clear you are both willing and able to carry out the threat, people become stubborn, sometimes at the cost of their own enlightened self-interest.

Whether you can make an actual threat in a principled way depends, of course, on what the threat is. If as a manager you have an employee who comes in late frequently, you can certainly say, "If this continues, here are the consequences." If someone is violating company policy, making it clear that you'll have to make a report if the behavior doesn't stop is clearly within ethical bounds and consistent with good character. There are a lot of threats that are fully legitimate by almost anyone's standards.

Even if the threat is legitimate, the way in which it is delivered is still important. Instead of the word "threat," think instead of the concept of "logical consequences." It's not a threat (at least in the emotionally loaded connotative sense) when you identify the desirable and undesirable consequences of a proposed course of action. For example, you might say, in a very calm and matter-of-fact voice, "Yes, you can certainly go ahead with your proposed reorganization. If you do, then I'll put forth my own proposal and I'll be talking to the vice president about it, and we'll see how it all comes out. Alternatively, if you and I can find a reorganization plan we both like, then we'll be able to present a united front and make the change much more smoothly."

The credibility of this statement rests first on whether your proposal and talking to the vice president is likely to scuttle the other reorganization proposal—in other words, the dimensions of the real threat. You avoid the emotionality issue by making sure that the other person has complete freedom of choice. He or she can take either action—go it alone or collaborate on a mutually acceptable version—on the reorganization plan, and all you've done is provided information about the consequences. People really like to have a choice, even if it's a "forced choice" in which only one option is desirable.

The same technique shows up in a lot of parenting books, on the grounds that children become inured to threats and that the idea of logical consequences gets better results; management books often recommend the technique for employee discipline, because the two worlds aren't that different. Logical consequences lessen the chance that the other person's back will go up and the stubbornness counterreaction will set in.

Dealing with Threats

Similarly, when the other person puts a threat on the table, the same two issues—actual and emotional—apply. A very valuable political (and negotiation) skill involves your ability to dissociate your emotions in a threatening situation. This is not easily done for most people, and hardly anyone does it perfectly. You can, however, improve with practice and with forethought.

When you perceive that the other person has made a threat, especially if it has the emotional impact of a threat, the first step is to paraphrase the threat into a logical consequence—say it back to the other person in the form of a question, as in, "Let me see if I understand what you're saying. If I understand you correctly, you are saying that if I go ahead with my proposed reorganization, your next step will be to file a formal grievance with the division vice president. Did I hear you correctly?"

Sometimes—though admittedly not always—when the threat is played back in a paraphrase, the other person will back down. "No, no, I mean that I'll want to make sure the vice president understands my point of view." Resist the temptation to gloat or smile, and say, "I understand. Now, let's see what we can do about working through this problem."

Other times, the person will say, "That's right. And I play golf with her every Tuesday, and when I tell her what's going on you'll be lucky to have your job at the end of the week." Your reply should be, "Well, I'd like to avoid having a public fight about this, and I'm sure you would, too. Let's see what we can do about working through this in a way that works for both of us." In other words, regardless of the response, you turn the conversation back toward problem solving and negotiation. Make it clear that you want to resolve the conflict in a mutually fair way.

Ultimately, there is no technique that will always work, and this is no exception. If the negotiations break down, though, there is some advantage at having been the reasonable and hard-working partner, not to mention that it is the principled and appropriate way to be. Besides, it works more often than it fails to work.

Notes

1. This term was originated by Fisher and Ury, op. cit.

2. Roger Dawson, *The Secrets of Power Negotiating* (audiotape) (Chicago: Nightingale-Conant, 1987).

3. Howard Raiffa, *The Art and Science of Negotiation: How to Resolve Conflicts and Get the Best out of Bargaining* (Cambridge, Mass.: Belknap Press, Harvard University Press, 1982).

Chapter 9

Tactical Politics—Politics and the Everyday Organization

With two thousand years of examples behind us we have no excuse, when fighting, for not fighting well.

T. E. Lawrence (of Arabia)

We've focused in these pages on understanding the political environment and on thinking about overall issues of power, environment, and goals. Office politics is also made up of tactical moves, small yet significant steps the effective politician plays each day. As with many of the issues we've discussed, these tactics can be employed both by principled and unprincipled persons. The maneuver is often the same; the details and motivations differ. In these descriptions, consider whether you ought to be applying these methods, and also pay attention to whether others are using them to further their own political objectives, whatever they may be.

The Art of Lunch

The "power lunch" is a well-recognized concept, even by those who tend to be otherwise oblivious to office politics going on around them. It does matter whom you go to lunch with, when and how long you go to lunch, where you go to lunch, and how you go to lunch. (Breakfast and dinner matter, too—more about that shortly.)

The core reason that meals matter politically is that they provide a relatively informal and personal way to build relationships, and relationships, as we've seen, are one of the keys to your overall political power.

Special rules and customs govern business meals, and, as with the other elements of the political life, a lack of awareness can cause you problems.

The Rules of Lunch

1. ***Don't go to lunch with the same people all the time.*** Develop a varied calendar of people with whom you go to lunch; try not to go out with the same people more than about twice a week. The people on your lunch list should include members of your department, your boss, some of your subordinates, key members of support activities that provide services you need, important power players throughout the organization, customers, and your professional network. It's just fine (even appropriate) that you have lunch with some of these people no more often than once a quarter; that may be all the relationship requires.

2. ***Don't go to lunch every day.*** As a busy professional, eschew a daily out-of-the-office lunch trip. Brown-bag at your desk, and catch up on routine paperwork as you eat. You want to send the message that all your work time belongs to work; your out-of-the-office lunches are part of relationship building and when you're in the office you're at work, even when you're at lunch. (Don't, of course, do lots of telephone work while eating; it's rude.)

3. ***Don't pay too close attention to the food.*** Business meals aren't about food, and it's bad form to spend fifteen minutes agonizing over a menu choice, then asking the waitstaff for details on how it is prepared. Order quickly and firmly; have a few favorite dishes in your mind so that you can order without delay. After a while, you won't even have to look at the menu.

4. *Observe your office customs about drinking.* The "three-martini lunch" is much less popular today, though there is significant variance among industries and organizations. It's politically a bad idea to drink more than others, and sometimes even to order something too different from what the others are drinking—a Fuzzy Navel among beer drinkers, for example. If you don't or can't drink, don't get into a discussion about it, especially with drinkers. (At office parties, the traditional drink for nondrinkers is ginger ale, which others generally assume is a mixed drink.)

5. *Use good table manners.* If you aren't sure about yours, get a good book on business etiquette and bone up. There are even workshops for the uncertain.

6. *Watch for overall office customs about meals.* In some organizations, lunch isn't the power meal—it's breakfast. Turning breakfast into a business session is a way of signaling the total commitment you make to work and the level of how busy you are; although the "power breakfast" is now so widely practiced that it's become somewhat of a cliché. Some organizations are sensitive about the type of restaurant and the size of the check; some favor the long lunch and others the short lunch; you need to observe whatever customs and rules exist.

7. *Make lunch dates in advance, but don't overbook your calendar.* The politically savvy people book lunch dates sometimes weeks in advance; don't expect powerful people to be ready to go to lunch at a moment's notice. (It's kind of like asking for a Saturday date on Friday.) Don't overbook your calendar, so you have the option of slipping in an extra person if a good opportunity opens up.

8. *Don't discuss business until it's time.* There used to be fairly hard-and-fast rules, such as "never talk business until dessert" or "until the third drink." The rules aren't nearly so certain today. Again, organizations and industries vary. In most cases, you have the option of waiting for the other person to bring up business, which can be a good cue. As a rule of thumb, don't hold actual business discussions until people have had a chance to relax and eat enough of their food; you may have had the experience of starting business discussions too early and being unable to get a chance to eat your meal.

Dog Robbing

The term "dog robber" is World War II–era slang for the personal attendant of a general or an admiral. His job is to ensure that his superior gets the best food and lodging, and to ensure this the attendant is willing to rob troops, widows, orphans, and even the dogs.[1] Obviously, as a principled person you're not going to go anywhere near that far, but the effective management of supplies, perks, and resources is a surprisingly valuable part of your political effectiveness.

One of the most powerful positions to hold in the U.S. House of Representatives, for example, is to membership on the committee that allocates office space, parking, supplies, and other goodies to member offices. Similarly, if you are responsible for distributing internal resources, you become a player almost at once.

It's generally a mistake to use that kind of position as an opportunity to punish those who won't cooperate with you. It's far more effective to treat everyone fairly and to treat people who take care of you even better. You normally have a professional responsibility to ensure that all workers get what they need to do their work, and if you don't fulfill that responsibility, you can find yourself—quite properly—in hot water. Besides, as a principled person (as well as a practical one), you want to build good relationships and improve those that aren't so terrific. There is a time and a place to make an enemy, and this is not it.

Consider stocking a "goodie dish" of candy so that people who need a quick afternoon sugar fix will wander by your desk or into your office. Most people will share a bit of gossip or information as payment for what they take, and you'll build relationships at the same time, all for a token investment. Similarly, bring an occasional box of doughnuts to a meeting at which you want people to open up to you, or simply as a random treat. These small acts of courtesy and kindness tend to pay off disproportionately, especially when combined with the other elements of good character and friendliness we've shown to be integral to effective office politics.

T.C.B.

Elvis Presley's inner circle wore rings with a lightning bolt and the initials "T.C.B.," which stood for "Taking Care of Business in a Flash." Obviously, we include the basic functions of your job here—political skills in the absence of quality of work may let you slide by for a while, but not forever. When the quality of your work is outstanding, the political strategies you employ will have far more impact, which we've described as one element of Respect Power.

The other area of T.C.B. is taking care of the business of others in your political environment. While arranging for a subordinate or colleague to get the travel advance he or she needs for a business trip is, objectively speaking, a low-priority task in terms of the other work on your desk, it is a very high priority to that person, and taking care of it (or alternatively, forgetting about it) will have a big impact on how that person perceives and reacts to you in the future.

The effective professional regularly prioritizes the work on his or her desk. When you set priorities, consider the political impact of each task. Small favors that mean a lot to other people may be legitimately high priority in terms of the long-term benefits of better relationships and a perception of trustworthiness and caring.

The High Art of Thanks

As President, George Bush continued a lifelong habit of writing thank-you notes. On one European trip in 1989, he took the time to hand-write forty thank-you notes to staff—several of his aides compared notes, and no two were the same.[2]

Just about every "how-to" guide about supervision and management emphasizes the importance of recognition as a motivator of human performance. It's equally important in the political sphere, and yet it is all-too-seldom practiced. Most career guides include a firm rule that you should always follow up an employment interview with a thank-you note; yet our informal survey of managers revealed that most of them could count on one hand the number of interview thank-you notes they'd received in an entire career!

Of course, that's one of the reasons the thank-you note is so disproportionately powerful as a technique—few people follow up on the recommendation to use it. Make sure you're one of those people.

For many of us, it's hard to get into the habit, and it may seem phony to you at first. Try the "ten-coin" technique to improve your skills at positive feedback. Place ten coins of any denomination in your right pocket. Be on the lookout for any opportunity to catch someone in the act of doing something you want. Provide positive recognition, and keep score by moving a coin to the left pocket. Work up until you are doing it ten times a day. Like any exercise program, it tends to be hard at first, then gets easier.[3] The feeling of phoniness is reinforced in the short run by people who wonder what you're up to, but in the long term, you'll see real behavioral change. Give this some time to work.

Find an opportunity to send out two or three hand-written thank-you notes a week; they can be very brief, but they have to be sincere and specific. For example, when you want to acknowledge a favor, congratulate someone, praise someone for a job well-done, or maybe in response to information or an idea. The list of ideas can go on and on. What you praise and what you recognize, you'll get more of. It's a principled and effective way to have a real—and sometimes dramatic— impact on human behavior.

Develop Talent

There is a secret game executives play for status points among themselves (and for the good of the organization, of course), which is to be the one who recognizes and develops tomorrow's leadership talent. This is the reason mentees get mentors, the reason some people get slotted into the kind of developmental opportunity that leads to promotion and others don't. Not only do you want to position yourself as one of those people, finding your patrons and helping them to help you; you also want to be one of those playing the game, developing the talent under you and helping them grow.

It's obviously good for the organization to develop tomorrow's talent, but it's less obvious why it's good for the developer of the talent. Isn't that just creating competition for yourself? It can be (think *All about Eve*), but, more often, your act in developing others will add to your power, influence, and support within the organization.

Which people on your team are "diamonds in the rough," needing some shaping and support to be suitable for advancement? (Make sure in this that you move beyond any personal stereotypes of race, gender, or ethnicity—it's actually a political shortcoming as well as a legal and ethical problem to advance only those who resemble yourself.) What do they need? How can you help them move into a position and ability level deserving of promotion?

This may involve personal counseling, especially if there are some people skill deficiencies they need to overcome. It often involves training, both classroom and on the job, and also requires developmental job assignments to give them hands-on experience and increased visibility in the eyes of management. Encourage people to raid your staff for your best people; after all, you can hire and train more. Encourage and support people who go for promotions, even at the cost of short-term problems in your own department.

This helps in several ways. First, it increases the morale and motivation of everyone else to know you're actively in support of their career aspirations. Second, the people who advance as a result of your support will tend to feel obligated to you, and it never hurts to have people who owe you scattered throughout the organization. Third, you'll be in the senior management game of grooming new leadership, and that will make you look more powerful and more promotable yourself. It's a win/win outcome.

Get While the Getting Is Good

There comes a time, unfortunately, in many of our careers in which we find that our current employment situation has become untenable. It's time to leave before we get pushed. It's not unusual for people to be in denial when their job looks likely to come to an end, and you can't afford to be one of those people. You need to recognize, first, when your job is in jeopardy, second, what you can do to get back on track; and, third, how to leave gracefully ahead of an involuntary departure.

Recognizing When Your Job Is in Jeopardy

Your job can be in jeopardy for any number of reasons, including these:

- There may be a real performance issue, some measurable and concrete deficiency in your ability to get the work done.
- There may be a personality conflict with someone who has more clout. (As you remember, this is the most common reason people are fired.)
- A major and highly visible project assignment for which you were responsible has failed.
- The company is downsizing, and your position is vulnerable.
- Someone has decided to use the downsizing as an opportunity to get rid of you.

Regardless of which of these reasons applies, the warning signs of an impending job removal are normally present quite some time before the actual termination takes place. If it's aimed at you as an individual, warning signs include:

- Reassignment of key responsibilities to other people
- Significant changes in attitude and demeanor in people around you, especially those who are normally "in the know"
- Your omission from major meetings to which you used to be invited
- A request that you train new hires in your core responsibilities

- Gentle hints (and sometimes stern written warnings) from your supervisor and others
- Moves by a new management team to busily move its people into key responsibilities, while others who, like you, have been around for a while are losing their jobs

If your job is in jeopardy because of a general downsizing, rather than because of something you did or are perceived to have done, there should be cues in the general environment to which you should pay attention. First, look for rumors or facts about mergers and acquisitions. If there is going to be one, what can you find out about possible overlaps in positions between the two organizations? Is your job something the company just won't need two of?

Keep your finger on the financial pulse of the organization. In our discussion of your personal spy network in Chapter 2 (Defensive Goals), we suggested such moves as owning a minimum of one share of stock. If you don't know how to read a balance sheet, either learn or pay someone to analyze the company's balance sheet for you. If you work for a publicly traded company that is followed by one or more stock analysts, read what they say. If you work for a privately held company, check such references as Dun & Bradstreet and Standard & Poor's. There are entire books to teach you how to find information on privately held companies. There are also ways to learn about public agencies and nonprofits. If the financial news is bad, layoffs are a late sign. Recognize the early signs to have the maximum opportunity to take action.

How to Get Back on Track

If there is a problem with your actual job performance, there are few excuses for not knowing well in advance that there is a problem. Sometimes, however, you have a different idea about the critical functions of your job than your manager has, and that can lead to your thinking your performance is satisfactory or even excellent, while your boss considers you borderline at best. Make sure you know what your boss expects of you, because that, ultimately, is what your job really is.

Feedback

Ask for regular feedback, including negative feedback. If the issue is performance, there is normally a significant lag between mediocre or poor performance and termination. Work on developing an action plan to turn your performance around; ask for help if you need it.

Style Issues

Sometimes the performance issue turns out to be a style issue. The work is satisfactory, but the way in which you do it gives a different impression to your manager. Some employees, for example, work so fast they get the work done in much less than a normal day and feel therefore that they can come in late—after all, their productivity is very high. In some organizations, this is acceptable. In others, an issue like tardiness is so important that the job performance is comparatively irrelevant. If you're tardy, that's unacceptable—period. You must not only do the job well; you must do it well in accordance with accepted methods, like it or not.

Similarly, dress and grooming issues sometimes loom disproportionately large. The hair battles of the sixties haven't gone away altogether; in fact, conflicts about different styles of dress and grooming have been with us for centuries. This can be particularly true in an organization where there is a pronounced age gap between senior management and the rank and file.

Relationship Issues

If there is a relationship problem, again, you should know about it. If someone powerful doesn't like you, try to neutralize the enmity if you can. Sometimes a little effort on your part can fix it. Sometimes, there was a specific thing you did or were perceived of doing (the Bob Dole/Bill Clinton conflict in our discussion of enemies in Chapter 4 (Enemies) is a good example). Perhaps an apology may be in order.

In some cases, no matter what you do, you can't lower the enmity. If the conflict is severe enough, and your enemy (even if he or she is not an enemy of your choosing) is strong enough, you must realize when your employment has become untenable and move on.

Sometimes you can work around an enemy if you can build a wide enough network of other relationships throughout the organization. If enough people like you, it may not be fatal that a particular person does not.

Departing Gracefully

When it's time to leave, don't wait to be pushed. We recommend you invest one hour each week in career planning, no matter how secure or happy you are. Don't wait until you are in need before starting a job-hunting campaign; that air of desperation hurts. The way to go is to think of yourself not as job hunting but rather as networking to build your career contacts, as research, as learning. Most of what's known to work in job hunting is the same behavior that's part of a proactive person's success. Here are some specific suggestions:[4]

• *Build a help network.* We tend to overlook the many sources of help, forgetting that even the legendary self-made man or woman seldom made it on his or her own. We need the strength and resources of others to meet our own goals. Besides, most important jobs require teamwork, and now is the time to get started.

Who can help: Survey your friends, acquaintances, supervisors, and business associates. Talk to them about your dreams and goals, and ask them what they might be able to contribute. You'll be surprised at the range of contacts and advice you'll get.

• *Make training part of your regular program.* Attend courses, workshops, and seminars. Take a few minutes to introduce yourself to the leaders or speakers. They always like to hear positive things about their presentation, and most of them are eager to share additional advice and tips with a participant who is willing to listen.

• *Go to meetings.* Get involved in professional associations and meetings where people in your desired field or industry hang out. Introduce yourself. Most people are happy to share; we all like a receptive audience.

• *Use the technique of information interviewing.* Use the "information interviewing" techniques developed by Richard Bowles in his seminal *What Color Is Your Parachute?* volumes, updated annually.[5]

Write letters to people who've achieved what you want to achieve. Many will write back, and some will be happy to advise you. Keep a list of your accomplishments at work. If the list is getting small, find something new to add to your responsibilities, and create an accomplishment.

Consider professional help, including career counselors, resume writers, and others who can look at your situation dispassionately and expertly and give you advice and technical help you might not be able to get anywhere else.

Most of us need some morale help, too. Friends, family, loved ones, partners of any sort can help keep our focus, energy, and positive feelings high.

One hour a week doesn't seem like a lot of time, and it isn't a lot of time. That's all you need to focus on right now. In one hour, you could work on setting career development goals. In one hour, you could read a couple of chapters in a good career development book. In one hour, you could have an introductory meeting with a career counselor. In one hour, you could attend an evening lecture by a notable in your field. In one hour, you could gather all the material you need for your resume. One hour each week adds up to more than a workweek each year; a more than reasonable investment for your success.

Notes

1. William Bradford Huie, *The Americanization of Emily* (New York: NAL/Signet, 1957), p. 13.

2. Andrew DuBrin, *Winning Office Politics: DuBrin's Guide for the 90s* (Englewood Cliffs, N.J.: Prentice Hall, 1990), p. 117.

3. Barbara Fielder, *Motivation in the Workplace* (Mission, Kans.: SkillPath Publications, 1996), p. 20.

4. Michael Dobson, "Federal Career Development: A

Strategy Guide," in Kathryn Kraemer Troutman, *The Federal Resume Guidebook: Second Edition* (Indianapolis: JIST Works, 1999), pp. 203–207.

5. Richard Nelson Bolles, *What Color Is Your Parachute: A Practical Manual for Job-Hunters and Career Changers* (Berkeley, Calif.: Ten Speed Press, 1999) (revised annually).

Chapter 10

Strategic Office Politics—Politics as Warfare

A prince . . . should have no concern, no thought, or pursue any other art besides the art of war, its organization and instruction. This is the only art that those who command are expected to master.

Niccoló Machiavelli, *The Prince*, 1513

You use office politics on a daily basis to handle your interactions with others, to defend yourself, and to find out what's going on. You also use office politics as a way to achieve longer-term goals. While many of the actions remain the same, when you move from the tactical to the strategic front there are some changes. In this sense, you approach office politics as would a military general planning a campaign. It's time to go to war.

War

The idea of war and warfare is used in many senses, some literal, some metaphorical. We speak of a war on poverty, or a war on drugs, or a war on disease. The language, strategies, and ideas of war have wide application in all human spheres and clearly describe the world of politics, office and otherwise. It's the warfare aspect that often makes a principled person particularly uncomfortable.

War, wrote the military scholar Karl von Clausewitz, "always starts from a political condition, and is called forth by a political motive. It is, therefore, a political act. . . . It is not merely a political act, but also a real political instrument, a continuation of political commerce, a carrying out of the same by other means."[1] Thinking of war as a political act means thinking of it in terms of goals: what you want to achieve, and how you can achieve it.

Power, terrain, communications, negotiation—the tools we have discussed so far are also some of the tools of warfare. There are valuable lessons in military thinking, even if one does not wish to fight, either literally or metaphorically. Learning some of these ideas will help your defensive ability, help you understand where the difficulties might lie in certain projects you might pursue, and show you the best way to achieve your objective.

War is something to be avoided, even in the minds of most military leaders. We're not recommending you go to war, seek out war, enjoy war, or in any way fight for the sake of fighting. You do, however, need to study that art to be an effective principled office politician.

Strategic Goals

Goals exist at all levels: immediate, medium term, long term. A goal-oriented professional, which we hope you are, has goals at all levels, all of which derive from a sense of purpose and from fundamentals of character.

Your overarching goals, your long-term goals, the goals that shape the tactics and behavior you should exhibit over long periods of time need to be looked at in a strategic sense. The age-old career counseling chestnut "Where do you want to be five years from now?" is an important question. If you don't have any idea, you're not going to take effective and fundamental steps in support of that goal you don't have.

But goal setting isn't enough. You have to develop and implement a strategy to meet that goal. You must normally overcome obstacles, and those obstacles often include other people, whose interests and goals do not always run parallel to your own. Through planning, analysis, and the application of political skills, your odds of achieving your goals increase.

Setting Political Goals

The types of strategic goals that involve office politics can be many, and you may be pursuing several at any one time. Goals can be personal; you may need to determine what steps you have to take to be promoted, to get a raise, or to increase your influence on key projects. Goals can also be organizational; you may wish to figure out how you can influence the strategic direction of the company, identify and overcome political obstacles to important changes that must be made, motivate and develop staff to make the organization more competitive and effective, or get the right people in the right position—and the wrong people out.

In Chapter 2, we discussed Reason Power, the purposes or goals for which you might choose to practice the techniques of office politics. Now, go back through your self-assessment and identify those purposes that have a long time horizon—at least six months, and up to about five years. For each such goal, answer the following questions:

LONG-TERM GOALS

Personal

1. Where would I like to be in my career in the next five years? Is it in this organization or elsewhere?

_____

_____

2. What daily/weekly/monthly political actions will help me achieve this goal?

_____

_____

3. Who can help? How can they help? How can I get their help?

_____

_____

4. Who is likely to hinder me? How can they hinder me? Why would they hinder me? How can I change their motivation? How can I block or defeat any moves they may make?

_____

_____

5. How can I increase or leverage my personal political power in support of my goals?

_____

_____

6. What short-term goals do I have that might conflict with my long-term objective? How can I balance such conflicts to get the best results?

_____

_____

7. What weaknesses or challenge areas do I have that might stand in the way of my goals? How can I overcome them?

_____

_____

Organizational

1. What major challenges does my organization face?

_____

_____

2. What internal political obstacles stand in the way of a solution?

_____

_____

3. What conflicts exist between organizational progress and the interests of key power players? Can those conflicts be negotiated or resolved?

_____

_____

4. What other visions or strategic goals for the organization exist other than mine? How are they different or similar, compatible or incompatible? Can differences and incompatibilities be strategically resolved through negotiation or brainstorming?

_____

_____

5. In what ways is my vision or goal for the organization better than competing goals? What problems or risks exist in my vision? How do others see the strengths and weaknesses?

_____

_____

6. How do the other political players in my organization distribute in the Political Environment (who are my allies, my opponents, my fellow travelers, my enemies, my neutrals)? How can I alter the position of people who are likely to oppose or hinder my efforts?

_____

_____

7. How can I present my vision in a way that minimizes opposition or resistance? How can I help others play a role in developing the vision? How can I meet the needs of others through modifying and adjusting my vision?

_____

_____

8. How do I lay the groundwork for the vision? Do I lay the goal out clearly from the beginning, or must there be a lot of advance preparation before the vision can be articulated?

_____

_____

9. Am I the best person to lead this effort, or is someone else better suited for that role? If so, how can I influence or lead that person in support of my vision?

---

10. Who will be hurt if I succeed? How can I minimize the collateral damage? Must I seek to have some people removed from their positions as part of my plan? If so, whom—and how?

---

11. What are the likely or possible problems or countermoves that others may make as my plan unfolds? What responses can I make, and how can I eliminate or reduce such problems ahead of time?

---

12. What are the advantages and benefits of success—to me, to others, to the organization as a whole? How can I present benefits in the strongest way?

Using the Exercises in Your Work

It's a bad idea to undertake major initiatives without a plan and without some careful analysis. Get in the habit of being a realistic and thoughtful goal-setter, and recognize that knowing the obstacles and the terrain is just as important, arguably more so than merely knowing the path from here to the objective.

Diplomacy

Before going to war on behalf of your objectives, try diplomacy and negotiation.

The negotiation issues we discussed in Chapter 9 are comparable to the diplomatic work that precedes a war, and also to the diplomatic efforts that take place during the war. You want to avoid the necessity of a pitched battle through effective negotiation. In negotiation, you're looking for a win/win outcome. As a principled person, and also as a practical one, you understand that the other side must get some of its critical needs met or there will be no cooperation toward a deal. At the same time, you must get your own critical needs met, or you can't call it win/win.

Sometimes there is no room for a negotiated solution, and sometimes the other side doesn't see the advantage in reaching one—it believes that its BATNA, or walk-away alternative, is higher or better than yours. In Chapter 8, we talked about the concept of logical consequences, which are a kind of implicit threat describing what will happen if people make choices that are unsatisfactory to you.

Logical Consequences

If you state that an action will have consequences, there had better be consequences, or your reputation for honesty and effectiveness with suffer. Most of us aren't good bluffers in the first place, and, even if we are, good bluffers know that they have to back up what they say a significant percentage of the time so that they will be taken seriously. If you have told a tardy employee that he or she will be suspended upon the next late arrival, and the employee is late the next day, if you say, "I'll give you one more chance," you've proven yourself unreliable. You will reap what you sow.

If there are going to be negative consequences for the other side if you fail to reach an agreement, then it's very appropriate for you to lay them out. In calculating people's walk-away alternatives, you might want to think of ways you can increase the negative consequences of "no deal," which worsens their walk-away alternative and improves your chance of a successful negotiated outcome. Don't always expect people to figure this out on their own; sometimes it's incumbent upon you to tell them.

Complex Negotiations and the Problems on Your Own Side

When people negotiate, they often discover to their surprise that the sides are not monolithic in their opinion. You may find yourself having more difficulty negotiating with your own side than with the other side. Let's take the North American Free Trade Agreement (NAFTA) as an example. As difficult as the United States's negotiations with Mexico and Canada were, they were relatively easy compared to the negotiations within the U.S. government. The negotiators at the table had a limited range of authority. They could reach a mutually satisfactory agreement with their counterparts from the other nations, but each side then had to ratify those decisions with its own government. And none of the governments had a monolithic view of the right and proper way to achieve a treaty. Virtually any provision had powerful interests for it and against it within each of the governments. The negotiators would negotiate with each other, then turn around and negotiate with their own sides.

What keeps a negotiation like this together (realizing, of course, that many such negotiations fail)? In any negotiation, there is a goal of mutual gain, and when we fail to reach agreement, we don't get that gain; we get our walk-away, instead. That's the incentive for the different parties to work together. Of course, if no agreement can be reached that is equal to or better than all parties' BATNAs, there is no deal possible. If you're a negotiator in the middle, trying to hold your side together while working with your counterpart on the other side, you have to do the preparation steps discussed above for *each of the parties on your own side*, identifying conflicts among them. Some of them may have interests that are in opposition to the deal, and there is no zone of agreement that will meet their needs. If those people are politically powerful enough, there will be no deal. On the other hand, if there is enough power on the side of those who will benefit from the deal, a deal then becomes possible.

Negotiating with Your Own Side

It's odd that your biggest negotiation problems can be on your own side, but that's very often the reality. We pretend our side is consistent in its opinion, and we often assume the other side is consistent in its opinion as well, but neither of these, often, is true. Negotiation is a political act, as we've seen, but participating in negotiation is also a political act and a political process.

In a two-party negotiation, whether there are one or many issues, each party has at least a theoretical veto power, which is the right to say, unilaterally, "No deal." Of course, there may be a cost to saying "no deal," and if that cost is high enough (your walk-away alternative is poor), the veto may be more theoretical than actual.

In a multiparty negotiation or a negotiation in which the front-line negotiators represent entire organizations, a variety of people may hold veto power in the negotiation. In the NAFTA negotiations, for example, the U.S. Senate possesses the constitutional right to refuse to ratify a treaty. Given that, under Senate rules, a relatively small group of senators can effectively block a piece of legislation, any document brought before the Senate would likely have had to be completely re-negotiated, with the ultimate result of "no deal." The solution was "fast-track authority," under which senators agreed in advance to make the vote a simple up-or-down, without possibility of amending the treaty. Of course, senators necessarily knew in advance that whatever treaty would be brought before it would have some provisions they felt were unacceptable, especially provisions that hurt their state's interests as they saw them. Why, then, would they vote to give the president fast-track authority?

The reason something like fast-track authority becomes possible is that the alternative to a negotiated and compromised deal isn't a perfect deal but rather "no deal." Don't make perfect the enemy of good. The vote for fast-track authority was a vote in recognition of the reality that an imperfect deal was expected to be better than no deal, with the Senate reserving the right to turn down the final treaty by majority vote if it found it unacceptable. This voluntary limiting of power was a strategic decision on the part of the senators.

War in the Executive Suite

Return to Oldsmobile

How does this discussion relate to office politics in general, your organization as a whole, and your situation specifically? Let's go back to the Oldsmobile scenario from Chapter 4. As the situation was reported in the business press, the division was experiencing lagging sales and perceptions of poor quality, and rumors began to spread that the Oldsmobile division might be shut down and the resources refocused on other areas.

Imagine that you are a member of the GM leadership team, and your opinion is that Oldsmobile should be sold off or shut down or otherwise eliminated. While the negotiations to, say, sell Oldsmobile might be difficult and complex, it is simple compared to the work of getting to the initial decision to sell it. This is a good example of the type of long-term strategic organizational goal we've been discussing. How would you approach such a project, given the issues we've raised?

Inside the organization, you will normally have some people in favor of such a move and others opposed. Given that tilting at windmills is an occupation that yields a pretty poor life expectancy, your first objective is to find out, on the basis of your political read of the situation, whether there's a chance of success. Back in 320 B.C., the Chinese military genius Sun Tzu wrote, "The highest form of generalship is to balk the enemy's plans . . . and the worst policy of all is to besiege walled cities."

Your personal BATNA, as opposed to that of the organization, is not to fight in the first place. If there is no chance for victory, or at least a solution that would be better than the status quo, then you need to look elsewhere to advance the interests of your organization. You will want to proceed carefully, sounding out potentially key players in a very hypothetical way, to find out where the support and the opposition lie.

Maximizing the Chance for Victory

Let's say that you conclude that, although it will be challenging, there is a chance that you could win the battle to do away with Oldsmobile. Your next goal is to maximize the chance of victory, ideally before the rumor mill tells the leadership of Oldsmobile that there's an executive cabal out to do them in. (Regardless of how noble, altruistic, and organization-centered your motives are, you're likely going to be considered an enemy, not merely an opponent, by the other side. Expect that you'll experience some attacks on the personal level.)

You'll want to have a number of meetings with key players, and watch out that you don't inadvertently recruit someone who turns into a double agent or mole for the other side. Ultimately, you'll have to persuade the very top of the organization that this is a necessary step. Look at less drastic alternatives. Is eliminating Oldsmobile the best possible way to go? Are there other options? You may start with an idea—cut Oldsmobile—and as your research and investigation continue you might discover that some other alternative can achieve the same goal with much less opportunity for political infighting.

The Use of Deception

If you decide to proceed, lay your groundwork carefully. Sun Tzu wrote, "All warfare is based on deception." Is this compatible with being a principled person? As in our discussion in Chapter 1 (Avoiding Extremism) of tactical dishonesty in communication, there are areas in which deception is clearly unethical, areas in which it's clearly ethical, and areas that are gray. There's certainly nothing shady about not stating your position before you've formulated your position—brainstorming can take place behind closed doors and it's appropriate no one should be the wiser. It's clearly dishonest to misrepresent yourself as an ally to infiltrate the other side and then use the information you gain to hurt those who shared it with you.

In between, there are such tactics as having meetings with decision makers of which the other side is unaware, providing information to reporters and business analysts outside the organization to marshal publicity in support of your goal, calling in favors to pull fence-sitters firmly into your camp, and so forth. It may be necessary—or at least highly desirable—to use tactics that fall into potentially questionable areas. Often, the distinction between an unethical and an ethical tactic is the integrity, professionalism, and organizational focus of the person using the tactic. Consider carefully your motives, how you would feel if someone else were to use the tactic on you, how you would feel if your use of the tactic were to become publicly known, the effect the tactic might have on your relationships with others (allies as well as opponents), and how your use of the tactic would be viewed long term. How would you feel if you learned of meetings to which you were not invited? If that's acceptable to you and within the sphere of normal organizational behavior, you may act accordingly (remembering of course the others may perceive things differently).

The Issues on the Other Side

How can you meet the needs and objectives of the people who will be hurt if you win? Eliminating a large division in a major company is going to impact a lot of people, hurting income, career potential, and a lot else. It may be that you think, "So what? I'm sorry people get hurt, of course, but this is a necessary step for the good of the organization." You won't be alone if you think that, and there's some justification for such an opinion. We generally think that cutting people with knives is a very bad thing, but surgeons do it every day and are rightly applauded for it. With certain diseases and injuries, cutting it out is the best thing to do, and the quicker the better.

The physician knows, however, that diseases can fight

back. So can people. Their pain, even if it's necessary and justifiable from the organization's perspective, is real, and their response must be part of your planning. To whatever extent you can reduce their pain and their upset, doing so will make it easier to achieve your goals. (On the other hand, remember Machiavelli's dictum about the best way to cause injury: "Commit [the injuries you must] all at once." It's not more merciful for a surgeon to use a dull blade and cut slowly.)

There are a variety of techniques available for eliminating people who are obstacles. Like all our recommendations, these techniques need to be applied carefully, in line with your principles and your character. Realize, too, that these techniques are in fairly common use, and, even if they are not suitable or appropriate for you, you need to be able to recognize these maneuvers in case they are used against you.

Techniques for eliminating people who are obstacles include these:

• **Promotion to oblivion.** A traditional maneuver to take out someone who has become a political obstacle is to promote him or her to a new position in the organization that carries a high title and possibly better salary but that is outside the line of power and has little ability to impact the rest of the organization. This shift dramatically weakens the other person's Role Power but can reduce the financial impact or injury to that person.

• **Strategic reorganization.** A reorganization not only changes the structure of work but alters the responsibility and power of individuals. Reorganizations are used strategically to remove certain powers from individuals and departments and to move them elsewhere, into more sympathetic hands.

• **Altering the chain of command.** A variation of the reorganization is the move that leaves the person in place but installs a new manager over the one whose power you wish to weaken. You must be sure, of course, that the new manager is in support of your objective.

• **Death of the thousand budget cuts**. It may be useful to weaken the power of the other side before beginning your attack. Rather than come out in the open with your plan to eliminate Oldsmobile, you might start by nibbling away at the division's resources and new projects through the budget process. As Oldsmobile's budget and resources decrease, so likely will its clout in the organization. Once softened up, it will be an easier target.

Flexibility

A successful alternative is still a success. Even if you finally conclude that going after Oldsmobile is the best thing to do, continue to study the alternatives and the opposite side, because once your plan leaks—and it will inevitably leak, and leak before you're quite ready—you can expect a counterattack with lots of resources. There will be deeply reasoned arguments and full-color graphs on the visible side, and an enormous press on the top managers and directors who will ultimately make the call.

When you are negotiating in an environment with many participants and many issues, flexibility needs to be your hallmark characteristic. In Chapter 8 you practiced a diagnostic exercise in which you took your own point of view and looked within it to see what goals were being served. If you were in favor of getting rid of the Oldsmobile division, what were your reasons? What was the goal? The organizational goals—all valid—might include lowering costs, focusing resources on opportunities for greater return, or streamlining the organization.

There is a huge advantage to accepting different methods of achieving a goal. For example, you can, without losing, choose to support any solution or combination of solutions that makes real progress toward those goals. If there are ways to achieve the goals without the elimination of Oldsmobile, you still get to count that as a victory from a negotiating perspective. You have lost, on the other hand, if Oldsmobile remains as a division of GM and no other progress has been made toward your underlying goals.

Tactical Planning

The war metaphor is often used to describe the conflict of company against company.[2] But it is the internal warfare of office politics that often causes the most stress. You must always remember that when people feel they have enough interests at stake, when the alternatives appear to be win or lose, they will fight, and they will fight to win.

People are most likely to resort to the tools of warfare when they feel—correctly or not—backed against the wall, cut off from other alternatives. The power of negotiation as a tool in office politics is that through negotiation you can help the other side feel more power and more control in getting what it wants and what it needs, thereby lowering tensions and moving toward a productive solution.

Winning a war is not necessarily the same thing as winning on the battlefield. U.S. forces in Vietnam were never defeated on the field of battle. But that was not the only place the war was waged. If you can't win a head-on fight, try to change the battlefield to one more suited to your strengths. Guerrilla warfare, warfare by public relations—even warfare by delay, as practiced by Saddam Hussein in the Persian Gulf War—are proven techniques.

A war is always about an objective, something you hope to gain. The Principle of the Objective governs these situations: You must know your objective and then figure out what you must do to achieve it, against whatever opposition may exist. Every choice you make must be about the underlying objective. If that slips from the center focus of your mind, the quality of your decisions quickly degenerates. When you keep the principle of the objective firmly in mind, you find it easier to see beyond the immediate battle and to keep focused on victory. It is a victory when you achieve your objective; it is a loss when you do not achieve your objective, no matter how valiant the battle. Or, as Vince Lombardi put it, "Winning isn't everything. It's the only thing."

Timing

When you are planning an offensive battle, which office politics is, you control the timing, and that can be a powerful advantage. Although the British military might at the time of the American Revolution was far stronger than that of the colonists, and popular opinion in the colonies themselves was hardly unanimous in support of American independence, the colonists still won. How? One ingredient was timing: The Revolution began at a time when Great Britain was facing a number of different military challenges around the world. It didn't matter that the total might of Great Britain far exceeded that of the colonists; all that mattered was what portion of that might could be spared to put down the rebellion.

The "death of a thousand budget cuts" strategy is a way to weaken your opponent in advance of the battle, and it works very well, especially if your opponent does not yet know you intend to fight. You can also look for exploitable situations. Imagine that the president of the Oldsmobile division leaves, and there is only an interim president in place. The interim president may be a lot less powerful than the preceding president. Perhaps there is labor turmoil, a lawsuit that is getting a lot of publicity, a merger that has gone sour. When the other side is weak and disorganized, your likelihood of success increases.

The Importance of Planning Your Campaign

Good military leaders are good planners, but they also know what planning is—and is not. Planning doesn't mean simply creating a road map; military planning always has to allow for the uncertainty that comes from not knowing what the other side will do. "No battle plan survives first contact with the enemy" is a traditional saying.

The best plans involve lots of understanding, insight into the way of thinking of the other side, and a healthy respect for the opposition. It's often a fatal mistake to underestimate the other side. It may in fact do less well than it might, but you're almost always better off assuming it will be at its best. Don't get too wrapped up in the details of your plan. If you've created a good plan to improve your understanding, you should find it easier to shift gears when necessary.

Getting Others on Your Side

Think about the five categories people occupy in the Political Environment model (see Chapter 4), and determine how to build and motivate your force in this endeavor. Parcel out your trust carefully, because if your plans become known, they are automatically easier to counter. Keep a lot to yourself; it will help you stay in control. Be prepared for change, because it is inevitable. Look for opportunities for peace, but remember that whatever you do in this conflict sets a precedent for the future; the wrong peace can lead to more wars.

Notes

1. Karl von Clausewitz, *On War* (London: Routledge, 1962), pp. 22–23.

2. Al Ries and Jack Trout, *Marketing Warfare* (New York: Plume/New American Library, 1986), p. 6.

The Rules

Nothing is as dangerous for the state as those who would
govern kingdoms with maxims found in books.
Cardinal Richelieu,
Political Testament, 1687

Every game has rules—official and unofficial—and so is it
with office politics. Rules are not always absolutes; sometimes
you have to know when it's right to break the rules. But this
much is true: Break the rules only when you have a strong
reason to do so.

Use the rules to focus your thinking, to give you a model
to analyze your current situation, to figure out some options
for a dilemma. Above all, use the rules to help you understand
what others are doing, why they're doing it, and what they
hope to gain.

Forty Rules of the Game

1. ***Deal with the way things are, not the way you think
they ought to be or want them to be.*** You may not think your
situation is fair or even reasonable. And you very well may be
right. You want things to be different, and maybe they can
be. No matter what, you must start where you are. As an exercise, start your political strategy process by writing yourself
an essay on why things are the way they are, who benefits,

and what factors stand in the way of change. Then—and only then—start making for plans for change.

2. **Put yourself in the other person's shoes: Always try to look at every situation from the point of view of the others who are involved.** To understand a political conflict and figure out what to do about it, look at it from three points of view:[1]

> *First position (mine):* How I see the problem from my own perspective.
> *Second position (theirs):* How I see the problem when I stand in the other person's shoes. (This is often the most valuable perspective you can have.)
> *Third position ("fly on the wall"):* How a neutral third party would assess the conflict.

3. **Understand the underlying game of politics.** Always remember that if you want to lead, if you want to manage, if you want to get things done, you will do so only through the instrument of politics.

4. **Establish your principles and ethics and always live by them, even when short-term advantages suggest otherwise.** In the somewhat arbitrary distinction between "politician" and "statesman," most people think of the "statesman" as a politician with principles. Not only is that the right ethical position, it's the right practical position as well. As we've emphasized, without a firm ethical compass, the game becomes an end in itself, rather than a means to an end, and the short term occupies more of your thinking than the long term.

Your principles can be one of your most effective political tools. Showing that you are a person of good character allows you to win the trust and confidence of others, even when they don't share your views and sometimes even when they strongly disagree with you. And the trust you build is a vital source of political power and effectiveness.

5. **Live _your_ principles and life, not everyone else's, but give respect to the official party line.** Your principles and your character have to come from within. You may refrain

from conduct others find normal and acceptable. You may choose to engage in conduct that others don't find acceptable, if your actions are in accordance with your own moral center. However, there's an "official party line" in every group that you must give at least lip service to in order to be accepted. It may be a myth like "Our people are better" or "Our product is superior," when those statements may not be true or may be irrelevant even if true. You have to say these words and then work around to a more realistic assessment; if you reject the assumptions, the result will be that no one will listen to you.

6. ***Deliberately acquire power and influence.*** Be clear in your own mind (although you shouldn't necessarily broadcast it widely) that your goal is to acquire more power and influence. Make sure that your mental attitude about the acquisition of power is positive. You have to want power, know why you want it, know how to get it, take the steps to get it, and use it effectively.

7. ***Know your reasons for being in the political arena— and know others' reasons, too.*** Knowing the dangers in acquiring and loving power for its own sake, you must be clear that, for you, power is something you get for a purpose. Understand your own purposes so that you acquire the right kind of power, acquire it the right way, and use it toward the right ends.

Identify the others in the organization who are also deliberate in their political strategies and actions. There usually aren't too many of them, and they tend to reach positions of power because they seek them. Learn their reasons, and you'll have insight into their actions.

8. ***Be a goal setter.*** "Are you a wandering generality, or are you a meaningful specific?" Zig Ziglar's famous question focuses on goal setting and is based on the reality that goals make you more powerful and more effective regardless of what you want to pursue. Make sure that you set goals for the short term, the medium term, and the long term. Review your goals on a regular basis. Make plans and strategies for achieving those goals.

9. ***Develop your own intelligence network.*** One of the necessary political skills in an organization is knowing how

to do your own intelligence work, which is the closest most of us can get to actual telepathy. Do you have your own internal spy network yet? In other words, do you have people who can—and will—tell you what's going on, what's behind seemingly strange requests, what people are really looking for? A lot of spying, by the way, is just learning to listen well and expanding your sources of information. An awful lot of information is publicly available—but it can tell you amazing things about what's going on behind the scenes.

10. ***Work toward win/win solutions.*** You almost always have to live with the people after the political battle is resolved. If they are angry or hurt, feel manipulated or abused, they remember—and you may pay the price in the long run. Not only is win/win the best way from the ethical point of view; it's the best way—period.

For win/win, you have to find out what the other person wants or needs and figure out a way for that person to achieve her or his goal in a way that helps you achieve yours. It takes brainstorming, creativity, and the willingness to consider other options, but it can be done.

11. ***Discover the hidden keys to the executive suite.*** Part of reading your own corporate culture is figuring out what the people who become executives have in common. Normally, there are three categories of characteristics: technical/job-related skills, interpersonal skills, and "old school tie." Technical and job-related skills include not only those related to the subject matter of the business but also related skills such as finance and project management. Interpersonal skills include public speaking, writing, negotiation, small group interaction, and relationship building. The "old school tie" varies from organization to organization: It can be a preference for people with certain educational or socioeconomic backgrounds or styles of dress, or even extracurricular hobbies, such as golf.

You will find people who succeed without having all three sets of characteristics. Those people normally have stronger than average skills in the categories they do possess. If you can't develop acumen in all three areas, work harder on the ones you do possess. If you find the door will nonetheless be permanently shut, go somewhere else.

12. *Take a stand.* The purpose and value of being political is to get something done, and if you don't take a stand—even at some personal risk—there's very little point in being political in the first place, except for personal defense.

Choose your stands carefully and deliberately; don't be the kind of person who gets backed into a corner and defends a stand he or she doesn't believe in the first place because giving in is inconceivable. Don't fight a battle you know you're bound to lose unless the principle is so fundamental that you can't live with yourself otherwise.

Separate the stand from the people involved. Try not to make the people who disagree with you feel stupid and venal—it doesn't make it any easier for them to come around to your point of view. Build relationships with those who oppose you. Look for common ground that allows you to achieve your goal in a way that does the least damage to others, and preferably helps them win, too. Listen to opposing points of view with an open mind, even if you end up rejecting them.

13. *Know who your allies, opponents, fellow travelers, enemies, and neutrals are.* It's important to study not just who people are but where they stand in relation to you. Remember that these stands are not necessarily permanent; you'll have some people who are allies on one issue, opponents on the next. Don't burn bridges. Why are your supporters supporting you? Why are your opponents opposing you? How much of it is the issue? How much of it is the personal relationship?

14. *Work to improve relationships and common interests.* The worst part of the Political Environment to locate people is in the enemy quadrant. While it may not be possible to avoid ever having an enemy, you can work to reduce the number of enemies you acquire and keep people from entering that quadrant in the first place. Relationship, confidence, and trust building should be ongoing activities, no matter what your political goal. Look for common interests and common goals as a way of laying the foundation for win/win outcomes.

15. *Remember your friends . . . and your enemies.* John F. Kennedy was attending a Boston dinner as a favor to a politi-

cal colleague. "I'll be happy to do it," he said, "but I want to be in and out. No meetings."

"I understand your wishes," his colleague said, "But we have some bishops who are hoping to meet with you, and a group of nuns in the next room."

Kennedy replied, "The nuns I'll see, but not the bishops. They all vote Republican."[2]

While Kennedy was obviously joking, some people behave that way deliberately. While vindictiveness and pettiness are not productive or principled, it's important that people understand there is a benefit to being your friend, and that benefit is not provided to your enemy.

16. ***Do favors for others and accept favors from others.*** Build up your bank account of obligations by going out of your way to be helpful and supportive of others. This lets you ask for favors later when you need them. Of course, others will want to do you favors to build up their bank accounts. Do accept these favors; don't look like someone who just stores up obligations to improve later leverage. The exchange of favors smoothes the organization and helps achieve overall organizational goals.

17. ***Be honest, or be quiet.*** Your word must be your bond, or your career as an effective office politician will be short, indeed. Your promise is very often the only thing of value you have to put on the table in a negotiation. If you have devalued your promises by previous action, you no longer have anything valuable to offer.

Silence is not dishonesty unless you're deliberately withholding something someone needs to know and ought to know. Silence is often the best policy.

18. ***If you don't have a stake in it, stay out of it.*** Avoid the Don Quixote syndrome of tilting at windmills. Pick your fights carefully, and don't get involved when there is nothing at stake for you. Some people have been known to make every little irritation into a huge matter of principle; don't become one of those people. Also, before you go charging in, make sure you do your homework. You may hear about some horrible injustice that makes you determined to act—but there also may be another side to the story. Check your facts first.

19. *Look for the WII—FM.* When you want to influence someone else's actions or behavior, you have to understand what's in it for the person. This goes back to the essential political skill: putting yourself in the other person's shoes. There is no skill you can practice that will bring you better results in the long run.

20. *Understand and respect the power of other people.* Other people possess power, and power must always be respected. It's not necessary to always like or approve of it, but because power is real, you must acknowledge it. Here are some questions to consider about other peoples' power:

- Is the power part of the person, or part of the position or situation?
- Is the power permanent or temporary?
- Does the person know how much power she or he possesses—or how to maximize it?
- What is the goal behind the power?

21. *Start with the relationship that exists and build from there.* This is a special case of the general rule that you should always accept the initial situation for what it is. If you want to improve a relationship with another person, you need to reflect on why you don't already have a better relationship with that person—and there's always a reason. Understand that small changes over time are much more likely to succeed than big changes quickly. Start with confidence-building and trust-building measures. Listen well. Put yourself in the other person's shoes. Accept your own contribution, whatever it is. Apologize, if you've done something to damage the relationship. Be patient.

22. *Avoid the double-cross.* Like a lot of political techniques, the double-cross may be effective on a short-term basis, but it leaves a damaged relationship behind. A person who double-crosses can't be trusted, and if you can't be trusted, you'll find it hard to be effective.

What if you do need to change a position you've already taken? What if what you planned no longer fits your situation? In that case, the best technique is often to bring the change out in the open. Give warning of your intentions. Explain what you're going to do and why you're going to do it. You may still make somebody mad, but you remain someone who has integrity.

23. ***Never make an enemy by accident.*** People are often sensitive—surprisingly so, especially when they don't seem to be sensitive to the feelings of other people. It is all too easy to find that you have mortally offended someone without ever having intended to do so. People tend to be self-centered, thinking that how others treat them and act toward them is deliberate and thought out, when in reality it's often accidental and careless. By being aware of other people, you can minimize the danger of giving offense and find out in time to make an apology helpful if you do.

24. ***Never attribute to malice what can satisfactorily be explained by stupidity.*** The reverse of this proposition is to develop in yourself an awareness that others don't necessarily mean to hurt you or abuse you by their offhand remarks or actions. When in doubt, ask: "I thought I heard a criticism (or dig, or something hurtful) in what you just said. Did you mean it to come out that way?" Often, the answer will be an immediate no, followed by an apology—and possibly improved behavior or sensitivity in the future.

25. ***Respect those who oppose you.*** For some reason, it's popular to trash your opponents, acting as if their opposition, or simply their group membership, makes them stupid or inadequate or worthless. Not only is this attitude unfair and possibly hurtful; it's also self-destructive. If you underestimate your opponents, they will be in a much better position to win. If you have to make a mistake, err in favor of overestimating the competition. It's safer.

26. ***Deal firmly and quickly—and proportionally—with threats.*** Remember the military definition of threat: the capability of someone to do you harm. Be aware of the threats to your goals and your position, and act immediately. Don't overreact to threats. You don't use a nuclear weapon to deal with a minor border skirmish. Sometimes, showing the other person or side that you're aware of what he or she has done will cause the person to back down or refrain from further

action. You normally need much less force to defend yourself or neutralize a threat when you act early.

27. ***Put the squeeze on when necessary.*** Earn a reputation for being supportive and for going to bat for others so that when you in turn need help, you can ask for it clearly and assertively. Remind people what you've done for them in the past, but don't do it in a way that makes it sound as if you feel guilty for asking for support in return. Sound firm and direct. Ask specifically for the behaviors you want; don't make people figure it out. If you'll be personally hurt or feel betrayed at their failure to help, say so, again in a direct, assertive manner.

28. ***Bend with the prevailing wind.*** This rule seems contrary to what you might expect from someone who operates on the basis of principles, but it actually is sound and ethical.

The historian and scholar Garry Wills has identified two prevailing models of leadership.[3] The first, the Periclean model, presents the leader as the "best man"—a person who is followed because of her or his superior qualities. The second, the Dale Carnegie model, is the leader as sales professional, who ingratiates and manipulates people into following. Yet neither model adequately describes the complicated relationship between a leader and her or his followers.

The strength of your leadership is subject to the extent your followers wish to go in a certain direction. If no one is following, you're not leading. The ability of many great leaders to move their organizations—or nations—in a certain direction is often a long and cumbersome process of push and pull, on the one hand saying what people want to hear and on the other taking a series of small steps in the direction of the goal. While it's tempting to simply stand up for what you believe, if you want something accomplished, you usually need support.

You must bend with the prevailing wind, because ultimately you cannot force people in a direction they don't want to go. But, like the willow tree, you keep coming back, moving slowly and imperfectly—and that's the only way to reach many important goals.

29. ***Examine job assignments for hidden traps.*** The most dangerous phrase to ever come out of a professional's mouth is "Yes, I'll do it!" said before the person truly understands what he or she has agreed to. When you say "Yes," you aren't agreeing merely to what has been said but also to every hidden assumption, wish, and fantasy your customers, internal or external, may have.

This is not to suggest that you should say "No," or even that you have the option to say "No." You can, however, ask questions and dig, all the time making positive noises, until you're ready to accept the assignment. Will this cause problems? Not necessarily. Many bosses would have a lot more respect for certain staff if they asked a few more questions at the beginning, rather than waiting until disaster struck.

Here are some questions to consider: Are there people in power positions who have agendas (hidden or clear) that affect the outcome, resources, priority, or methodology of the project? Who are the key players in this assignment, what are their relative powers, and what do they want? Put yourself in their shoes and look at the problem from their perspective. What will success for the project mean for them? Will it advance their careers or harm them? What personal benefits will they acquire from the project's success or failure?

30. ***Study the political environment, looking for factors that affect how people will act.*** The historian and author Tom Clancy has identified an odd fact about recent military history: Almost every war since the Industrial Revolution has been initiated by the side that ultimately lost.[4] Going to war, therefore, is not a rational act. The thinking behind the decision to start a war—the *why*—is not necessarily important, but the *what*—the objective—is, because if you can determine the objective, you can figure out how to deny it to those who oppose you. People get so wrapped up in their own goals that they often forget that somebody else might try to stop them from achieving them.

Obviously, you don't necessarily want to deny someone her or his objective, unless that objective is destructive to you or your interests. Often the best way to resolve the conflict is to help the person achieve a goal, if you can do so in a way that benefits (or at least doesn't harm) you.

31. *Learn how to manage change.* One of the major purposes in acquiring and wielding political power is to achieve change. Tom Peters observes, "The most important and visible outcropping of the action bias in the excellent companies [we studied] is their willingness to try things out, to experiment."[5] However, it's usually a bad tactical approach to try to make too many changes in too short a period of time. Pick one or two major areas, and work on those first. As you feel comfortable with them and as you see how they work, add more. Gentle and consistent pressure over time is your best friend in accomplishing change.

Just remember that your credibility and power to make these changes must be earned. It's not enough merely to be right that a proposed change is desirable; you have to earn the right to make the suggestion in the first place, and you do that through demonstrating that you're on top of the situation just the way it is.

This quandary—that being right isn't usually enough—is a source of never-ending frustration for a number of people. You'll notice them in every organization, hard at work selling their ideas, becoming increasingly frustrated, disenchanted, and negative about management, and never understanding that their own performance and credibility dramatically affect their ability to achieve desired change. Don't let yourself become one of these people. You avoid that situation by mastering the basics and building from there.

32. *Know the organization's internal image and how it relates to the real world.* One disadvantage of propaganda is that the person who generates it all too often ends up believing it. The cognitive dissonance between an organization's internal image and how it is perceived by the outside world has destroyed many companies. Effective politicians work very hard not to believe their own propaganda.

Make a habit of overestimating your competition, internal and external. Study them. With external competition, such as rival companies, gather data on them. You should have a file of their catalogs and press releases, clippings of newspaper stories and magazine articles, printouts of their Web sites, photographs of their trade show booths, and at least one share of stock if they're publicly traded. Go to their annual meetings, and get and read their annual reports. Have your broker keep you up to date on their status in the industry.

33. ***Respect the chain of command.*** The chain of command is one of management's many borrowings from the military. In a traditional organization (or military unit), each person is responsible to one immediate supervisor, and that supervisor is in turn responsible to a higher-level supervisor or manager, and so forth to the top of the organization. Lines of authority are clear in this type of structure.

Violating the chain of command means bypassing one or more intermediate levels of supervision to get job assignments or decisions from a higher level. Although it may be tempting as a short-run strategy, especially if you're not getting the support you need or want from your immediate boss, this behavior has several drawbacks.

- It smacks of a child trying to corner one parent or the other alone to get a favorable decision after the other parent has already said "no."
- It shows lack of loyalty to your own supervisor, which not only harms that relationship but also raises questions about you in the minds of higher levels of management.
- It shows lack of understanding about the organizational structure, which also raises questions about you in the minds of others.

34. ***Promote your accomplishments.*** Don't assume that others are spending their day looking for your accomplishments and achievements. It's up to you to sound your own trumpet. Announce when you've accomplished something, send a short, clear memo to your boss if that's appropriate. Look for high-visibility assignments, and volunteer for them. When you go to a trade show or convention, write a report when you get back on what you've learned. Keep a file of your achievements, and make sure your boss sees it at performance appraisal time. There's no need to be pushy; this is actually helpful to your boss as well as to you.

35. **Protect your reputation.** Your reputation is your primary political asset and must be defended at all costs. There are two sources of potential damage to your reputation: other people and yourself. Of the two, the most important to worry about is damage you cause to your own reputation. When you find that others are trying to damage your reputation, your own behavior will help others decide whether to take the attack seriously. If someone has lied before and is accused of lying, the accusation may well be believed, even if it is false. But if someone with an absolute reputation for telling the truth is accused of lying, it's much less likely the accusation will stick.

36. **Learn something new.** Part of your political strategy should be to develop the asset of yourself. There are many valuable reasons to practice the discipline of lifelong learning; political success is one of them. Because your respect power is a key element of your total power, learning new disciplines, new skills, and new insights develops that source of personal power.

You can't get promoted to high levels without political skills, but that doesn't mean political skills alone are sufficient. You must be able to do the job if you want to keep it. (Some people do get promoted into positions they can't handle because of their political skills—but this is a short-term accomplishment only.)

37. **Keep your word, both positively and negatively.** "An honest politician," said Simon Cameron in 1860, "is one who, when he is bought, will stay bought." There will be times in which keeping your word will get you into trouble or compromise your short-term interests, but the damage caused by breaking your bond will be significant and not to be taken lightly. This does not apply to changing your mind, which you are completely entitled to do, as long as you don't leave others in the lurch.

Equally, when you make a threat or provide someone with a statement of logical consequences, you'd better deliver, because failure to follow up is also a failure to keep your word.

38. **Go to lunch with different people.** Lunch isn't about food; it's about relationships. Use the time wisely to cultivate

a wider network of contacts. You don't have to talk business—in fact, you frequently shouldn't. If you eat lunch with the same people every single day, you are limited in your potential power.

39. *Think several steps ahead.* Military theory, chess, and politics have in common the need to think several steps ahead. The first rule is to stop and think in the first place. The second rule is to think about the other person's goals and strategies. The biggest tactical mistake people make is to assume that their opponents are just going to sit there and do nothing. The third rule is to take your time, whenever possible. Let your plan roll around in your mind for a while; you may find something wrong with it, or you may come up with a better idea.

40. *Take time to plan.* Many people have the wrong idea about planning—they think you plan because you expect things to work out according to that plan. When they don't (and they usually don't), you conclude either that you're a bad planner or that planning doesn't work. Neither is true.

You don't plan because you expect reality to conform to your plan. Instead, you plan because the act of planning forces you to be better prepared for the unforeseen. Remember, no matter how well you plan, the uniqueness of each situation virtually ensures that you will not anticipate everything. Plans never happen exactly as planned.

The real value of planning is that it helps you decide whether or not your plan reflects your project reality. Plans provide two key advantages: First, the process of planning is educational. If you don't make a plan, you don't understand the situation. Second, a plan always serves as a benchmark, a way to tell where you are relative to your destination. A roadmap is useful even when you get lost; a plan is useful even—especially—when your project goes off track.

Notes

1. Fisher, Kopelman, and Schneider, op. cit., pp. 32–33.
2. O'Neill, op. cit., p. 59.

3. Garry Wills, "What Makes a Good Leader?" *Atlantic Monthly*, vol. 273, no. 4, April 1994, pp. 63–80.

4. Tom Clancy, *Debt of Honor* (New York: G. P. Putnam, 1994), pp. 415–416.

5. Thomas J. Peters and Robert H. Waterman Jr., *In Search of Excellence* (New York: Warner Books, 1982), p. 134.

A Final Word

In this book, we've talked about the nature of office politics, the reasons for its existence, and the fundamental ideas you need to cope and even prosper within its confines.

Certain skills—and office politics is among them—can't be mastered, in the sense of knowing everything there is to know. You can spend your life working on your political skills and improve them, but you will still find yourself with more to learn.

Before you rush to put the ideas in this book to work in your own organization, take a week or two to simply observe. How does the behavior of other people relate to the models you've studied? What are their goals? What are the unique features of your current landscape?

Start small. Don't implement your grand strategy right away. Try a few smaller ideas to get comfortable. Use some defensive ideas to improve your self-protection. Build allies, mentors, and confidants.

And remember, politics is all about people. Many of the same skills you use to build good friendships also help build political allies. There *is* a principled solution. And you can find it and prosper.

Bibliography

Alessandra, Tony. *Mastering Your Message* (audiotape). Mission, Kans.: SkillPath Publications, 1997.

Andersen, Richard, and Helene Hinis. *Write It Right: A Guide for Clear and Correct Writing*. Mission, Kans.: SkillPath Publications, 1993.

Bennis, Warren, and Burt Nanus. *Leaders: The Strategies for Taking Charge*. New York: Harper Perennial, 1985.

Berglas, Steven. "Entrepreneurial Ego: Liar, Liar, Pants on Fire." *Inc.*, August 1997.

Block, Peter. *The Empowered Manager: Positive Political Skills at Work*. San Francisco: Jossey-Bass, 1987.

Bolles, Richard Nelson. *What Color Is Your Parachute: A Practical Manual for Job Hunters and Career Changers*. Berkeley, Calif.: Ten Speed Press, 1999.

Bramson, Robert M., Ph.D. *Coping with Difficult People*. New York: Anchor Press/Doubleday, 1981.

Brown, Jerry, and Denise Dudley. *The Supervisor's Guide*. Mission, Kans.: SkillPath Publications, 1989.

Burley-Allen, Madelyn. *Managing Assertively: How to Improve Your People Skills*. New York: Wiley, 1983.

Burton, Mary Lindley, and Richard A. Wedemeyer. *In Transition: From the Harvard Business School Club of New York's Career Management Seminar*. New York: HarperBusiness, 1991.

Caro, Robert. *The Power Broker: Robert Moses and the Fall of New York*. New York: Alfred A. Knopf, 1974.

Caroselli, Marlene, Ed.D. *Meetings That Work*. Mission, Kans.: SkillPath Publications, 1992.

Caroselli, Marlene, Ed.D. *P.E.R.S.U.A.D.E.: Communication Strategies That Move People to Action*. Mission, Kans.: Skill-Path Publications, 1996.

Clancy, Tom. *Debt of Honor*. New York: G. P. Putnam, 1994.

Clarke, Colleen. *Networking: How to Creatively Tap Your People Resources*. Mission, Kans.: SkillPath Publications, 1993.

Clausewitz, Karl von. *On War*. London: Routledge, 1962.

Collins, Jim. "The Long View: The Learning Executive." *Inc.*, August 1997.

Crosby, Philip B. *Quality without Tears: The Art of Hassle-Free Management*. New York: Plume, 1985.

Dawson, Roger. *The Secrets of Power Negotiating* (audiotape). Chicago: Nightingale-Conant, 1987.

Dean, John W. III. *Blind Ambition*. New York: Pocket Books, 1976.

Dobbs, J. R. *The Book of the SubGenius*. New York: Simon & Schuster, 1983.

Dobson, Michael S. *The Juggler's Guide to Managing Multiple Projects*. Newtown Square, Pa.: Project Management Institute, 1999.

Dobson, Michael S. *Practical Project Management*. Mission, Kans.: SkillPath Publications, 1996.

Dobson, Michael Singer, and Deborah Singer Dobson. *Coping with Supervisory Nightmares*. Mission, Kans.: SkillPath Publications, 1997.

Dobson, Michael Singer, and Deborah Singer Dobson. *Managing UP!* New York: AMACOM, 1999.

DuBrin, Andrew. *Winning Office Politics: DuBrin's Guide for the '90s*. Englewood Cliffs, N.J.: Prentice Hall, 1990.

Dudley, Denise. *Every Woman's Guide to Career Success*. Mission, Kans.: SkillPath Publications, 1991.

Elgin, Suzette Haden. *Success with the Gentle Art of Verbal Self-Defense*. New York: Prentice Hall, 1989.

Ferrero, Guigliemo, and Corrado Barbagallo. *A Short History of Rome: The Monarchy and the Republic*. New York: Capricorn Books, 1964.

Fielder, Barbara. *Motivation in the Workplace*. Mission, Kans.: SkillPath Publications, 1996.

Finkler, Steven A. Ph.D., C.P.A. *The Complete Guide to Finance & Accounting for Nonfinancial Managers.* Englewood Cliffs, N.J.: Prentice-Hall/Spectrum, 1983.

Fisher, Roger, and William Ury. *Getting to Yes: Negotiating Agreement without Giving In.* Middlesex, England: Penguin Books, 1981.

Fisher, Roger, Elizabeth Kopelman, and Andrea Kupfer Schneider. *Beyond Machiavelli: Tools for Coping with Conflict.* New York: Penguin Books, 1994.

Friedman, Paul. *How to Deal with Difficult People.* Mission, Kans.: SkillPath Publications, 1991.

Fuller, George. *The First-Time Supervisor's Survival Guide.* Englewood Cliffs, N.J.: Prentice Hall, 1995.

Fussell, Paul. *Class: A Painfully Accurate Guide through the American Status System.* New York: Ballantine, 1983.

Gaddis, John Lewis. "Living in Candlestick Park." *Atlantic Monthly,* vol. 283, no. 4, April 1999.

Garreau, Joel. *The Nine Nations of North America.* New York: Avon Books, 1991.

Goleman, Daniel. *Emotional Intelligence.* New York: Bantam Books, 1995.

Grotjahn, Martin, M.D. *Beyond Laughter: Humor and the Subconscious.* New York: McGraw-Hill, 1966.

Grout, Pam. *The Mentoring Advantage.* Mission, Kans.: SkillPath Publications, 1995.

Heinlein, Robert A. *Space Cadet.* New York: Ace Books, 1948.

Huie, William Bradford. *The Americanization of Emily.* New York: NAL/Signet, 1957.

Humphrey, Watts S. *Managing Technical People: Innovation, Teamwork, and the Software Process.* Reading, Mass.: Addison-Wesley, 1997.

Keegan, John. *A History of Warfare.* New York: Vintage, 1993.

Kennedy, Marilyn Moats. *Office Politics: Seizing Power, Wielding Clout.* New York: Warner Books, 1980.

Kirchner, Paul. *Everything You Know Is Wrong.* Los Angeles: General Publishing Group, 1995.

Korda, Michael. *Power: How to Get It, How to Use It* (audiotape). New York: Simon & Schuster Audio & Video, 1986.

Kouzes, James M., and Barry Z. Posner. *The Leadership Chal-

lenge: How to Keep Getting Extraordinary Things Done in Organizations. San Francisco: Jossey-Bass, 1995.

Lewis, H. W. *Why Flip a Coin? The Art and Science of Good Decisions*. New York: Wiley, 1997.

Liddy, G. Gordon. *Will: The Autobiography of G. Gordon Liddy*. New York: Dell/St. Martin's Press, 1980.

Machiavelli, Niccoló. *The Prince*. London: Everyman Library, 1995.

Mackay, Harvey. *Swim with the Sharks without Being Eaten Alive: Outsell, Outmanage, Outmotivate, and Outnegotiate Your Competition*. New York: William Morrow, 1988.

Marlette, Doug. "Iago Lives!" *Esquire*, August 1997.

Martin, Judith. *Miss Manners' Guide to Excruciatingly Correct Behavior*. New York: Warner Books, 1982.

McCullough, Colleen. *Caesar's Women*. New York: William Morrow, 1996.

McGraw, Robert. *Learning to Laugh at Work*. Mission, Kans.: SkillPath Publications, 1995.

O'Neill, Tip, with Gary Hymel. *All Politics Is Local (and Other Rules of the Game)*. New York: Random House, 1994.

Pachter, Barbara, and Marjorie Brody. *Climbing the Corporate Ladder: What You Need to Know and Do to Be a Promotable Person*. Mission, Kans.: SkillPath Publications, 1995.

Pardoe, Blaine. *Cubicle Warfare: Self-Defense Strategies for Today's Hypercompetitive Workplace*. Rocklin, Calif.: Prima Publishing, 1997.

Peters, Thomas J., and Robert H. Waterman Jr. *In Search of Excellence*. New York: Warner Books, 1982.

Poley, Michelle Fairfield. *Mastering the Art of Communication: Your Keys to Developing a More Effective Personal Style*. Mission, Kans.: SkillPath Publications, 1995.

Pollan, Stephen M., and Mark Levine. *Lifescripts: What to Say to Get What You Want in 101 of Life's Toughest Situations*. New York: Macmillan, 1996.

Puzzo, Mario. *The Godfather*. New York: Signet/New American Library, 1969.

Raiffa, Howard. *The Art and Science of Negotiation: How to Resolve Conflicts and Get the Best out of Bargaining*. Cambridge, Mass.: Belknap Press, Harvard University Press, 1982.

Ries, Al, and Jack Trout. *Marketing Warfare*. New York: Plume/ New American Library, 1986.

Rubin, Harriet. *The Princessa: Machiavelli for Women*. New York: Currency Doubleday, 1997.

Stein, Richard J. *Learning to Manage Technical Professionals: Crossing the Swamp*. Reading, Mass.: Addison-Wesley, 1993.

Stone, Wilfred, and J. G. Bell. *Prose Style: A Handbook for Writers*, 2nd ed., New York: McGraw-Hill, 1972.

Tannen, Deborah. *Talking from 9 to 5: How Women's and Men's Conversational Styles Affect Who Gets Heard, Who Gets Credit, and What Gets Done at Work*. New York: William Morrow, 1994.

Tannen, Deborah. *You Just Don't Understand: Women and Men in Conversation*. New York: Ballantine, 1990.

Troutman, Kathryn Kraemer. *The Federal Resume Guidebook: Second Edition*. Indianapolis: JIST Works, 1999.

Warren, Ellen. "Where Do You Stand?" *Chicago Tribune*, July 1, 1997.

Weisbord, Marvin R. *Productive Workplaces: Organizing and Managing for Dignity, Meaning, and Community*. San Francisco: Jossey-Bass, 1987.

Wills, Garry. "What Makes a Good Leader?" *Atlantic Monthly*, vol. 273, no. 4, April 1994.

Index

About the Authors

MICHAEL SINGER DOBSON is an author, consultant, and popular seminar leader in project management, communications, and personal success, who brings a unique practical perspective to what works in the real world. He has trained people in well over 1,000 organizations on three continents on topics ranging from project management to career strategies. His down-to-earth style and practical advice comes from his management career positions, including vice president of Discovery Software, Inc.; vice president of marketing and sales of Games Workshop, Inc.; and director of marketing and product development for TSR, Inc. He was a member of the research team that created and opened the Smithsonian National Air and Space Museum, the world's most popular museum. He is the author of the business books *Practical Project Management*, *The Juggler's Guide to Managing Multiple Projects*, and *Exploring Personality Styles* and coauthor of the military thriller *Fox on the Rhine*.

DEBORAH SINGER DOBSON, M.Ed., is vice president for human resources for GATX Terminals Corporation in Chicago and was cofounder and executive director of ERIS Enterprises, Inc., a Maryland management consulting firm. An expert in organizational development and management effectiveness, she has consulted for numerous Fortune 500 companies in the areas of quality, team building, leadership, and cultural diversity and has lectured on the topic of training return on investment strategies.

The Dobsons have coauthored the book *Managing Up!* (AMACOM Books), the book/video/audio series *Coping with Supervisory Nightmares,* and the video and audio program *Training Skills for Team Leaders.* They live in the Chicago suburbs with their son Jamie and two shelties.